Managing Rental Properties for Maximum Profit

Revised 3rd Edition

Greg Perry

PRIMA PUBLISHING

This book is possible only because of the
Master Landlord, my father, Glen Perry.
Thanks, Dad, you're the greatest.

Published by Prima Publishing, Roseville, California. Member of the Crown
Publishing Group, a division of Random House, Inc.

PRIMA PUBLISHING and colophon are trademarks of Random House, Inc., registered with the United States Patent and Trademark Office.

Library of Congress Cataloging-in-Publication Data

Perry, Greg M.
   Managing rental properties for maximum profit / Greg Perry.— Rev. 3rd ed.
      p. cm.
   Includes index.
   ISBN 0-7615-2531-9
1. Real estate management—United States. 2. Rental Housing—United States—
Management. I. Title.

HD1394.5.U6 P47 2000
333.5'068—dc21   99-059675
                                                                           CIP

02 03 04 05 HH 10 9 8 7 6 5 4

Printed in the United States of America
Third Edition

Visit us online at www.primapublishing.com

Contents

Acknowledgments

MY COWRITERS ARE all the tenants I have had over the years who continually teach me how to improve my landlording approach. It seems that the more I care about my tenants' needs, the better tenants I have. I now believe that good tenants are always out there and it is the landlord's responsibility to bring out the best in them. Only when landlords provide safe, clean, affordable housing will tenants be the "good" kind that landlords dream about.

Readers of this book's earlier editions have also sent me many households of advice that I appreciate dearly. We landlords seem to have similar problems and shortcuts, but we rarely get a forum that allows us to share our views, ask for advice, and offer suggestions along the way. This book provides that vehicle both for me and for the many readers who have written to share their experiences.

David Richardson helped steer me in the right direction for this revised third edition. David helped me when I needed help and stayed out of my way when I wrote. Such trust is often rare in the writing business and I want David to know that I appreciate his help. The good people at Prima always give me freedom with my books' content, and that makes a writer happy. I also want to thank the other editors who turned my manuscript into a decent book, namely Chad Caruthers and Leslie Ayers.

My family stands behind me the most, and their support is the only reason I have any success in life. My beautiful bride, Jayne, travels around the globe with me and cleans rental properties when we're home. She probably never expected to have such contrasts in her life, but I suspect she is rarely bored. Glen and Bettye Perry, my parents, are the keys to my life. No other son could dream of the support they provide.

To my readers, the landlords and would-be landlords out there (landlording gentlemen and landlording ladies), I hope you pick up a few skills from this book to add to the bag of tricks you currently use. If you approach rental ownership with trepidation, my goal is to calm you with this text. Landlording requires energy and patience, as well as some very basic computing skills that can help keep you ahead of the game. However, it also includes lots of relaxation time once you streamline your efforts.

Introduction

PEOPLE OWN RENTAL properties for different reasons. Of those who do, some owners are happy with their rentals, while many are not. The rare ones who do love the business are those who through trials, tribulations, and insight have developed money- and time-saving techniques to turn the part-time business of rental property ownership into steady monthly cash flow. Perhaps the genesis of this book arose because I wanted to show landlords that rental properties could be rewarding in so many ways.

Some readers may pick up this book out of desperation. These frustrated landlords have almost abandoned all hope of enjoying their landlording duties. Other landlords have found ways to put their properties on autopilot (often without hiring a rental management company) and might want to hone their landlording skills even further. Some readers may not yet own rental properties, but they are curious about the business and want to know what to expect. Although no book can be all things to all people, this book attempts to help people in these three categories:

- Frustrated landlords: reluctant rental property owners who bought a second home or inherited one, could not sell the property or did not want to, and now need help renting the extra place.
- Happy landlords: those rental owners who successfully own and manage their properties.

- Would-be landlords: investors who want to acquire rental properties or inheritors who are about to come into the possession of rental property.

Whatever your landlording success has or has not been, you will find ample help in this book to start you on the path to easy landlording.

There are other books on the market that offer landlording advice for the big-time landlord, the owner of apartment complexes, and rental corporations. This book is intended for the small-time landlord, someone who owns only one or a handful of properties. There are so many individual landlords out there who want some hands-on advice. This book is meant for them.

Meanwhile, the small-time landlord has pinched some profits from the large-scale property management companies. In many markets, the small investor can be more successful on a per-unit basis than a large rental property company that specializes in gigantic apartment complexes. As a smaller-scale landlord, you can offer more individual services to attract tenants who want a more personal renting experience. After all, when tenants rent from a landlord who owns one to twenty houses, they usually deal only with the landlord/owner and one or two workers who may perform repairs on an as-needed basis. Unlike the large apartment complexes, the landlord that owns single or multi-unit dwellings often can provide a fenced area for small, outside pets and safer areas for children to play.

Landlording can be an extremely enjoyable, profitable, and relaxing career. The book you now hold is teeming with landlording advice, tips, warnings, and shortcuts. It's not a get-rich, no-money-down, fancy marketing manual but a book of hands-on advice, immediately helpful to anyone who is a landlord or who wants to become one.

To achieve landlording success, you must be a *caring* landlord. This book's primary goal is to show you how to streamline your landlording activities while still being the landlord your tenants expect. Too many rental owners are absentee landlords, never seeing their property or spending a dime on its upkeep. However, you can be an absent landlord without being an absentee landlord. Unfortunately, many people do not know until it is too late that rental property ownership and management is a part-time job. You can treat that job as an active investment instead of a chore you dread if you follow a few simple guidelines. In addition, if you enjoy your landlording experience your tenants will more likely enjoy theirs and they will stay longer. Vacancies are the bane of the landlording business and some landlords cannot afford for a unit to sit empty for a full rental cycle. With this book's help, you'll rarely have vacancies that last more than a few days and your tenants will be the long-term kind (two years of tenancy is long-term in today's rental environment). Your income will be more stable and your tenants' renting experience will make them appreciate your property more than they have ever appreciated any other rental home.

THIS BOOK'S GOALS

This book shows you the many ways you can prepare your properties to minimize maintenance. This in turn lowers your costs and lessens your time requirements. This book also teaches you how to find good tenants in only a few hours, how to keep them, and how to buy properties that attract them. You will learn how to remove the not-so-good tenants, while still maintaining the peace you desire and the respect all tenants want. Most important, this book shows you how to make money without spending a lot on property upkeep or constant tenant recruitment.

In order to ease into a successful landlording career, you must do your homework. Preparing the rental properly, attracting the best tenants, and buying more properties in the best rental locations are the keys to loving your very part-time job of landlording. If you already own a rental property, I assure you that you'll find treasures within these pages that will become time- and money-saving realities for you. If nothing else, this book will demonstrate the importance of owning and regularly using computers and the Internet. Computers are much simpler to use than ever before. Even if you don't want to use one, your competing landlords will, and you can fall behind the competitive curve quickly if you don't keep up.

PLEASE SHARE YOUR IDEAS

I'm open to suggestions! This is not a finished landlording text by any means. Future revisions will include comments and suggestions made by you, the readers, as you continue to share your experiences with me. Different towns, different homes, and especially different people can provide lots of good material that should be shared with other landlords across the country. I welcome your ideas and suggestions to provide readers of future editions with timely advice on tenant care and the enjoyment of rental property.

Take some time out of your landlording schedule to share with me your own landlording nightmares, solutions, and short-cuts. I would be grateful to hear from you. If I include your material in future book editions, I'll send you a free copy for your library. Jot down a note on a postcard or letter and mail it to:

Greg Perry
P.O. Box 35752
Tulsa, OK 74153-0752

Please enclose your return address with your correspondence. I cannot answer all the mail, but I read everything and respond to a great deal. Thank you in advance for your help. Readers of future editions will benefit from your experiences as I hope you benefit from the information within these pages.

CHAPTER ONE

Getting Good Tenants

IF YOU ENJOY landlording you will be more successful than if you don't enjoy the job. The happiest landlords are those with the best tenants. The best tenants are those who are the happiest and most pleased with their rental experience and with their landlord or rental property manager. If you've experienced bad times with your rental property, the odds are good that those problems were people oriented; more specifically, those problems were tenant oriented. Bad tenants will make you wish you had never seen that property. Good tenants will help you forget that landlording is a job. Seek good tenants! If waiting for the right tenants means keeping your house vacant for an extra month, then wait. You don't want to lose a single month's rent, and good landlords rarely do, but serious tenant problems can cost you a lot more than one month's lost rent.

Problems arise when you rent to people who do not meet your income and rental history requirements. You do not want late-night calls from bothersome tenants asking when you will paint their back fence. You especially do not want tenants who put you at the end of their bill-paying obligations. You want tenants who pay on time and take as much pride in their dwelling as you do.

The first step in becoming a successful landlord is to find responsible tenants. If you have proud tenants who are reasonable with their requests and pay on time, you will enjoy your job as a landlord. Landlords who own rental properties with good tenants have time to acquire several more properties and slowly build their rental empire. Landlords with tenant problems, however, *never* seem to have time to themselves; they are always dealing with problems that prevent them from enjoying the benefits of property management.

A wise real estate agent once described the three most important factors in selling real estate:

1. Location
2. Location
3. Location

If those are the three most important factors in selling real estate, the three most important factors in renting property are:

1. Advertise properly
2. Advertise properly
3. Advertise properly

Good tenants bring you landlording success, so you must attract them. Advertising ingenuity will attract the best tenants. The key to successfully acquiring good tenants is to draw a large pool of potential tenants from which to choose. The more potential renters you attract the better chance you have of finding great tenants. More available tenants make your job easier—the chances are greater that more people will fulfill your rental requirements than if only a handful of people wants your place.

Do not waste your time and money on unproved advertising methods. Stick with the basics and you will soon have more would-be tenants than any of your competing landlords. This chapter demonstrates how successful landlords advertise effectively and increase the number of good and interested tenants.

ADVERTISING

Most of the time, getting a tenant is simple. You must advertise in the classified advertising section of your newspaper. No other method consistently proves itself with successful results. Other ways to advertise exist, but newspaper advertisement is easy and works best.

Some landlords achieve success with other forms of advertising, but their methods are often costly, time consuming, or less effective than those of the landlords who follow the pack and advertise locally in the papers. For example, instead of advertising in a newspaper, you could place a sign in front of the house that lets drive-bys know it's for rent. But the next day you'll get a call from neighbors who complain that some crazy kid put your sign in their yard. Signs often work, especially in neighborhoods where neighbors watch your place closely, or in a multi-unit dwelling with others already living there, but signs can also invite trouble.

> **TIP**
>
> Nothing works as well as newspaper advertising to draw a large pool of prospective tenants.

Some owners put "For Rent" signs in the front window of their rentals. These signs do not get stolen as easily as those pitched in the front yard. Those crazy kids will probably not even see such a sign, but neither will most of the people who drive past the property. Those who do see it are often in too much of a hurry to stop and read its details. The reason the real estate salespeople put their signs right out by the curb is because they are most visible there. The same principle applies if you use a sign as part of your tenant-hunting process.

Besides being less effective in some cases than classified ads, signs in the yard or window of your property pose potential safety problems. You should not tell the world that your home is vacant. A sign makes it obvious. You want to announce the vacancy to as many would-be tenants as possible, but you do not want to invite vandals and vagrants. Granted, an ad in the newspaper clearly labels your house as an empty target, but people scanning those pages are generally interested in finding a home to rent.

Of course, some rental markets attract more tenants with signs than with newspaper advertising. If your area supports an advertising scheme not discussed in this book, you'll still be able to adopt this book's methods to suit your area. You will find in most cases that the fundamental landlording process, tips, warnings, and shortcuts detailed throughout this book will work very well in your area.

To attract even more potential tenants, you can also pin messages on community bulletin boards, advertise in university lounges, and offer your rental in trading newspapers that normally sell washing machines and used cars. Some landlords with time on their hands stack fancy fliers on the racks outside of grocery stores. There is nothing inherently wrong with any of these methods. They each get the word out and attract more people than a newspaper advertisement will by itself. Nevertheless, you will probably find that the extra time and energy are just not worth the results.

In today's computer age, access to the Internet is often only a few clicks away. The Internet provides several ways to advertise virtually anything, including rental properties. Chapter 12,

"Record Keeping and Computerizing Your Rental Properties," introduces ways to use a computer in your rental business and Chapter 13, "Can the Internet Help Landlords?," explains how to find useful information online. On the other hand, the Internet offers a global reach that is probably overkill for your needs. You don't want to target the whole world in your ad, you want to target a specific type of renter in a specific region. For the time being, the Internet will likely offer little or no advertising benefit for the small landlord, so it is still best to stick with the ads that target prospective tenants in your area.

The time-tested means for the successful landlord to find tenants is always local newspaper advertising in the "Rentals" classified section. The classifieds are the first place future tenants look. When they do look there, you want to grab their attention at the start and hold on tight.

Your Newspaper Ad

"How do I word my ad?" is a question many landlords ask every time a rental falls vacant. The answer is easy if you want to minimize your troubles: *Put every detail in the ad that the would-be tenant would want to know.* Include the property's address, the number of bedrooms, the air conditioner/heating status (central, forced air, lots of blankets needed, or whatever), supplied appliances (stove, refrigerator, dishwasher, garbage disposal), garage, type of flooring, fireplace, garage or carport, the monthly (or weekly) rent, the deposit, your pet policy (Do you allow them? How many and what kind?), your children policy (Adults only? How many people can live in the place?), your waterbed policy, and terms of the lease (six months, one year, and so on).

The smart landlord knows that a good ad costs more than a bad one, but a good ad produces quicker, better results and costs less in the long run. Put yourself in the shoes of a would-be tenant: You know exactly how much you can pay and you know the smallest house you want to rent. Those two pieces of information should be in almost every ad.

```
For Rent: 3-bedroom, 2-bath house. $575/month, $350
deposit. Call 555-4321.
```

Consider the ad displayed here. It costs very little and seems to tell the would-be tenant everything that he or she needs to know. Would you rent this home if you were a tenant? You cannot answer that. This ad does nothing except raise more questions. Guess who gets to answer those questions—in the form of phone calls—twenty-four hours a day? That's right, you do. This type of ad begs every other reader to call you for more information. The only reason *every* reader will not call (only every other one) is that the other half will scan the classifieds until they spot a more informative ad that answers their questions without requiring that they pick up a phone. To get the most prospects you've got to minimize the prospective tenant's tasks. The less work potential tenants have to do to find out about your place, the more likely they are to pursue your home.

This book strongly urges you to save money in every way you can. Your properties are supposed to be investments. However, an investment that loses money is not only a headache but a liability. Nevertheless, the ad is the one place you should spend whatever it takes to give your readers every necessary detail, so they do not have to call you for information. If a reader must call, both you and the potential tenant are doing more work than necessary.

Tell the Reader Almost Everything

If you truly want to maximize your time and minimize your hassle, keep only two details out of your ad: your name and phone number. No matter how thoroughly an ad describes your property, some people will still call to ask you something trivial. Even worse, some will ask questions that you already answered in the ad! Stop this at the source by leaving your name and phone number out of the ad. You can only go so far; once you realistically describe everything about the property, you have done your job.

Without your name or phone number, how will your would-be tenants get in touch with you to see the inside of the property? You will show them, of course. Only now you are working smarter than before.

The most time-consuming task involved with owning rental properties is answering questions about your ad and showing the property. The day your ad appears in the paper, you may get thirty callers, twenty of whom will want to see the inside of the property. You do not have time to handle all these calls or to show the property twenty separate times. The way to avoid running to and from your properties is simple. But surprisingly few landlords have hit upon it: Hold an open house.

> **TIP**
>
> Comprehensive ads cut down the time you spend with prospective tenants. The less time you spend getting renters, the more time you have to acquire properties, fix things that need fixing, or simply enjoy more time away from your properties.

Holding Your Open House

The typical rental property owner places an ad in the newspaper that includes his or her phone number. When a prospective tenant calls to see the property, the owner must get in the car to show the home if the would-be tenant wants to see the house immediately. Invariably, as soon as the owner gets home from one showing, she or he gets another call to show the property again.

In times of depressed housing markets, owners seem happy to oblige would-be tenants. If a potential tenant wants to see the property at 4:35 in the morning, many owners feel that's better than having to cover another month's mortgage payment. But such housing slumps should not require that you cater to the whims of every caller who wants to see your property. Even though callers are potential renters, if you ever want your rental empire to grow, you cannot spend your time showing a home twenty times to twenty different people. Even worse, you don't want to pay someone to make twenty trips. You picked up this book because you want to be a smarter, more successful landlord.

> **TIP**
>
> Save time and trouble: Don't put your name and number in the ad!

In place of your name and phone number, put the date and time you will show the property. Think about the instant advantages. Wouldn't you like to make one trip instead of twenty? This strategy alone will save many landlords a tremendous amount of time—not to mention gallons of gas—starting today.

Reserve several hours on a Friday afternoon and during the day on a Saturday for your property's open house. Scheduling the open house between 4 and 6 P.M. on a Friday afternoon lets you catch people who drop by after work. Early Saturday afternoon is also a premium time for home seekers to go looking. Whatever time you pick, be sure to prepare the house for viewing by cleaning it thoroughly and touching up all the details that will catch people's eyes. Chapter 2, "Preparing Your Rental Property," describes many things you can do to turn the home into a showcase.

Most landlords find that the first of the month is the best time to offer homes for rent. Renters' leases often start on the first of the month and expire at the end of the month. If you can hold an open house during the last week of the month, you will get the largest pool of visitors because they will be able to move the following week, assuming they've given their current landlord proper notice.

More people will see the property during your open house than if you use any other method. Prospective tenants appreciate the fact that they do not have to meet you alone. Because an open house can involve several people, would-be renters can maintain more distance between themselves and you than if you make a special trip to see each one individually. Women who do not want to risk meeting a stranger at an empty house especially appreciate this.

Because you clearly posted the open house hours in your ad, people can fit it into their schedules, instead of trying to negotiate a mutual meeting time. One spouse can drop by after work, then bring the other back if interest is high. But if they have to call you for an individual viewing, the entire family might want to come, perhaps to find that the house is somehow inadequate. In addition, you will have to conform to the schedule of every caller. If you hold an open house one evening and the next weekend afternoon, you'll be available during a time when most tenants will be able to see your place or send a spouse to do the same.

> **TIP**
>
> Hold an open house at a time that is convenient for you and most working people. Successful landlords do not make twenty-five trips to show the home to twenty-five potential tenants.

Not only will you draw a larger number of prospective tenants at an open house, and not only will you save time and gas, but the prospective tenants who attend your open house will be *more interested* in your property than the typical prospective renter. Think back for a minute about the contents of good, comprehensive ads that describe everything pertinent about a property. A comprehensive ad lets prospective renters know exactly what to expect from your property before they ever attend the open house. From the ad, they know that the property's features match their needs. They know the deposit and the terms you expect. They know the address; most of them will have driven by before your open house just to "scope out" the property. They liked what they saw on the outside or they would not be at the open house. You will know, therefore, when prospects appear at your open house that they have a higher interest level than if you had run a more standard, less comprehensive ad.

Chapter 3, "Open House and Tenant Selection," includes several open house tips and outlines your role during open houses. You want open-house attendees to feel comfortable and know you're there to answer questions and pass out paperwork. You do not want to be a pushy salesperson. A well-maintained home will say more about you as a landlord than anything else you do or say.

Tenants will come to your home with a confirmed interest and also to make sure that you honestly described the rental, and that your place is clean and in good shape. This is when you grab them—when your house is sparkling. After reading this book, you will know how to add all the extra touches that make people want to rent your property at first sight.

By placing a proper ad and holding an open house, you will find yourself with only two problems:

- What will you do with the extra time on your hands?
- Out of the large number of people who are begging for your property, how will you choose a tenant?

Landlords across the country would love to have those problems!

Before continuing, please know that I give you this advice after years of working and reworking methods of rental property management. Be assured that you will find many good tenants by using these methods. Although there are many other ways to get good tenants, this is one that proves most successful time and time again.

No method is perfect. There *is* one set of renters that you may miss with the open house approach. There are certain people who will call the number in every rental property ad in the Sunday paper to ask specific questions. But they will not bother to read the ads first. You've had people call before and ask how many bedrooms and how much the deposit is when you put those facts right before your phone number, haven't you? I find it interesting that people do this—and it happens among all types of renters. Instead of reading the details in the ad, they prefer to ask questions and make an interactive decision on the phone. But if you don't supply your phone number, these renters cannot call you and will not show up at your home. Nevertheless, I prefer to avoid these renters and leave my number out of the ad. It's possible that I'll reach these renters with one of my other advertising methods, such as a posting on a community bulletin board, but I don't worry about them too much because plenty of other prospects come to my open houses.

A Simple Ad with a Catchy Header

For a catchy advertisement model, read the effective rental ad displayed in this section. You can change the details, but keep the format the same whether you are leasing a home or a duplex in a large city or a small town. Notice the phrase centered in boldface letters at the top. Most newspapers will add the extra line for you for a small extra charge. Your ad will stand out because most owners do not want to spring for that extra line. Competing (and less savvy) landlords will be placing a second ad when you are signing your first lease.

Don't Miss This One!

Beautiful, clean 3-bedroom, 2-bath home, carpeted, dishwasher, laundry hookups, central heat/air, separate dining area, ceiling fans, miniblinds, fenced backyard, 2-car attached garage, great neighborhood, 1 outside pet OK, up to 2 children OK, waterbed OK, close to schools, 6-month lease minimum, $575/month, $350 security/cleaning refundable deposit. 1013 S. Illinois. Will show this Friday 4-6 p.m. and Saturday 1-3 p.m.

The headline phrase is an attention-getter. Put any catchy two- to four-word expression here, but make sure it fits well centered across the top of the ad. You might want to try the following:

- Like New!
- Stable Neighborhood!
- 10 Mins. from Downtown!

- Country Living!
- Dream Home!
- BEST DEAL!
- I Welcome Pets!
- Newly Remodeled!

Do not overdo the advertisement, but do supply succinctly every bit of needed information. Remember, since you will not put your name or phone number in the ad, you must supply potential renters with all the details they want to know.

I used to put the phrase "safe neighborhood" in the ads because I only buy properties in neighborhoods that I would feel safe living in, and I want potential renters to know that the neighborhood is not crime-ridden. Unfortunately, the litigious nature of today's society has frightened me into leaving this information out of ads. Although your neighborhood might be safer than many others, you cannot guarantee that a problem won't occur as soon as a tenant moves into your property. Phrases such as "safe neighborhood" might open you up to lawsuits if problems

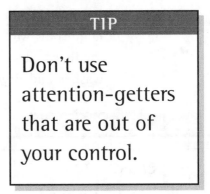

TIP

Don't use attention-getters that are out of your control.

arise. The phrase "friendly neighborhood" conveys the same idea, but does not create a problematic description that can come back to haunt you later. File away the ads that work well over the years so that you can keep track of the wording that attracted the most would-be tenants to your open houses.

Keep Your Ad Honest

Proudly describe everything pertinent about your rental property, but do not exaggerate or misrepresent it. Otherwise you will lose trust (and most of your would-be tenants). As soon as ad readers see the inside of the property, they will know whether you told the entire truth in the newspaper.

Landlords before you have lied to many of your ad's readers over the years. Prospective tenants might be apprehensive and mistrustful of you before they see your rental. Think of how pleasantly surprised they will feel when they find that your ad is 100 percent accurate. If anything, your ad undersells the coziness and pride of ownership that your home displays. The would-be tenants' trust is impossible to gain after you lose it, so capture it at the beginning when it is easiest to snare. Try to think like a salesperson and determine how a negative can be turned into a positive. If your home has no washer and dryer hookups, you might put "Minutes from Laundromat!" in the ad or, at least, in the flier that you hand out at the open house. Tenants who want washer and dryer hookups will almost certainly rule out your home immediately when they do not see them listed, but if you mention that laundry facilities are in close proximity to the home, the price and condition of the home may make the hookups less important. Adjust this concept to suit the specifics of your property.

> **TIP**
>
> Advertise the truth and reward your tenants.

If you can cut costs without sacrificing quality, pass those costs on to your renters by setting your rent levels slightly below that of your competition. But if you require higher rent than surrounding properties, make certain that your home is sparkling clean and offers enough amenities to warrant the extra rent.

I prefer to undercut my competition. I'd rather have a larger pool of prospective tenants to choose from, and I'd rather have fewer vacancies. Nevertheless, financial conditions sometimes necessitate raising rents above those of competitors. This book will show you how to make your rental a showplace so prospective tenants will be happy to pay the extra rent. Your property will no longer be a time-consuming headache but something to be proud of.

Throughout this book, you will find ways to lower the cost of being in the rental business, but the original cost of the home is what dictates the rent you must charge. As you buy more properties (and you will after reading how easy property management can be), be open to low-cost housing with good structures located in better neighborhoods. Generally, a fix-up home is much cheaper in the long run than a home that is ready to move into, even if you hire someone to make every repair. Chapter 10, "Finding and Buying More Properties," offers lots of advice on finding the perfect low-cost rental property.

This book is not a magic formula for success. But if it does nothing more than teach you to develop your own techniques for money-saving, pride-of-ownership, fully occupied rental properties, my goal for the book will be surpassed. The magic comes from your own pride in your property, which will shine through in your ad if you are honest with readers.

By the way, if you own property in a rent-controlled district, my prayers are with you. Have you ever wondered *who* writes the rent-control laws and who sets the limits on such rentals? Elected officials stay as far from such activity as they can. Somehow, government-funded legal service attorneys draft these rent-control regulations. Forget all you learned in civics class about the government's legislative branch drafting laws! The lawyers draft rent-control laws, and they do not have to answer to you, to me, or to anyone else in the public realm. The bottom line is that you as a property owner are almost always going to have income problems in rent-controlled districts. If you're looking to purchase a rental property, stay away from areas that are zoned this way. If you already own property in these areas, see what you can do to live with the situation, but *do not* keep your property at a loss because too many deals are waiting for someone like you elsewhere.

RENTERS ARE EVERYWHERE

The combination of effective newspaper advertising and the open house will find you a good tenant, but there are other avenues to explore as well. The easiest and cheapest advertising available is word of mouth. Although it does not reach the large audience that a newspaper does, its benefits are appealing if you target the right people.

Be selective with any word-of-mouth advertising. Your friends and coworkers care about you, so tell them about an upcoming vacancy. If a friend or coworker sends you a rental prospect, that person is probably a better candidate than a complete stranger. You still run some risk, but the risk is smaller.

Although this may surprise some landlords, I have often gotten great rental recommendations from previous tenants and from tenants who are moving out. More than once, I've had a tenant give me notice that they are moving out and tell me about a relative or friend who needs a place to live. As long as the recommended person meets your rental requirements, you've got a winner: The friend or relative has surely seen your place and has not heard anything negative about you as a landlord.

Know your primary competition. Such competition is not always easy to define, but the longer you own the property, the more obvious the competition will become. If your tenants often move because they purchase their own home, you are probably doing everything correctly. If your tenants tend to move to another rental unit, you will want to know what incentive they have to move. Perhaps their family is growing and they need more room. If so, you're not at fault. If another location is offering a better deal, a cleaner place, or a better neighborhood, you will have to adjust your property somehow, perhaps in the rental amount, to keep people longer. A vacancy that lasts for a month can become extremely expensive if you have a vacancy once a year.

As long as my tenants give me fair notice and do not break the lease when they move out, I always thank them for living in my place and tell them to contact me if they ever need a reference. In addition, I ask them *right then* if they know of someone who might want to live there. If you own a multi-unit dwelling such as a duplex or a fourplex, ask the remaining tenants if they know of someone who wants to live in the unit to be vacated. Most of the time, your other tenants' expectations will be higher than yours, because they will have to live next door to whomever they recommend. Therefore, if other tenants suggest someone, you should be sure to pursue that candidate.

If eventually you rent the property to a friend's or former tenant's recommended candidate, send a crisp $20 bill and thank-you card to the person who recommended the new tenant the very next day. Don't go overboard with the thanks, but quietly let that person know that you are grateful for his or her help. The money does two things: It genuinely shows your appreciation, which is its main function. It also increases the chances that the next time you have a vacancy, that person will want to help you find another tenant. Two people searching produces many more potential renters than you could by yourself.

You must still be in control of the rental situation, no matter how well-meaning your friends are. Use common sense. Even though your friend probably has your best interests at heart, only you know who can and cannot rent your property. Follow your guidelines for smoking/nonsmoking, minimum income, number of family members, and so forth. The candidate your friend recommends should exceed your minimum qualifications for rental, just as a stranger off the street would have to do. In Chapter 3, "Open House and Tenant Selection," you will read some guidelines for selecting tenants in a legal and orderly fashion.

> **TIP**
>
> Let your friends, coworkers, and former tenants know when you have a vacancy. Thank them with a small cash gift if they save you time and money by supplying you with a tenant.

Advertising in Surrounding Towns

Rarely will you have to place an ad outside your property's town. A well-written, comprehensive ad attracts renters like nothing else. However, occasionally local economic conditions and timing may work against you. If you hold several open houses but still feel that the candidates do not measure up, consider advertising in surrounding towns for the next week's open house.

Many people work outside their hometowns. You may attract someone who works in the town where your property is but lives farther away and is tired of the commute. Or you may be the answer for a family who wants to move closer to relatives living in your area.

Be cautious about doing too much advertising too early, however. The comprehensive ad and open house will provide a good number of rental candidates. But if you also place ads in many different places the first week or two of advertising, you run a big risk of spending much more than necessary to get a qualified tenant. Even though surrounding areas may offer good prospects, most of your lookers will be from the town in which the property is located. Over time, you will learn how large an area your ads must cover to get enough prospects at your open houses.

USING A RENTAL SERVICE

Should you consider a rental service? Most landlords consider hiring their job out to another agency several times throughout their property management tenure, especially when a bad tenant slips past all precautions and rents their home. Many real estate companies offer a management service for rental properties. They will advertise, show your home, handle complaints, collect the rent, order the repairs, and send you what is left of the rent (if anything) after they do their job.

There are two drawbacks to using a rental service: The first is loss of income. The property management firm has to make a profit to survive, so it will charge what it needs to maintain its profit margins. Remember, though, that you too have to make a profit to survive. By the time you pay the mortgage, taxes, and insurance, you may not always have enough to pay the rental service. But because you are locked into a contract, you will have to pay. Even when the service does nothing during a given month, you still have to pay the monthly fee. Most require a percentage of the rent, with additional charges for any and all repairs, advertising, and showing time. Generally, you can expect the agency to want half of the first month's rent and 10 percent of each month's rent thereafter. The agency cannot and will not guarantee that your home will be occupied, so you have no security when using the service that your home will rent for longer or for more money than if you were handling it yourself.

One advantage that many rental agencies can provide is a staff that might be more up to date on fair housing laws and antidiscrimination laws than you are. I say *might be.* Be warned that if an agency illegally discriminates against prospective tenants, *you* are also responsible for the consequences. By law, the agency will be considered your agent, so whatever it does, you are also presumed to do. I don't like losing control over such aspects of property management.

> **TIP**
>
> Manage your own properties for maximum profit and control.

More important, you lose contact with and eventual control over your property. Most property management companies offer high-quality rental services. Despite that, nobody takes pride in your own property as much as you do. There is no way to ensure that the rental service will handle all problems exactly to your liking. By the time you finish this book, you will see that managing your own properties is easy and cheap and demands an extremely small amount of your time. If you have had lots of problems managing your properties in the past, you may be willing to pay most or all of your monthly profit to a rental service, but I urge you to finish this book before making that decision.

Since I mentioned the drawbacks of hiring property managers in this book's previous edition, I have received cards and letters from people who use the services and from people who own such services. All of these cards and letters suggested that I rethink my advice. Despite their good arguments, I cannot advise the typical

CHAPTER TWO

Preparing Your Rental Property

YOU CAN RELAX during the open house. At the open house, you do not actually show the home because the home shows itself. As a result of your effective ad, most of the people who come to the open house will have driven by at least once before. In fact, you invited your ad's readers to do so by including the address—and you should hope that they did drive by before coming to the open house. That way, you know they like the outside of the home. If the inside is attractive to them as well, they will want to rent the house.

Your open house will give prospective tenants a good or bad first impression—the choice is yours. A good impression of the outside will disappear if the inside is dirty. At the same time, a bad impression of the outside will be hard to reverse, no matter what the inside of the home looks like.

You can do many wonderful and inexpensive things to make people want to rent your house. This chapter focuses on making your home a "must have" for everyone attending the open house. (For advice on how to completely renovate your home, see Chapter 11.)

If you have not attracted enough interested prospective tenants in the past, you've done one or two things wrong:

1. You overpriced your home, or
2. The home was in poor, sloppy, or dirty condition.

Learn how to make your property stand out from the competition. Show those would-be tenants why your house should be their future home.

CLEANLINESS IS PARAMOUNT

Clean the house—or delay the open house. If you do not make sure that the home is clean for open house, you are in the wrong business. There is no excuse for dirty carpets, walls, counters, or sinks. The only people you want as renters are those who are turned off by dirt in their home. If you show a dirty house and someone wants to rent from you, you are fortunate (extremely rare), you just attracted problem tenants, or your rent is just right for a dirty place, which means that you could clean the home and ask for a lot more.

No matter how wonderful the previous tenants were, don't wait until the open house to determine the condition the former occupants left the property in. As soon as the previous tenants move out, check the house to see what needs to be done to put the house in tip-top condition. I know of landlords who tell new tenants that they can clean the house themselves and have part of the first month's rent—or, worse, some of the deposit—deducted. These owners are inviting trouble by making it clear to the tenants that you do not place a high priority on cleanliness and collecting rent or security deposits.

It's to be hoped that your former tenants left the house in move-in condition. Good tenants will. Nevertheless, some landlords pride themselves on never giving back a cleaning deposit, even to a deserving tenant. They feel that the cleaning deposit is their payment for having to find another tenant. But tenants can challenge these landlords in court. One landlord had a problem on his hands when a savvy tenant who wanted his deposit back took photographs of the clean house along with the daily newspaper to prove the date of the pictures. This landlord had to pay a large penalty to his ex-tenants in addition to the original deposit.

A majority of court cases where owners and tenants are involved end up as a win or compromise in favor of the tenants. Do not invite trouble. Be fair with the deposit. Never use the deposit to compensate for normal wear and tear, which includes but is not limited to a reasonable number of wall holes for pictures. For long tenancies, even new paint and carpet replacement can be considered normal wear and tear.

Don't try to squeeze extra pennies from tenants by keeping their deposits if they leave the home clean. You should always intend to give back every dollar of your tenants' deposit. When you are able to do so because your tenants cleaned the house adequately prior to leaving, your job becomes easier. Remember, you want to spend as little time and money as you can to manage your property. When tenants move in, tell them that you want to give them back their entire cleaning deposit. Tell them you have done so many times with former tenants who took care of the house and left it in as

> **TIP**
>
> Prospective tenants always see dirt; they rarely notice cleanliness.

good as or better condition than when they moved in. When tenants give notice that they will move out, encourage them to clean up and cheerfully mention that you will return their deposit if they do. No matter how much notice a renter gives, your job is easier and you save money in the long run if you have nothing to repair and very little to clean.

At the open house, every spot on the wall, every piece of lint on the carpet, and every fingerprint on the faucets will stand out in potential renters' eyes—and you do not want tenants who don't care about cleanliness! If would-be tenants want to move into a clean home, they are more likely to keep it that way. Be wary of people who want to rent the home virtually sight unseen. Typically, these people have bad rental histories, and they're taking advantage of the fact that some landlords have problems finding renters—although you should no longer consider yourself one of those desperate landlords.

> ### TIP
> Desirable prospective tenants will look in every nook and cranny.

Tenants who are good enough for you will inspect your home thoroughly. These caring tenants will look in every closet, open every cupboard, open and sniff the refrigerator, look in your sinks, judge the toilet's sanitation, and notice every speck of dust and grime.

Whether or not the former tenants left the house clean, you must take responsibility for making sure the home is ready for immediate occupancy. Take pride in the job you do. When you begin to look at your rental as a problem, you lose interest and your attitude shows to potential tenants. But when you see your home as an investment, as only a minor time-consumer (it can be), and as your second home if needed (you never know), you will go the extra mile to prepare the home for showing. You want top-quality renters. You want to lure the best renters away from the huge apartment complexes and the corporate landlords. You can—and the first step begins with a broom.

We naturally put more effort into preparing a home to sell than we do preparing a home to rent. I've been treating my open houses lately as if I were showing the places to sell. I'm not looking for renters but people who like my home enough to buy it. If I feel satisfied that I've prepared the home well enough to sell it, I know I've got the home in top-notch rental condition. When my open-house guests decide to rent, they like the home well enough to buy it if the home were for sale for a fair price. They are not settling for a second-rate place to stay until they locate something better. When they see my place, at the price I'm asking, they've just found the one that is "better."

> **TIP**
>
> Treat the rental home as if you were trying to sell it.

When you go to clean the house, bring everything you need to clean it so you do not have to make extra trips (to like landlording you must spend as little time doing it as possible). Following is a list of cleaning supplies you should take with you to spruce up the home for open house:

    vacuum cleaner with an empty dust bag
    furniture polish (for natural woodwork, cabinets, doors, and
        baseboards)
    broom, dustpan
    spare lightbulbs
    mop
    bucket
    rags, sponges, towels

cleaners, disinfectant
glass cleaner
toilet bowl brush
rubber gloves
trash bags
smoke alarm batteries
nail hole–patching compound
sandpaper
touch-up paint
common tools (screwdrivers, wrench, hammer, nails)
air fresheners

If you have more than one rental, it may be more convenient to keep the needed cleaning supplies and equipment in a ready-to-go box. This will save you the time of gathering these items when you need to clean one of your rentals. And be sure to re-stock your box when you run out of materials; you don't want to drive all the way to a property and not have something you need. I have found that the best time to restock my supplies is immediately after I finish cleaning a home. I know exactly what I'm low on or out of, and I can stop by the store to restock on my way home. That way if I'm surprised by a quick move-out, I can be assured that I have everything I need to prepare the home as quickly as possible.

Disinfect all toilets, baths, and sinks. Let bleach stand in any white porcelain that has become discolored. If bleach does not take off the dingy color, you may have to purchase a stain re-mover for the job. Many landlords replace worn-out porcelain sinks with stainless steel sinks, which clean easily and do not discolor. If white porcelain chips away from a sink or toilet, paint stores sell cover-up paint that will last for a while. (Don't use regular paint on porcelain fixtures.) You'll learn more about problem sinks and toilets in Chapter 11.

If you have difficulty removing stains from the toilet bowl, chances are good that mineral deposits have built up over the years. The only solution is to rough them off. First, drain the bowl by turning off the water and flushing the toilet. (Most toilets have water valves close to the floor behind the toilet.) Sprinkle pumice powder on the stains and rub with a hard brush (but not one with steel bristles) or a coarse rag. You will not mar the surface of the bowl, but you will remove the stains with a little effort. Mineral buildup is common in older toilet bowls, especially ones that have not been used in a while.

If your house has a garbage disposal, run a lemon through it before each open house. This replaces with a pleasant aroma any odors that may be lurking in the drain. Some baking soda helps keep the drain fresh, too.

Remember to put fresh air filters in the air conditioner/heating unit. These filters need to be replaced about every two to three months— you can get by with every six months, but that's stretching the limit. Most people go much longer than that between replacements. Dirty filters make the units work harder, the home will not heat or cool as fast, and your tenants will have higher utility bills and less money when the rent comes due. By changing the filters when you prepare the house for showing, you gain two or three months before you have to change them again. Better yet, buy a few extra and leave them in the house. They are very inexpensive and are often available for even less

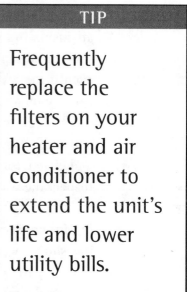

TIP

Frequently replace the filters on your heater and air conditioner to extend the unit's life and lower utility bills.

in two-for-one sales. Show the new tenants how to change the filter to keep their heating and cooling bills low.

Check the Details

Before preparing the home to show, walk through the home with a pencil and paper and inspect everything. Make sure every door and window opens and closes easily and quietly. A sticky door quickly gets torn away from its hinges from the extra force necessary to open and close it. Make sure the locks work. Make sure windows stay up when opened. Check for air leaks under outside doors and windows. A bead of caulk around a window seal and an insulating strip at the bottom of a door improve a home's soundproofing and air efficiency. Check the doors and windows even if they were fine the last time the rental was vacant; caulk can dry up and weather stripping can come loose.

Flush all toilets and turn on all faucets. Check for water leaks and drips. Open and close all windows. Turn on all ceiling fans and listen for rubbing on the bearings or unbalanced blades. Inspect the water heater closet and the heating and air closets for leaks. Raise and lower any miniblinds and window shades looking for cracks and bad pulley systems. Today's large-scale building supply warehouses stock replacement parts. Often, you can replace parts of a system without replacing the entire system. If you need a miniblind rod or a ceiling fan light globe, you can often find them without replacing the entire miniblind or light fixture. These replacement parts save time as well as money because you do not have to spend the time removing the old item and putting up a new one.

You will do your renters a favor if you put screens on the windows. Your tenants can turn off the air-conditioning and enjoy the spring and fall without getting bitten by insects coming through screenless windows. Uniform-looking screens improve the appearance of the outside of the home as well. Window screens are not expensive. You can often find like-new screens at junkyards, but brand-new screens are also inexpensive. Be sure to measure each window before you go to the store, since windows in a house vary in size. If the existing screens are coming loose, you can buy a repair strip, called splining, and a screen repair roller. (Chapter 11 describes screen repair in more detail.) Screens come in several colors, but the most common colors are silver and black. The more traditional you keep colors the longer your home's color scheme works.

Be sure to put ample toilet paper in every bathroom. Some people will ask to use the bathroom when they come to the open house, and, if you do not let them, be assured they will not rent the home. Put a bar of soap and a towel in the bathroom so open house guests can wash their hands. And don't forget to turn on the water if the previous tenants had the water company turn it off when they left.

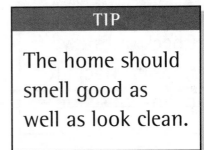

TIP

The home should smell good as well as look clean.

Remove kitchen and bathroom odors by thoroughly cleaning with a lemon-based disinfectant. Unless you clean the offending surfaces and appliances, you can only temporarily hide the odors. After cleaning, a room deodorizer will help enhance the clean scent—but do not purchase a strongly scented one. To some sensitive noses, that would be worse than the original problem. Sprinkle carpet freshener into the carpet before you vacuum. Freshener works wonders.

If you supply a refrigerator (and you should in most areas because renters usually do not lug one around), put a fresh box of baking soda in it. Put the old box to good use by pouring it down the kitchen and bathroom sinks to freshen the drains. Almost everyone at the open house will open the refrigerator. Because renters are used to seeing soiled, smelly refrigerators with cracked shelves in the houses of other landlords, surprise your prospective tenants with the fresh, clean look and smell of your refrigerator.

Some landlords understandably like to minimize utility bills when their rental is vacant. If you choose to turn off the refrigerator during the house's vacancy, prop the door open. Even many clean refrigerators will produce mildew and begin to smell bad if left off and closed for more than several days.

Patch large nail holes in the walls and clean or paint over dirty spots on the walls and baseboards. Everything that catches would-be tenants' eyes can register as a negative. Tenants will not notice smooth, clean walls, but they will see every blemish.

> **TIP**
>
> Check out new housing tracts for open-house ideas.

For more ideas about how to spruce up your rental for an open house, go by an open house in a model home in a newly developed neighborhood. You will see that the electricity and water are on and the home is inviting. The selling agents often put flowers somewhere in the house to help you feel at home, which is exactly the reaction the seller wants. That's also exactly how you want your open-house guests to feel.

Utilities in Vacant Rentals

As mentioned, you must keep the basic utilities on while you show the home. You will need those utilities anyway to prepare the home properly. You must have water and electricity to clean the home well. During the winter months, keep the heat on also.

This keeps the pipes from freezing while nobody is there to keep the place warm. You don't need to leave the heat on high when the house is empty, but leave the thermostat set at a temperature that will keep the cabinets warm so pipes have less chance of freezing.

In cold-winter areas, have a plumber or electrician install heat tape on the water pipes in the crawl space (if the home has one). Heat tape has wires that connect to an electrical source. When the temperature falls below a certain level, the heat tape charges and warms the pipes so they do not freeze and burst (a broken water pipe is extremely costly and never fun to

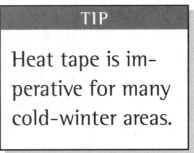

TIP

Heat tape is imperative for many cold-winter areas.

repair). The good thing about heat tape is that it works whether you are there or away as long as you keep the electricity turned on. When tenants move in, the heat tape continues to work, even if the tenants go out of town during a cold spell.

When a tenant vacates your property, you must have the utilities turned on in your name as soon as possible. The sooner they are on, the sooner you can prepare the home for showing and the sooner the rent will roll in again.

You will have to grit your teeth and pay the utility companies' hookup fees. Most utilities do not actually turn service off and on, but they do need to send a meter reader out to get a final reading for the previous tenant so they can transfer the billing to your name. Nobody likes to pay for this, but the utility companies must pass the cost on to someone—and that someone is you.

Many utilities now offer a "leave-on" service designed specifically for landlords. When you sign up for leave-on service, you tell the utility company the location of your property (or properties). When the company receives a shutoff notice from the former tenant, the company automatically transfers the service to your name. The utility company charges you less for this service than it would if you called each time to request a transfer. Not only is it cheaper, but also during the winter months the home will remain heated even if the tenants quietly move out without telling you.

If you sign up for the leave-on service, your only responsibility is to inform the utility company whenever a new tenant moves in. You do not want to pay for the new tenant's electricity and gas any longer than you have to. As soon as you call, the utility company will stop billing you for future usage and will transfer the subsequent charges to the new tenant after they verify occupancy.

I had a problem with a leave-on policy once that you should remain aware of. I moved without remembering to tell my utility company to change my leave-on policy's billing address. This would normally be no problem because the U.S. Postal Service forwards all mail for one year. I had no vacancies that entire first year, however, so I never received a forwarded leave-on utility bill that would have reminded me to change my billing address. Fourteen months after I'd moved, I sold one of my rental properties. The utility company did its job and left the utilities on and mailed me a bill. The bill was never forwarded because the one-year limit for forwarding had expired. The utility company couldn't find me so the account went delinquent. The first I heard of this was when a collection agency called me two years later to collect this past-due bill! After realizing what had transpired, the utility company removed me from its delinquent list, I paid the past-due bill, and I changed my billing address for the leave-on policy immediately. Although it was my job to inform the utility company about my new address, it didn't make a lot of effort to find me, either. I moved four miles from my previous address, on the same street, in the same city, with a listed phone number, and I had utility service under my name at my new address. The utility company found it easier to turn the matter over to collection than to look me up in the phone book. Fortunately, the entire matter was cleared up once I realized what had happened.

If the home is all electric, or if you simply have an electric water heater, you must leave the water on whenever the electricity is on. Although it does not pose a safety danger, the heating element will burn up if the tank is allowed to go dry. A plumber or electrician can replace the heating element, but you do not want to pay for the repair—especially since the problem is so easy to avoid.

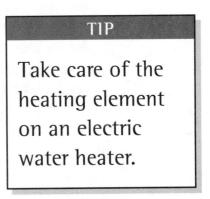

TIP

Take care of the heating element on an electric water heater.

To be safe and to avoid unnecessary utility bills, turn off the breaker to the electric water heater as soon as you finish cleaning. You do not need hot water to show the house. In addition, if the electricity happens to go off while the house is still vacant, the heating element on the water heater will remain intact.

Finally, leave on some lights, both inside and out, while the home is vacant. A dark house invites problems. A well-lit house also looks more appealing to potential tenants who drop by after reading your ad.

Hiring Cleaning Help

Every landlord considers paying someone else to do all the cleaning and fix-up work. Although this book shows you how to manage your properties on your own, without relying heavily on outside services and spending lots of money, there are times when hiring others makes sense.

You might first consider "hiring" your own family. Involve your spouse and children if they are willing. Pay your children to run the vacuum and wipe the walls. Promise your spouse an extravagant present if he or she helps! Whatever you do, make the property's work upbeat and fun. Take a portable television or radio with you. At noon, take your family for a lunch-break pizza party. This is their property, too, and their future partly depends on its rentability. Offer your children a percentage of the rent and tell them that the more appealing the house is, the more rent you can charge, and the more income they'll make. Your kids will be more ambitious than you are!

A side benefit to family members helping is that they learn the trade. Owning rental properties is a rewarding sideline investment or career. Not only will your younger family members be apprenticing under you, they will also learn about the business so that you can later go on vacation and leave someone else in charge. When they are older, perhaps they will want to manage their own rentals, or you can hire them to manage some of yours while you renovate one or two new purchases a year.

If you have no family, or if your family cannot help, consider hiring others to clean, paint, and prepare the home for occupancy. The cost is tax-deductible to you as the owner of the home. Even more important, the job will be done faster than if you did it by yourself and the income can begin sooner. House cleaning services can be in and out of your house faster than you would be able to clean the half-bathroom. They are well-trained and know how to make a home shine in record time. Given that their fee is tax-deductible and that they work so fast, you should never rule them out. By the way, successful house-cleaning services know to start at the top; they start with ceilings and high woodwork on the top floor and work their way down. When you clean your home, remember how the pros do the job and you'll soon see all sorts of advantages to the system. Remember that local church groups, college fraternities and sororities, and local youth groups are always looking for short-term group fundraisers as well.

The key is to let others do what they do best while you continue to do what you do best. If you manage your property well, inspect the details, ensure cleanliness, attend to the extras, prepare for the open house, and do all the other tasks needed to make sure things run smoothly, eventually you will rent to high-quality, paying tenants. If you like to clean, paint, or do other home-improvement work, by all means do those things. The money you save is nice, and more important, you develop an increased sense of pride in your property. However, even do-it-yourselfers need to hire help now and then.

SAFETY FIRST

You, your insurance agent, and your tenant will be happier if you purchase at least two smoke alarms. If you own a two-story house, be sure to get at least one for each floor. Make sure that each bedroom door is close to a smoke alarm. There is no excuse to forget smoke alarms, and if you don't install them, you open yourself up to a lot of liability if there ever is a fire.

When preparing the house for showing, be sure to check the batteries in the smoke alarms. Electric alarms do not require batteries, but an electrician must install them. Battery-powered smoke alarms are cheaper than electric alarms and have test buttons that demonstrate the battery's life. Even if the battery is still good, replace it if it's been a while since the last replacement. Dust can "confuse" a smoke alarm, so be sure to remove the cover and dust or vacuum every smoke alarm when you prepare the home for showing.

Surprisingly, many owners in the rental business never think to provide a fire extinguisher. A fire extinguisher placed under the kitchen sink may be the best investment you make. Every time you prepare your home for showing, check the extinguisher's gauge to make sure it is fully charged.

> **TIP**
>
> Place a five-pound, all-purpose fire extinguisher under the kitchen sink.

Resist the temptation to "test" the fire extinguisher by shooting it. Instead, rely on the gauge. If you shoot an extinguisher, even for a short burst, the pressure will slowly leave it over the next week or so. If you do not use it, the extinguisher will remain at full pressure for several years. I've had extinguishers that kept their fully charged state for ten years or more, so when you amortize the cost of an extinguisher over the life of the rental unit, the cost is virtually nothing compared to the protection they can provide. Large fires begin as small fires—and small fires are easy to put out with the right extinguisher.

If the fire extinguisher has been in the home for a year or so, gently shake it to mix the contents a little. Although shaking is not required, it's recommended to keep the contents from settling on the bottom.

If the gauge shows that the extinguisher's pressure is gone, replace it with a new one. Although many extinguishers can be repressurized, the cost of this service is almost as high as a new purchase, especially for small home extinguishers. Besides, the contents of new extinguishers are fresher and they tend to hold their pressure better than older ones that have been repressurized.

Smoke alarms and fire extinguishers are a lot like insurance: You hope they are a waste of money and that you never have to use them. Also consider installing carbon monoxide detectors if your home contains a fireplace or wood heater. Although carbon monoxide rarely is dangerous to the structure, your tenants can get sick or worse if they do not properly ventilate when they burn wood.

Every time you walk in and around your vacant house, look for loose carpet, weak door hinges, sagging flooring, loose stair steps, exposed wiring, and anything else that might pose a danger to tenants. Each house has a different layout and a different set of potential problems.

If the cable TV wire or phone cord is loose, buy a package of U-shaped staple tacks to secure the wiring along a wall. Keep in mind, however, that there are materials (such as Formica) that cannot be nailed or tacked. A few drops of clear glue along the wire, temporarily held against the wall with tape until the glue dries, will secure the wire in place.

If you own a two-story home or townhouse, make sure the stair railings are secure. If you need to install a handrail, buy a kit at a home-improvement store. Although many people do not realize they're for sale, handrail kits are available at most home-improvement centers.

> **TIP**
>
> Fasten loose wires to walls and baseboards.

If you follow these suggestions, your tenants will recognize that you take safety seriously. This adds to your image as a caring landlord, and the better renters will appreciate your style. You are showing that you care about them and the home. Landlords who do not maintain their properties and do not limit hazards around the house often attract tenants who have the same low concern for the property. Have you ever rented from someone who provided fire extinguishers? Some, but not all, states require them by law, but even in those states that do require them, many landlords and tenants don't think to get them. Providing a functional fire extinguisher will make you stand out in a crowded and somewhat lazy field of landlords. In addition to fire extinguishers, cover all bases with carbon monoxide detectors. These detectors can detect hazards that the human nose cannot pick up. Your renters will stay healthier if they are warned of carbon monoxide before the fumes affect them.

PAY ATTENTION TO THE EXTRAS

You are only looking for one good renter, but that good renter is worth some investment of your time. No matter how good or bad your area's rental market is, you are in constant competition with other landlords to rent to good people. You must make your home stand apart from the crowd. You are in business, and the renters are your customers. You must attract better quality, long-term, paying renters away from other landlords.

You might be surprised by how little it takes to make the home attractive to renters. By cleaning the home and adding inexpensive extras to the house, you draw more would-be tenants to your open houses. Whether your rent is slightly lower or higher than that of your competition (it should never be much different from a competing house, but remember that lower rent attracts more would-be renters), the property will speak for itself if you go the extra mile to distinguish your place from the others.

The key to owning and managing rental properties is to minimize the time and effort you put into them on an ongoing basis. To achieve this, you must invest a little extra effort up front, when preparing to show the home, thereby attracting the best renters you can find. Spend as much time as is necessary to turn the property into a clean, well-kept, welcome attraction to renters. The more renters you attract, the higher the minimum income and rental history standards you can set and the fewer problems you will have down the road. Wouldn't you rather put all your time into the home at one time, before renters move in, than spread a lot of time over several months of phone calls? When you prepare the home properly, you'll have more free time in the future to look for other homes to buy or to enjoy some free time.

Carpet Can Make the Home

You must vacuum the carpets and spot clean them where needed. Steam clean the entire carpet if soil and deep stains make it necessary. When tenants look at your carpet, they are not checking for dirt, although they will always see it if it is there. They are picturing themselves and their children lying with pillows and blankets on the floor in front of the television set.

Your rental will have no appeal if the carpet is stained and worn. Depending on the age of the house, the rent you are asking, and the time since your last renovation, your carpet might not be brand-new, and it doesn't need to be. But it must be clean, which is much more important to renters than the carpet's age.

Of course, if your carpet shows heavy signs of wear, or if its color or style is too dated, you should consider replacing it. When you buy carpet, look for traditional styles and colors. A nonsculptured, small nap, light tan carpet is always appropriate and goes with any tenant's furniture.

Look around for bulk discounts on carpet, especially if you have more than one rental property. Ask the carpet company's manager if you can find a durable style and color for a good price. If the manager will sell at a discount, buy more than you need. You will eventually use it. Leave your name and number with the store so they can call you if something comes in that fits in your price range.

After a while, every rental unit you own should have the same carpet. Think about the advantages of such consistency: If you ever need to replace the carpet in a room or a portion of a room (such as in a closet where the carpet was soiled beyond cleaning by oily shoes), you will have a matching remnant.

Carpet does not have to be expensive to have a nice look and feel. Your tenants are much more interested in its cleanliness than in its cost or style.

> **TIP**
>
> Replacing worn-out carpet will improve the rentability of your home by 300 percent.

Clean the carpet after each occupant leaves. The fresh smell and the uniform look of the nap will help attract new tenants. The sooner you get new tenants into a vacant home, the faster your pocketbook fills up.

Ceiling Fans Pay for Themselves

Install a ceiling fan in each bedroom and living area. Purchase fans with ample lighting so your tenants will be comfortable with the lights. Shortsighted landlords cringe at the thought of buying two or three ceiling fans for each rental house. But ceiling fans make a great first impression because they help fill the empty rooms. And tenants realize they can use the fans rather than the air conditioner on days that are merely warm rather than sweltering (ceiling fans cool rooms by approximately 7 degrees). Be sure to tell your tenants (perhaps in the New Tenant Information Sheet described in Chapter 3) about the reversible fan motion. Few people know that this feature helps warm cooler rooms.

Most inexpensive ceiling fans have attractive wooden or wicker blades. Many allow you to put different material on each side of the blade so you can get the look you want. These days you can purchase attractive ceiling fans with bronze or brass light kits for a reasonable price at most home-improvement or department stores.

Choose a ceiling fan appropriate to the size of the room. The number of blades (three, four, or five) really doesn't matter, but their width does. Typical sizes are listed below:

> **TIP**
>
> If you have more than one rental property, consider buying a carpet-cleaning machine or cleaning attachments for your current vacuum.

Fan Blade Size	Room Size
42 inches	up to 100 square feet
52 inches	100 to 400 square feet
56 inches	more than 400 square feet

Hang the fan eight to twelve inches from the ceiling. Anything closer will not allow the air to circulate properly.

Get a sturdy ladder and someone to help you hang your first ceiling fan. Before you start, make sure you flip the main breaker off or disconnect the fuses in the house. The first ceiling fan you install will be the most difficult; you will have no trouble with the rest. The instructions are easy to follow. Be sure that you hang the fan securely so it stays up. A loose fan could damage your ceiling and (worse) fall during use.

The only problem you might experience with a ceiling fan is noise. Every once in a while, you will install a fan that makes a rubbing noise as it spins. There are several things you can do to stop this noise. The first and easiest is to tape a quarter to the top of each blade, one at a time. If a blade is unbalanced, a quarter on the offending blade (or the one opposite to it, depending on the problem) often quiets the fan.

> ### TIP
>
> Buy a ceiling fan that features reverse motion. During the cold months, a backward spin helps distribute warm air in the room.

If the quarter trick does not work, you may not have hung the fan's body vertically in its bracket. A bubble balance will let you know whether the fan is exactly vertical. You may have to remove the cover that hides the hole in the ceiling to make sure you hung the fan according to the instructions.

If you simply cannot stop the noise, completely remove the fan and rehang it. Although this is an extreme solution—and rarely needed— it might do the trick if all else fails. Only after rehanging the fan a second time and finding that the fan still makes noise should you take it back to the store for a replacement.

Miniblinds Boost the Visual Value

Miniblinds spruce up a home's windows; they last for years, help conserve energy, and look great. Most renters will not hang drapes in windows that already have miniblinds, preventing the window frames from getting drilled full of holes to put up cheap curtain rods.

Along with a clean, neutral carpet and ceiling fans, miniblinds impress would-be renters. Not only do miniblinds look good, they sound even better in your newspaper rental advertisement (not many landlords will bother to install miniblinds; those who do will not think to put them in the ad).

Miniblinds are inexpensive at department stores and are adjustable for a range of window sizes. Be sure to take your window measurements with you when you shop. You will not find heavy-duty, designer miniblinds in a wide range of colors at a department store, but you don't want those anyway. Choose a neutral color, like cream.

Installing miniblinds is similar to installing ceiling fans—it's easy after the first one. If you make a mistake on your first attempt, chalk it up to experience.

Once you see a room with its windows covered by miniblinds, you will wonder why you never thought of them before. You may even want them in your own home if you don't already have them. They always look neat, they open and close easily, and they allow you to let in (or keep out) varying degrees of light.

THE OUTSIDE PRODUCES THE FIRST IMPRESSION

You should maintain the outside of your home as carefully as the inside. People will come back for your open house only if the outside is clean and tidy. When you prepare the home for showing, take along trash bags and put in them every piece of trash you find around the outside of the house.

Cut the lawn. You do not necessarily have to edge it or get rid of all the weeds, but the lawn should be mowed and look neat. Wash any dirty windows, repair holes in the screens, and make sure that working lightbulbs are in the front and back porch light fixtures. Leave these turned on for security while the home is vacant.

If your property has a garage, clean it thoroughly. When you show the house, interested renters will want to look in the garage. If a previous tenant left any oil on the floor, a bag of generic cat litter will absorb it; you should throw away old tires and anything else not nailed down. Your new tenants will want an empty garage with as much room as possible for their cars and storage.

Use Consistent Colors

If needed, touch up the exterior of the home with an outside-grade paint. Not only will your home look better, but the paint will help protect and extend the life of the wood. Light trim on a darker colored home is generally much more appealing than dark trim on a lighter home. Lighter trim increases your home's visual size by widening the look of the front.

If you have more than one rental property, try to paint each the same color. The theme of consistency prevails throughout this book. The best color to paint your rental house is the same color you paint your own home. As you add properties to your rental empire, paint them the same color, too. The only time this probably won't work is if you have two homes next to one another.

TIP

Paint every rental property you own the same color.

This tip alone will save you time and money. Whenever you need to touch up paint, you will always have an extra gallon of the right color in your garage. You might even consider buying it in bulk. With each house the same color, you will use up the paint over a period of several years, especially if you continue to purchase more rentals. Freezing affects many paints, so read the labels and store them properly.

This same advice holds true for the inside of the house. You do not have to paint everything in the house such as the trim, walls, and baseboards the very same color, but whatever color scheme you choose should be your choice for every home you own. Your renters will not know that every house is painted the same, and it does not matter if they do unless the houses are next to each other.

Being able to touch up paint and match the color at any time is a wonderful maintenance improvement. If you currently have one or more houses painted different colors, choose the color you like best. When you see paint for sale, take your color's match-up number (which appears on the last can you used) and stock up. The next time you paint another house, use that color. You will be glad you did.

Shutters Improve the Outside Appearance

A pair of white plastic shutters costs very little, never needs painting, takes eight minutes to install, and immediately makes a home look larger and friendlier. If you have a rental home without shutters, put them up now. You do not need them on the back windows, but place them on the front and on any side windows that are visible from the street.

Before you install shutters, stand back and take a good look at the outside of the home. After putting them up, look again. You will think you are looking at a different house. The need for shutters cannot be overemphasized, and yet many people would never think to put them on a rental house.

Plastic shutters have a wood-grain texture. You can install them with an electric drill and six sheet-metal screws (one in each corner and two in the middle). Select white shutters. They will go with any color you ever paint the house, and they make white house trim come alive, especially on houses with a cream-yellow or colonial blue background. If you have extra wood shutters or get good buys on them, spray paint them twice and hang them firmly.

TIP

Plastic shutters last longer than wood shutters and need no maintenance.

There will be times when the effort you put into a rental house is reflected in your own home. One landlady thought the shutters looked so good on her rental house that she went out and bought some for the home she lived in. However, she fell into a trap common to owners: She bought the most expensive wood shutters the store had to offer because she didn't want to put the cheap plastic shutters on her own home. But after one of the shutters continually fell because of its weight and the wind, and after painting the shutters twice in two years, she had them ripped off and replaced with the same cheap plastic shutters she had used on her rental home. She has never had a shutter problem since. One more thing: Not one of her guests has ever, to her knowledge, walked up and knocked on a shutter to see whether it was plastic or wood. Nobody knows or cares whether you have cheap plastic or expensive wood shutters, but you will appreciate the plastic ones for many years to come.

The idea is that your rental properties should be important not only to you but to your tenants and their guests. If you treat your properties as well as you do your own home (which doesn't always mean buying the most expensive materials), you will attract better tenants—and better tenants take care of a home longer and cause fewer problems for you.

Flowers Draw More Renters

The day before your newspaper ad appears, buy planting flowers from the local discount store. Plant them in the ground in front of the home, or in attractive plastic outdoor planters, if you have a condo or apartment. You do not have to be a flower expert to cover a small area with color. You also do not have to maintain them. Good tenants will take care of the flowers once they move in.

Don't spend a lot of money on the flowers. But do buy one bag of soil and some peat moss to put around the plants. This shows that you put some care into the outside (even though it took very little time and money).

In the fall and early winter months, weed the flower beds and get rid of the dead flowers. A clean, empty flower bed with mulch looks better than one with weeds and dead flowers.

SUMMARY

You want tenants who will keep your house clean, but you must give them a clean house to begin with or you should not expect the same in return. If you follow the advice in this book—and, more important, if you learn to develop your own rental improvements and shortcuts—most of your tenants will leave the home cleaner and in better shape than when they moved in.

Beware of the attitude, "It's only a rental house, why should I put more effort or money into it?" The effort you put into your rental property is an investment—a good one. Put effort into making that home livable, clean, and safe. Put effort into finding good tenants who will take care of the home and who can pay the bills. Your tenants will only be as proud of your home as you are. The effort you put in up front and the money you invest in ceiling fans, miniblinds, shutters, and other extras will result in a house that is easy to rent to tenants who will stay a long time. Over the years, you will have fewer phone calls, fewer expenses, and a happier life of landlording.

Your tenants will love renting your house! They will live in a clean, like-new (but maybe old in actual age) home in which everything works. They will like their quiet neighborhood (the only kind you should buy in). And you will let them know they can call you and get respect. Most important, they will know that you are proud of your property and that you expect them to be proud of it as well.

CHAPTER THREE

Open House and Tenant Selection

YOUR OPEN HOUSE is today and the rental is ready for visitors. You cleaned the carpet, scrubbed the sinks, put up the shutters, installed the miniblinds, fixed the problems, and checked the appliances. You have made the home a showplace. When the time comes for open house, arrive early, turn on enough lights to brighten the rooms, open the miniblinds to show just enough of the outside to liven the rooms, and open an outside door for several minutes to freshen the air. You are now ready to welcome the guests.

You do not have to be the world's most outgoing person to present a good first impression. Remember, people are there to see the house—you are their secondary concern. Make them comfortable and answer their questions, but stay out of their way and do not come on too strong. Don't wear formal attire, but be well-groomed and casual. If you have prepared the home properly, it will sell itself. When the lookers are ready for the next step, be there to hand them rental applications and describe your expectations of tenants.

This chapter focuses on the open house and also explains how to select tenants from the prospects that apply. After the open house, you should be left with a stack of applications. You must sift through the applicants in a fair and legal manner, attempting to find the best qualified to live in your home.

DURING YOUR OPEN HOUSE

Stay alert: During your open house, you must be aware of many things. Be friendly to your guests but not pushy. Keep an eye on children without seeming to dislike them (you would be surprised what damage boisterous children can do!). If your property has outside stairs, make sure they are free from obstacles that could cause people to fall.

During the open house, appear professional but casual. Don't look too dressy unless you're offering a high-end property. Don't dress down: You want to appear professional so would-be tenants know that you are able to respond quickly if there are problems with the property. Don't drive a car that's considered by the average renter of your kind of property to be too fancy; you don't want to appear as the rich landlord (even if it's true!). Be courteous, but allow the would-be tenants to look around the home on their own. Be there to answer questions, point out the property's good points after they've had a chance to look it over, but don't be pushy. If you've prepared the house the way this book suggests, your home will sell itself—you'll merely be a guide.

Putting a sign on the front door during the open house that reads "Come in!" is a nice touch. If you're talking to other guests when new guests arrive, you won't have to interrupt the conversation to answer the doorbell or a knock. You might say, "Thanks for coming by, feel free to look around and [...]ns you may have. Here is an information sheet t[...]ls." Hand them a sheet that describes the rent, d[...] es-sentials (most of which were in your ad if [...]per advertisement), then let them go from there[...]

Put salt on the steps and porch if ice [...] problem. If the weather is snowy or rainy, [...] doormats both outside and in. You do not [...] the first looker to soil the carpet, because [...] will reflect poorly on you no matter how often you explain it. Hard rain requires that you have a spare umbrella on hand for the open-house guests who want to look at the backyard. I have

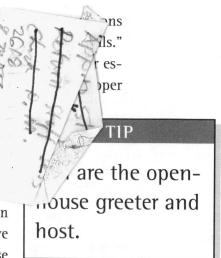

TIP

[...] are the open-house greeter and host.

not found weather to be a huge factor during open houses: Just as many people seem to show up during good weather as during bad. It has been my experience that if the ad is effective and the property is priced fairly, there will be plenty of open-house guests.

Thank everyone as they leave, even those who seemed to take no interest in your property. This is basic courtesy; you should respect everyone who takes the time to attend the open house. In addition, a little friendliness on your part might win people over who are on their way to see another property with a less pleasant landlord. As they leave, tell them about the next open-house date (if you plan one or feel there is a chance you will need one) and wish them well in their house hunting. Show them they can come back simply to ask more questions if they wish, without feeling like they're imposing. The more time they spend with you is less time they will spend at a competing property and the more likely you'll win that tenant.

As prospective tenants view the home, answer all their questions as fully and truthfully as you can. These people need to

> **TIP**
>
> Show copies of past utility bills that represent typical high- and low-usage months.

know as much as possible about the house to make a wise decision. This may be their home for the next few years, and the more interested they are in it, the more they will want to know about it.

Ask the previous tenants or the local utility companies to give you copies of a few utility bills for summer and winter. When you fixed up the home for rent (you will find lots of improvement tips in Chapter 11), you made sure there was adequate insulation, and the utility bills will demonstrate this. If your home is in close competition with another, the lower utility bills may make the difference.

THE RENTAL APPLICATION

Do you use rental applications or guesswork for tenant selection? You may be surprised at the number of landlords who select tenants without using rental applications. These landlords have only vague criteria for renting, usually coming down to who wants it first or who has the most expensive clothes or the flashiest car. There are several problems with choosing rentals this way. You run the risk of renting to someone with inadequate (or no) income, or even worse, someone with a poor rental history (property damage, drug use, and so on). The most critical problem is the legality of such a free-form system.

Smart landlords take precautions against legal headaches. This book is not a substitute for a good attorney, but it has lots of advice for avoiding legal problems. You open yourself up to discrimination lawsuits if you do not set rental standards, follow those standards, and show proof that you did so.

The rental applications that you will request from potential renters help show that you were fair and impartial when you finally decided upon a tenant. You may never be called into court for discrimination, but if you are, a stack of applications goes a long way toward proving how you made your choice.

It is possible (and recommended) to discriminate legally, as long as you show that you were fair across all applicants. You know that, according to the Fair Housing Act, you cannot discriminate on the basis of race, creed, religion, or physical impairment. If you do, you will almost certainly be challenged at some point in your landlording career, and you will be hard-pressed to defend yourself.

There are many forms of discrimination that are not as severe and are perfectly legal. The rental application can supply the information you need to make a final decision based on these other factors. You will need to decide how many, if any, pets you let your tenants own. If you allow pets, you can limit the size and type of animal. You can suggest no children (your ad should read, "Prefer adult tenants only"), but you cannot discriminate against them. You can, however, place a limit on the number of people living in the house (two per bedroom is a standard maximum, but check local statutes).

> **TIP**
>
> Keep all rental applications for at least two years.

You can require that a tenant net or gross a certain level of income. Many landlords require a monthly income of two or three times the monthly rent. Smoking, criminal history, and rental recommendations are legitimate considerations as well.

As a rule of thumb, guard against anything and everything the law specifically states is discrimination and be fair and consistent about the other requirements you impose. You will find the best information on discrimination at your local library, where you can look at a copy of your state's Landlord and Tenant Act (most states either have such a statute or follow a neighboring state's policy) as well as the federal Fair Housing Act.

> **TIP**
>
> Go to the library and photocopy your state's Landlord and Tenant Act.

Some landlords do not rent to unmarried couples. This policy has been upheld by some courts and rejected by others. If you follow this policy, you might have a difficult time justifying why you rented to two unmarried women or two unmarried men the following week. Two-parent families are often more financially secure and stable, so most landlords would like to have them as tenants. But in this day and age, a two-parent family is not always going to be available.

A fenced-in backyard (and allowing a dog or cat) attracts more families than an open backyard. The stability of the tenants over the years repays the cost of the fence. A garage appeals to families, but if you don't have a garage, consider installing a low-cost carport if room is available on the side of the house or in the driveway.

If you do rent to unmarried couples or to two people of the same sex, each tenant on the lease should qualify individually. A married couple's stability and legal bond lessens that requirement's importance and makes it easier for you to justify renting to families if that is your intent. If one party of an unmarried couple does not meet your financial and rental history requirements, that person cannot live in the house. In fact, if one does not qualify, then the couple does not either because a lease is inseparable.

Too often, one person in an unmarried relationship decides to split, leaving the other with the lease and the rent payments. Both parties are equally responsible; you have full legal recourse to go after whomever is left holding the rent for the full amount of the lease. Of course, the same can happen with a married couple but, again, the legal marriage bond gives you more stability and more legal room to collect from the person who leaves.

I know of one landlord who supplies neither a refrigerator nor a stove. He says that he only gets a certain level of interested renters due to the fact that lower-income tenants don't often own such appliances. I don't agree with that tactic, although it seems to work well in his area. I have had extremely good tenants and only a handful of them had their own refrigerator, and to my knowledge none of them had a stove. People generally only purchase these large appliances once they buy a home, and previous homeowners rarely turn to renting again. The best all-time tenant I have known—*me* when I rented apartments as a young adult while owning a house that I rented out to others—never had a stove or a refrigerator until I bought my first home to live in. I think you will lose too many decent applicants if you don't supply a stove and a refrigerator. The home's area and the level of competition for renters dictates which other appliances, such as a dishwasher, are optional and which are not optional.

Figure 3-1 shows a sample rental application that works well. Adjust the application to suit the circumstances of your own property. Tell each applicant to fill in all the blanks that apply. Take plenty of applications and pens with you to your open house.

FIGURE 3-1. A sample rental application

```
** Application For Rent **
1013 SOUTH ILLINOIS, MIAMI, FLORIDA 41127
** PERSONAL INFORMATION **
Name:_____ Social Sec. #_____
Phone:_____ Address:_____ How long?_____
Landlord:_____ Phone:_____ Rent: $_____
Previous address:_____
Landlord:_____ Phone:_____
Previous rent: $_____ How long?_____
Pets?_____ How many, what kind?_____ Smoker?_____
List names of each person who will live here: _____
_____
Emergency name and phone:_____


** WORK INFORMATION **
Occupation:_____ Present employer:_____
How long?_____ Gross income: $_____ Supervisor:_____
His/her phone:_____
Previous employer:_____ Supervisor there:_____
Other sources of income:_____


** BANKING INFORMATION **
Savings bank and acct. #_____ Checking acct. #_____
Credit card: Type:_____ Acct. #_____
Credit Reference: Name:_____ Acct.#_____


** AUTOMOBILE INFORMATION **
Car makes:_____ Models:_____ Years:_____
Financed where?_____
```

***The above statements are accurate. By signing this application, I author-
ize reference disclosure for purposes of leasing the property at the address
listed above.

Signature:_____ Date:_____

Note: ID is required with this application. This speeds the process and
guards against possible problems later.

Let the applicants know that they can either fill out the application on the spot or they can fill it out later and bring it back. Applicants who are in a hurry can relax, since they don't have to fill out the application immediately. Also, many people will not have with them all the information you request. You should consider bringing a local telephone book with you to help applicants find phone numbers. This makes your job easier later because you won't have to look up information the tenant did not remember, such as addresses or phone numbers.

Letting prospects take the application with them also gives an easy out to people who cannot afford your rental, who do not like your house, or who were just looking around to test the waters. They will not feel obligated to apply. Many will take an application and never return it; you might not want to rent to them anyway. People with lousy rental histories rarely want you to know about their former landlords. Such renters are looking for the landlord who does not ask for references.

Most people will probably fill out the application at the open house. Many will want to rent your home and will have no problem applying then and there. As they turn in the applications, you must ask for one more item: You must check their identification to make sure the application matches the applicant. State on the application that you will do this (as shown in Figure 3-1) so they will not be caught off guard. Pleasantly explain to them that you trust them, but occasionally people fill out an application falsely, for someone completely different with a good credit history (such applications check out, but the renters often end up being unable to pay).

If would-be tenants balk at the idea of filling out an application, don't rule them out without explaining why you need the application. Many people have rented several houses and have never had to fill out an application. They might hesitate because they're suspicious of what you'll do with the information on the application. Explain that car rental companies would not rent a car without a credit check or a valid credit card and that your home is worth much more than a car. Let them know that you could not turn over your home to people you don't know without checking their rental and financial histories. Explain that you will use the information only to select renters and that the information will remain confidential. If applicants still don't want to fill out an application, tell them that they can probably find another landlord who does not use applications and thank them for coming anyway.

> **TIP**
>
> Request identification with each application turned in to you.

As you meet people and collect applications, you will make some initial judgments (but do not make a final decision until you verify the applications). If you feel that certain candidates can pass your minimum requirements, casually tell them before they leave that you need everyone who will be on the lease to see the home before you make a final rental decision. This will typically be a spouse or a roommate. More than once, half of a couple wants the home, but after you cancel the next day's open house and the newspaper ad, the other half, who sees the house later, doesn't want it. If you can get both people to the property during open house, and if they both like the place, your chances of landing and keeping them increase.

Checking the Application

Most landlords do not subscribe to a credit-checking agency, because it's expensive unless you pass the charge onto each interested looker. The general rental market is very competitive and your tenants will not expect to pay for a credit check except in high-demand areas. If you feel you must subscribe to a credit-checking service, you will have to pass the cost onto the prospective tenants. Many will not pay the credit-check fee. Ease the burden of those who are interested by refunding the fee to the applicant to whom you rent and explaining that you will do so when prospects apply.

The Internet, however, provides a way for you to pull up a credit report quickly and inexpensively. You'll learn about the Internet in Chapter 13, "Can the Internet Help Landlords?". You can request a credit check in a matter of minutes. You'll have to register and show a legitimate reason for needing someone else's credit report. As a landlord, you have that legitimate reason. You can also access the services of a credit-reporting agency by telephone, but you will not receive the reports as quickly or as cheaply as you can online.

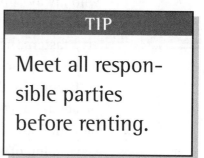

TIP

Meet all responsible parties before renting.

Even if you do not use a credit-checking service, your applicants have no idea whether you do or not. Luckily, most people are fairly honest on their applications. If you are good friends with a real estate agent or a banker, he or she may be able to perform a credit check for you, but do not count on it. Typically, they must have a valid reason to request a credit report, and a favor for a friend is difficult to justify.

The most important information that applicants supply is their previous rental history. No matter how good their income is, or how small their expenses are, their former landlord is the best reference possible. He or she should tell you whether the tenants paid on time and whether they left the home in good, clean condition.

If applicants hesitate to give you their current landlord's name and number, that does not always signal that they are bad renters.

Actually, good tenants feel bad that they are leaving their landlord; they don't want to "break the news" until they know for sure that they have another place. Explain to the applicants that you will only request a "credit check" from their current landlord, without indicating that it is an inquiry for a new rental. I've had many tenants call to tell me sadly they are leaving. Assuming they have kept their part of our lease, I let them know that I regret their leaving but I wish them well. Of course, I also tell them that I pay a finder's fee for recommendations I rent to, so they should let me know if they know of anyone looking for a home to rent.

Keep in mind, too, that there are unscrupulous landlords who always give other landlords excellent references for their bad tenants. This practice gets the tenants out of their property faster. The selection of a tenant is not a science, and you must weigh several factors.

Driving by the applicants' current residence can tell you a little about how they take care of it. If your tenants are supposed to mow their own yard, you will get an idea of how well they would stay on top of mowing. A car or two up on blocks will show you what your property could look like. The current fair housing laws actually give you permission to inspect the *inside* of a prospective tenant's residence, but they require one stipulation that can haunt you if you don't follow the guidelines: If you don't inspect each and every applicant's current home and you refuse to rent to one based on your inspection, you open yourself up to a discrimination suit. Since you cannot possibly inspect the inside of every applicant's home, it's better to avoid this practice.

Call the applicant's employer to make sure the applicant has worked for the duration and in the capacity stated on the application. Not all employers give salary information, but you can ask whether the salary specified on the application is "within the salary range." The longer that applicants have worked in their current company, the more stable they are. Be sure to ask for the payroll department or the primary payroll clerk. Many an applicant has been embarrassed when the person who happened to answer the credit-check phone call leaked the employee's salary information.

Call the applicant's bank to ensure the account information is correct. Ask the bank to tell you how long the account has been open. Generally, banks will not give specific balances over the phone, but they will verify account numbers and will usually tell you the age of the account. Be sure to verify any loans the applicant told you about and ask whether there are any others. If you do business with that bank, you may have leverage to learn additional information.

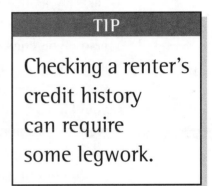

TIP

Checking a renter's credit history can require some legwork.

You have no way to verify a lot of the information on the application, but ask for it just the same. Although applicants might leave a few lines blank, usually they'll try to be as complete as possible, especially if they like your property and have a good credit history. The good news is that better tenants fill out more complete applications—they have less to hide!

It is extremely difficult to compute an applicant's net income. You should base your minimum income levels on gross income unless you have access to a credit-reporting agency with very accurate records. Most applicants will underestimate their expenses without intending to lie, because it is difficult to remember every little expense. About the best you can hope for is a solid gross income and a responsible tenant.

You cannot discriminate against renters based on physical handicaps. Of course, many owners realize that people who are self-sufficient but who have a handicap often make excellent tenants. Depending on when your property was built, you may have to conform to the regulatory requirements of the Americans with Disabilities Act (ADA). The ADA is quite strict, often requiring expensive building changes to accommodate people with disabilities. I'm someone who might be considered "obviously and physically disabled" by the bureaucracy behind the ADA due to several handicaps, but I believe the ADA intrudes unnecessarily on people's daily lives. As a rental property owner, however, we must pay attention to the law's far-reaching implications. Take my advice when I tell you that you need to check out the federal, state, and local ADA ordinances that affect your property before you consider it ready to rent. The ADA's requirements are growing exponentially as each year goes by; if you ignore it, do so at your own peril. For information about how the ADA affects your kind of rental business, call the hotline at (800) 514-0301 to request information. The ADA's Web site (*www.usdoj.gov/crt/ada/adahom1.htm*) is quite comprehensive, too.

Do not bring up HIV, AIDS, or other serious illnesses on applications or when deciding between tenants. You cannot ask for such information and you cannot use the information in your decision if you already know about it. Some landlords may fear the presence of infectious diseases in their multi-unit dwellings, but at this time the law does not allow you to ask prospective tenants about this subject.

If two or more applicants have adequate rental histories and both seem equally qualified to rent your property, rent to the one who applied the earliest to show that you were impartial. This is not a law, but it is wise to do everything you can to avoid legal hassles, and the first-come, first-served rule further demonstrates your impartiality. Be sure to call the other qualified applicants to let them know your decision and tell them you would like to keep their applications on file for a while. Ask them whether you may call them if the chosen applicant decides against renting the home or the next time a vacancy comes up.

Keep all of that vacancy's applications together, even after deciding on a tenant (the date on each application will show the time period). You want to have a full record of each candidate's application. On the top application in the stack, attach a page that explains your rental policy and the selection criteria (the minimum income level and so forth) you used during that application period.

Do not feel obligated to hold the second day's open house if you select a tenant from the first day's applicants. You would only be wasting your time as well as that of the other people who walk through the house. A small sign in the window saying "Sorry, but this home is already rented" takes care of the lookers who come by the next day. Be sure to cancel your newspaper ad as soon as you inform the new tenant of your decision.

Although your new tenants will probably have to give notice to their current landlord, if they have not done so already, you must get a deposit from them as soon as you can to hold the home. When you inform applicants that you have selected them, ask to meet with them to get the deposit and discuss the lease. The applicants do not actually have to sign the lease then, but you can go over some of the lease's details when you get the deposit. You will need to agree on the exact terms of the lease (the day of move-in, the day rent is due, and so forth) before you can write the lease.

Discussing the Deposit

Explain to the new tenants that the deposit means you will hold the home for them and rent it to nobody else. However, you should also explain that the deposit is nonrefundable *if they back out of the deal.* Once the lease goes into effect, the deposit will become their refundable security/cleaning deposit; but until they sign the lease, the deposit is for your mutual protection. It keeps you from renting to someone else and keeps them from changing their minds.

Be sure to check local ordinances for deposit limits. Most states limit the amount you can charge. Many landlords rightfully question such laws, but you are stuck with them. Certainly, you do not want to be sued over charging a deposit that is too high.

The sooner you get the deposit and agree to the details of the lease, the sooner you will rest easy that another job is almost done. Wait to get the deposit in your hands before telling the other applicants you rented the home; if the tenant and the deposit fall through, you will still have a backup applicant. Of course, courtesy dictates that you do not keep people waiting more than a day or two for your decision.

I like to get a cash deposit, but many tenants prefer to write checks and I let them. If given a choice, take the cash. The cash helps lock the tenants into your place even more than a check they can stop payment on. I always go straight to the tenant's bank and cash the deposit check if the bank is nearby and open. I've never had a problem with a bad deposit, but if there's going to be one I want to know before the tenant begins moving in.

Place the deposit in a special *escrow* account. This precaution alone awards more court judgments in the favor of the landlord than any other thing you can do. The deposit your tenant gives you *is not your money.* You cannot spend it for any reason unless the tenant moves out and violates the lease's deposit description. Be sure to specify that the deposit is for *cleaning and security.* If you do not specify this, tenants can claim it is a cleaning *or* a damage deposit only (they will choose the opposite of the one they violated).

The only thing you can do with the deposit during the tenant's entire tenancy is put it in an escrow bank account. This sounds intimidating if you have never done it before, but it is easy.

Typically, all you do is open an account with your name followed by the word *escrow*, like this:

Julie G. Wilson – Escrow

The day you get the deposit, place it in your escrow account. There's nothing to keep you from withdrawing the money any time you want, because you are the owner of the account. The bank will not stop you. However, the escrow account shows a judge, if needed, that you put the deposit money aside separately from your own money. Putting the deposit in an escrow account costs you nothing and guarantees that the deposit will be there when the tenant moves out. It does not mean the tenants will receive the full amount, or any of it at all if they leave the home damaged or in disarray. Escrowing the deposit simply puts the tenant's money away until the legal time comes (after move-out) for you to decide how much to return to the tenant.

Since so few landlords escrow deposits, a judge has a surefire way of determining how accurate and lawful a landlord is. Although it takes much more to win an eviction lawsuit, proof of an escrowed deposit helps your case a great deal. If you do not escrow the deposit, you commit a misdemeanor.

> **TIP**
>
> Get a full deposit immediately after choosing a tenant.

You can keep any interest earned from the escrowed deposit. Some landlords give this to the tenant as well, especially if the deposit is high relative to that of competing homes. Of course, this interest is income and if you keep it, you must report it as such. I always keep the escrowed interest, but it never amounts to much. If I were to rent high-priced homes—something that I wouldn't do very much because the rental investment potential in them is so poor—I'd want to return to my renters at least one-half, and possibly all of the interest the deposit earned, so that would-be tenants wouldn't balk at a high deposit. If I didn't return all of the deposit because of something the tenant left in bad condition, I'd return interest earned only on the part of the deposit that I return.

Consider keeping your deposits in a high interest–bearing account. I keep my deposits in a long-term account that pays higher interest than regular savings. I'm penalized if I withdraw the money, but I don't have to worry about that, as I'll explain. As I buy additional properties and rent them, I place the deposit in the account for each property. If I increase a deposit, I place the difference in the account. When a tenant moves out, I simply refund the deposit from my other funds. I've held the tenant's deposit in the special account and I can withdraw (with a large interest penalty) from the escrow account if necessary, but I have never had to. The long-term account not only separates the deposit from my regular funds but the interest is higher than a regular savings, and I've protected the tenant's original deposit better than most landlords do. A money market fund might be a good place to park deposit money because you won't be making frequent withdraws from the account as you might a regular checking account. The money market holds its principal and usually pays higher interest than other savings and checking accounts. The *Wall Street Journal*, often in its Thursday editions, lists the highest money market rates in the country, along with phone numbers you can call to get new account applications.

By the way, if I had a policy that returned the interest earned on the deposit, I'd probably return the fair market value of interest on a

> **TIP**
>
> Don't pocket the deposit; hold it in escrow.

standard savings account. If you go to the trouble of opening a money market account, you deserve to keep the bonus interest the account earns.

Some landlords like to give tenants a price list of repairs, such as an hourly cleaning and painting charge or the price of replacement keys, window screens, and even lightbulbs. The landlord can use such a list to help ensure against damaging move-outs. When the tenant knows how fast the deposit will be eaten up by cleaning and painting, you are more likely to get the property back in good shape when the tenant leaves.

Wrap Up the Details

You also want to find out the name of each person who will be on the lease. Explain that each person on the lease is responsible for the full rent, even if the others move out. The more people on the lease, the safer you are. In addition, verify the number of adults and children who will be living in the home. Put this number into your lease in case you later find out the tenant has moved some relatives in and forgotten to tell you! In most cases, you would be wise to get a credit application for all the parties on the lease, including unmarried couples.

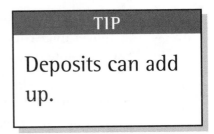

TIP

Deposits can add up.

Do not turn over the key until you receive the first month's rent. This is critical: If you turn over the key earlier, your tenant can legally move in and take possession. Most landlords require a deposit to hold the property, then turn the key over on the date of the signing of the lease and the payment of the first month in full. This ensures that your tenants have a reason to take care of the home (you hold the deposit), and you have the first month's rent instead of an empty promise. Chapter 4, "Welcoming Your New Tenant," explains in detail the process of turning over the key. The deposit is enough to hold the home until the tenant meets you with the first month's rent. Keep in mind my earlier advice about driving directly to the tenant's bank to cash the deposit check—if that first check bounces, you do not yet have a tenant.

SUMMARY

Successful landlords show properties only once, understand how to use rental applications, and take the time to process applications in a legal and orderly fashion. At your open house, you are there simply to answer questions; you let the home show itself. If tenants show interest, ask them to fill out a rental application and have plenty of pens handy.

One of the easiest ways to avoid legal problems is to choose your tenants carefully and fairly. Check the local ordinances governing rental properties. Determine the legal minimum rental standards that an applicant must meet to rent your property. If you have more than one rental house, each one can have different rental standards depending on monthly rent, size, and layout.

Once you decide on the tenants after checking out the information on their application, you must prepare them for their stay in your rental. Set up an initial meeting at the house and walk through all your rent procedures and expectations. The next chapter explains how to start off on the best foot with your new tenants.

CHAPTER FOUR

Welcoming Your New Tenant

AT THIS POINT, the difficult part of rental ownership is over. After preparing your rental beautifully for open house, you probably had a hard time choosing from the many well-qualified applicants. As you're beginning to see, landlording is rewarding and actually generates pride of ownership when you properly prepare a home, write an effective newspaper ad, and hold a productive open house.

By the time you sift through all the applicants and decide on the proper tenant, your work is almost done. After you let the tenant know of your decision to rent, you have one final but very important job to do—perform the new-tenant interview.

Your tenants are a captive audience when you meet with them to hand over the house keys and have them sign the lease. It is during this time that you want to set the ground rules for the tenants' stay. Sign an effective and binding lease, outline your rent expectations, describe your tolerance for noise and property damage (none), and explain your maintenance policies to your new houseguests.

This chapter focuses on the steps you must take to ensure as carefree a landlording career as possible. The tenants want the home, you selected the best candidates (by following the tips in Chapter 3), the tenants paid the deposit—and you are almost ready to take a breather from your landlording responsibilities.

PRESENT THE NEW TENANT WITH A VACANT HOME

Perhaps it goes without saying, but you must ensure that the premises are vacant at the time your tenant is to take possession of the property. No matter what the lease says, and no matter what you and the tenant agree to at the open house, if the tenant is unable to move in because the house is not vacant, the tenant can terminate the lease and has full rights to the deposit. An interesting side note is that if a former tenant still has possession illegally, either you *or* your new tenant can sue to evict the illegal possessor. Obviously, though, getting the previous tenant out is really your responsibility.

The New Tenant Interview

Select a time when both you and the new tenants have half an hour or so to discuss the details and sign the lease. The new tenant interview is vital. Without it, your relationship with your tenants will be more strained; with it, you start off together on the right foot. Nothing but time will guarantee wonderful tenants, but the time you spend on the initial interview will pay in dividends throughout their tenancy. I always offer to meet the new tenants at a location that is most convenient to them, perhaps halfway between work and home, or at a café, or at the home they are about to rent (if it is vacant). I want to show them that I am available and attentive to their schedule. I maintain a business relationship, but the relationship is always a friendly one. This is easy because the new tenants are almost always excited about the prospect of moving into a new home.

The new tenant interview gives you the chance to meet your tenants one-on-one. If a tenant has a family, attempt to get both husband and wife at the interview. Not only will two remember details better than one, but getting both signatures on the lease is better than getting only one. Of course, if you are renting to more than one unmarried party, you must meet with all of them since each must sign the lease.

TIP

Treat the new tenant interview as a business meeting. Set priorities and goals, receive the first month's rent, sign the lease, and state your requirements clearly.

Below is a list of items to cover in the new tenant interview, all of which we will discuss in this chapter:

- Welcome the tenants.
- Review the details of the lease.
- Sign the lease (two copies: one for you, one for the tenants).
- Accept the first month's rent.
- Turn over the keys. Stamp the keys with a "Do not duplicate" warning so that other locksmiths will not duplicate the key. Such warnings help keep extra keys out of circulation when your tenants move out (although it's not a guarantee that they won't be copied), and you can track more accurately the number of keys you've given out for each property.
- Discuss the rent-collection policy.

- Review the walk-through checklist plus any other information you want to share with the tenants.
- Show the new tenants the location of smoke alarms, the fire extinguisher, the toilet plunger, and the utility shutoffs for the electricity and water.
- Walk through the house and around the outside with the tenants to acclimate them to the home.

This is the tenants' first and last chance to understand your requirements. They may not fully realize that fact unless you someday have to evict them. Hopefully, the eviction process and your tenants will never meet. Nevertheless, make sure every tenant on the lease understands what you expect. Be friendly but businesslike during the interview. This is the tenants' last chance to back out or to agree to your terms.

> **TIP**
>
> State your do's and don'ts in the tenant interview.

Suppose someday down the road a neighbor calls to complain about loud parties, trash, property damage, excessive drinking, or even drug use on your property. Take care to check out the facts before you act harshly. If the neighbor's complaint has merit, your eviction procedures should be swift and firm. Chapter 7, "Handling Tenant Problems and Problem Tenants," explains the process of eviction. Invariably, such problem tenants will ask for a second chance. But there is no room for a second chance with extreme behavior, especially if good relations with good neighbors are important to you, and they should be. When you give such behavior second chances, you only help condone and promote the activities. You do your neighbors a disservice if you do not act against such behavior. Be sure that you can look tenants in the eye at such time and state that their second chance was during the new tenant interview when you told them you could not and would not tolerate illegal or disruptive behavior.

During the interview, explain that the lease dictates your objections to certain behavior. Spell out that you will never tolerate loud parties, unapproved animals, any illegal activity, and all the other policies you may want to list. Tell the tenants that you like them and that their rental history was excellent, or you would not have rented to them. Stay friendly while listing your requirements. A good line to begin with is, "I don't necessarily think you will participate in such activities, but I tell these things to all my new tenants. I want to let you know what I will do if you *(fill in with your list of pet peeves)* or if you miss your rent payment one time."

Introducing the do's and don'ts this way takes the personal aspect out of the discussion. You are telling your tenants that you trust them fully. However, you do not know them very well yet, and to be safe, you tell all your first-time tenants what you expect from them and what they should expect from you. This also gives you the chance to put your actions down on paper in the form of the lease.

Attempt to arrive early to the new tenant interview. This shows how serious you take your property management. Being "fashionably late" is rude to your new tenants and shows sloppiness on your part. Don't expect your tenants to come through if you don't shine.

TWO COMMON LEASE AGREEMENTS

There are two types of rental agreements that landlords use most commonly, and you should make either available depending on your area and your home's rentability. Most rentals require a typical six-month to one-year lease. The other common type is a month-to-month lease. If you and your tenants do not sign a lease agreement, a generic month-to-month lease is implied in most states. Your state's Landlord and Tenant Act (a copy of which is available at the local library) will verify this.

There are advantages to each kind of lease. A long-term lease, whether it is for six months, one year, or longer, locks in the rent amount for the tenant. You will not be able to raise the rent during the lease period, unless of course the lease provides for such a contingency. Locking in the rent lets your tenant forecast costs over the coming months without fear of a rate increase. This is attractive to many renters, especially those in areas of high housing demand.

Some tenants prefer a month-to-month agreement. With this kind of lease, each month either you, your tenant, or both have the right to change any terms of the lease; you can even write a brand-new lease with completely different stipulations. However, if the other party does not agree to change the lease, the original agreement is considered complete and either party has the right to give thirty days' notice to the other.

> ## TIP
>
> A long-term lease protects the rent amount for tenants and implies longer occupancy for your property. A month-to-month lease is attractive to good tenants whose job or family requirements favor relocation soon.

Many landlords fear a month-to-month lease, but such leases are a little more effective in some areas, especially those parts of the country with low renter demand. A month-to-month lease gives tenants the opportunity to move any time, with no strings attached, with only thirty days' notice. Many tenants like this freedom. What they do not always realize is that without a longer-term lease, you (the landlord) can increase rent rates as much and as often as you think the market will bear.

Some wise landlords give their new tenants a choice between a month-to-month lease or one that is longer term. To the landlord, there is really little difference, except that the month-to-month lease may require slightly higher rent since it is short term. Just as a bank will pay higher rates for a long-term certificate of deposit than for regular savings, month-to-month landlords rightly need a slightly higher rent since the tenant can move with only a month's notice at any time. The risk to the landlord is greater with a month-to-month lease and a higher rent justifies the extra risk of more frequent move-outs.

Consider also the tenant who gets transferred or married or simply tires of your place and wants to move. Even a long-term lease will not keep such a tenant in your home. Despite the lease, the tenant will move out and most courts will only award you damages for the time it took you to find a new tenant to replace the one who broke the lease. You will probably not go to small-claims court over the matter anyway. Instead, cut your losses and put your energy into the more productive task of finding another tenant.

Inertia is another reason month-to-month leases are just as attractive to landlords as longer-term leases. Most people dislike moving. Once tenants move in with a month-to-month lease, the odds are good that they will stay for many months and maybe years. They like the

> **TIP**
>
> A month-to-month lease generally demands higher rents than longer-term leases for the same property.

freedom of the month-to-month and dislike moving. You will have justified higher rents since your vacancy risk is slightly higher, but most of the time, month-to-month tenants will stay just as long as those with longer-term leases.

Both types of leases are similar. They differ only in the payment amount and the termination of the lease. Both leases contain the same legal and landlord requirements.

The Contents of the Lease

The lease you and your tenants sign will be a binding, legal agreement. Take it seriously and show the tenants that you do. You do not have to be a lawyer to write an applicable lease, and your tenant does not have to be a lawyer to understand it. You can modify the sample lease (presented a little later in this chapter) to suit your own needs. A lease should simply answer the standard who-what-when-where-how questions:

Who are the tenants and the landlord?
What is being rented?
When will the tenant–landlord obligation begin and end?
Where will payments be made?
How are the landlord and tenants going to stay happy?

I go through my leases with my tenants *before* I give them a key. You do not have to read the entire contract to your tenants, but describe the highlights, even if it means walking through the lease paragraph by paragraph. This is the most important part of the new tenant interview. Everything you require should be in the lease. Although the lease binds both parties, current landlord and tenant laws favor tenants. It is not difficult for tenants to walk away from a lease, and many times (assuming the tenants leave your property in good condition), it will not be worth your time to go after them for the lost rent—lease or no lease.

A more detailed lease, as opposed to one that is less detailed, *generally* favors the landlord (you). The more you and your tenants agree to in writing, the more tightly bound the tenants are to your rental policies. Unless your lease contains unreasonable terms, tenants are likely to agree without reservations to your requirements.

> ### TIP
> Give tenants plenty of time to read the lease, but only after you discuss its every detail with them.

Not every clause in your lease has to be legally binding. Again, your lease must be reasonable, and it *is* a legal document. If you want the tenants to do anything, such as check the fire extinguisher's gauge weekly, state that in the lease. But if a blazing fire demolishes the house, there is probably little you can do to hold your tenants responsible if they did not check the extinguisher. Nevertheless, the gauge-check requirement in the lease gets tenants' attention—most people take seriously the documents to which they sign their name—and they will probably try to comply, thereby helping to maintain the safety of your property.

A Sample Lease

This section contains a sample residence lease agreement (see Figure 4-1). Modify the lease to suit your own needs. Over time, you will add and delete clauses, requirements, and details. Since tenants will sign the lease at the new tenant interview and you will go through it with them in detail, it's a good idea to include everything that you want the tenants to understand before they move in.

FIGURE 4-1. A residence lease agreement

Page 1 of 5   (initials) _____ _____

* RESIDENCE LEASE *

This lease, made and entered into this ___ day of _____, by and between _____, of _____, _____, hereinafter called the "landlord," and _____, of _____, _____, hereinafter called the "tenant."

The landlord owns the following described real estate and premises, situated in _____ County, _____:

_____

The landlord rents and leases to the tenant the described premises, from the ____ day of _____, for _____ months.

The tenant promises and agrees to pay the landlord as rental the total sum of _____ payable as follows: _____ for the security/cleaning deposit paid to landlord at the execution of this contract. The entire security/cleaning deposit will be refunded to the tenant within ten (10) days after tenant's normal lease termination or move-out, whichever comes last, if the property is left in move-in condition, and will be escrowed in a safety bank account until such time. The security/cleaning deposit's refundable amount will be prorated accordingly if the property is left in less than acceptable condition.

The sum of _____ is already paid for the first full month's rent of occupancy (_____). The sum of_____ payable on the first (1st) day of each and every month of the lease term (_____ full months) until this lease has expired to complete the full sum payable.

No part of said money shall be due and payable until the tenant has been placed in the actual possession of said premises with the keys needed to gain access. This has been done as of this contract's date.

FIGURE 4-1, cont. A residence lease agreement

Page 2 of 5   (initials) _____   _____

It is agreed that the tenant will keep and maintain all portions of the building let to him or her by the terms of this contract in as good a state of repair as the same are turned over to tenant. This means woodwork, walls, floors, ceilings, windows, screens, doors, carpet, shades, electric, grounds, plumbing, and outside storage, all of which may be inspected by the landlord on notice from the tenant of intent to vacate and in no event will this lease terminate unless the foregoing is acceptable to the landlord. Normal use without evident mars will not constitute violation.

The tenant agrees to be responsible to pay for the repair of any damage done to any of the buildings or grounds by any of tenant's family or guests. If the tenant notices any signs of property damage or signs of any negative physical attribute, including but not limited to water leaks, extreme floor or wall or ceiling cracks, insect infestation, appliance breakdown, or roof damage, the tenant will immediately notify landlord by phone or by written notice.

The tenant agrees to keep the property clean in and around the house and agrees to maintain proper sanitation of the area by preparing trash for pickup by the regular trash service of the surrounding neighborhood, unless other arrangements have been made and agreed to in writing by the owner.

The tenant agrees to keep the lawn, landscaping, trees, and shrubs neat, clean, mowed, trimmed, watered, and maintained as needed to ensure a healthy and visually appealing homestead, unless different arrangements have been agreed to in writing between landlord and tenant.

The tenant agrees to hold the landlord from any and all expense for lights, heat, water, or any other expense incident to the occupancy of said property, unless specifically agreed to in writing. The tenant agrees to keep these standard utilities connected and their corresponding bills paid in a timely manner as required by the following utility companies:

FIGURE 4-1, cont. A residence lease agreement

Page 3 of 5   (initials) _____   _____

_____

_____

If ANY utilities are not kept current, the tenant agrees to terminate this lease and give up the property's occupation at the landlord's discretion.

The tenant shall not engage in, or allow any other person, pet, or animal to engage in, any conduct that will disturb the quiet and peaceable enjoyment of the other tenants, neighbors, landlord, or use the property for any purpose whatsoever that violates the laws of the United States, the State of _____, or the City of _____.

The tenant will keep no pets of any kind, inside or outside the property, without a separate and written consent of the landlord.

Time is the essence of this contract, and should the tenant default in the payment of any installment of the principal sum herein named, the total principal sum shall become immediately due and payable and the landlord shall be entitled to possession of the premises, at landlord's option in accordance with the _____ Landlord and Tenant Act, and the landlord shall have the right to store and/or dispose of such property in accordance with said Act, and thereafter the tenant shall be liable to the landlord for any amounts uncollected from such disposition, and the expenses therefor, including a reasonable attorney's fee.

The property herein leased will be used for residential purposes only and for no other object or purpose and this lease shall not be sublet without the written consent of the landlord.

In the event of assignment to creditors by the tenant, or the institution of bankruptcy proceedings against the tenant, such events shall cancel and hold for naught this lease, and all the rights thereunder, and possession of said property shall immediately, by such act or acts, pass to the landlord at landlord's option.

FIGURE 4-1, cont. A residence lease agreement

Page 4 of 5   (initials) _____   _____

The tenant shall pay a late fee of _____ in addition to each monthly payment that is paid after the _____ day of any month within the terms of this lease. Starting on the _____ day of the month, a late fee of _____ per day will be added to the existing late fee due.

The tenant will waive tenant's rights under the _____ Landlord and Tenant Act if the rent and all late charges are not paid in full by the _____ day of the month, immediately relinquishing possession of the property to the landlord at the landlord's request.

The tenant agrees to pay all rents and fees with a personal check, money order, cashier's check, or cash. If a personal check is ever not honored by the landlord's bank, for any reason whatsoever, the tenant agrees to pay a check charge of ten dollars ($10) then pay with cash until the expiration of this lease term.

The tenant shall check each and all smoke alarms weekly, replacing the battery as needed with an alkaline battery to ensure that adequate warning is provided. Also, the fire extinguisher's gauge will be checked monthly to make sure the extinguisher gauge indicates a full charge of pressure.

The tenant agrees to keep the window screens on the windows at all times, paying a twenty-dollar ($20) service charge plus parts, if a screen is removed or damaged in any way, for its replacement.

The tenant will let no more than _____ guest(s) stay overnight for a maximum period of seven (7) consecutive days in any two-month period without written consent from the landlord. This limitation does _____ apply to immediate children of the tenant.

The tenant _____ keep any water-filled furniture at the property without the landlord's written consent.

FIGURE 4-1, cont. A residence lease agreement

Page 5 of 5   (initials) _____   _____

The tenant agrees to keep no more than _____ vehicles, including but not limited to trucks, motorcycles, and cars, on the premises. These vehicles must be both operable and currently licensed. The tenant agrees not to repair any vehicles on the premises if the repairs will take more than twenty-four (24) hours, without prior written consent from the landlord. Tenant agrees not to keep off-road vehicles, including but not limited to boats and trailers, without prior written consent from the landlord.

Landlord has obtained insurance to cover the landlord's interest and liability, but does not insure tenant's belongings or negligence.

The tenant will return any and all property-related keys upon lease termination and will give up five dollars ($5) per nonreturned key out of the security and cleaning deposit.

The tenant further agrees that after the expiration of the time given in this lease, the _____ day of _____, without notice from the landlord, to give possession of property to landlord, and upon tenant's failure to do so shall become liable to the landlord for an additional one-month extension of this contract upon notice from the landlord.

Contact the landlord at _____
(phone: _____).

IN WITNESS THEREOF, the parties hereto have hereunto set their hands the day and year first above written.

_____   _____

_____   _____
     (Landlord or Agent)   (Tenant(s))

Notice that the sample lease includes the following:

- The property address, date of signing, and landlord and tenant names are clearly stated. This information is critical for the lease to stand up in court, if necessary.
- The language is clear but specific. None of that "party of the first part" or "the rentor or rentee" legalese. The tenant is called the "tenant" and the landlord is called the "landlord." (You might want to change the term *landlord* to *owner.*)
- Most standard lease agreements include the total amount of money the tenant must pay over the life of the lease. This includes deposit money that might be refunded to the tenant at the lease's termination. The money paid at the date of signing and the monthly rent amount are also clearly stated in the early paragraphs. Spell out all dollar amounts to deter fraudulent changing of numbers.
- The late-payment penalties and the eviction rules upon nonpayment are specified.
- The lease is comprehensive, even down to the number of cars the tenants can have in the driveway.
- In the upper right-hand corner, both parties initial each page. The page number appears here, and the total number of pages is indicated as well.
- There is a location for the signatures of both landlord and tenant. If there is more than one tenant on the lease, each tenant should sign.

Depending on the layout of the home and the tenants' or your special needs, you may have to greatly modify this sample lease. Most landlords opt not to use the preprinted lease agreements available at office supply houses because they are too formal and rigid and contain too much convoluted language. By writing the lease yourself, you include the wording and requirements that suit your own situation.

To be safe, take your lease to an attorney for review before you offer it to the tenant. You will not necessarily have to get an attorney's opinion every time you make a change to the lease, but a trained eye should definitely look at the first pass. After that, show it to a lawyer only when you make major changes. (Or have the attorney review your lease changes as often as makes you comfortable. Some people's tolerance for risk-taking is greater than others'. Keep your leases legal, but keep your costs down as well.)

TIP

A lawyer's eyes are probably better than yours for reviewing your lease!

If you run the lease by an attorney, be sure to inform the lawyer that you want a lease that is clear to the layperson but is still binding. Tell your lawyer that some clauses are for effect and that you realize they may not be legal requirements, but you feel better including them in your lease. For instance, if tenants go too long without paying the rent, the sample lease states that they waive their rights under the state's Landlord and Tenant Act. In reality, people cannot sign away legal rights. Even after signing that lease, they still have those rights according to the laws of the land. Nevertheless, it is not illegal for you to ask them to waive their rights upon nonpayment, and if the paragraph encourages them to pay on time, so much the better.

As with contracts, leases are just pieces of paper as long as both parties fulfill their promises to each other. Most of the time, your lease is a legal, binding obligation that you'll never look at again. However, when a problem tenant pops up, you will be glad you included every foreseeable clause in the lease. The more you both agree to, the stronger your position becomes if you have to go to court.

When you meet with the tenants and review the lease, you or the tenants might spot an error or needed correction. Feel free to mark out any unacceptable wording or clauses that do not pertain to a certain tenant. Do this by drawing a line through the clauses in ink. Both you and the tenant should initial each marked-out passage in the margin next to the change.

If you opt for a month-to-month lease, only the financial conditions have to change. Instead of specifying the full multi-month rental terms, you only have to specify that the lease renews monthly. Still specify the deposit amount, late fees, and every other clause in the normal multi-month lease. For example, Figure 4-2 shows a month-to-month lease. Most of the clauses in both leases are identical except for the wording on rent payments and lease renewal.

Chapter 12, "Record Keeping and Computerizing Your Rental Properties," tells you how to use a computer, if you decide you need one. A computer is of greatest use to a landlord for lease writing and lease maintenance. Word-processing software makes changing the lease and printing it a breeze.

TIP

Nothing beats a computer at changing and printing your leases.

Retyping a lease from scratch every time you want to make a change takes too much time and is too prone to error. If you are the kind of person who will never use a computer, no matter how "easy" they have become to use, consider hiring a friend or word-processing service to keep your lease on their computer's file. When you need to change the lease, it can be done quickly and

FIGURE 4–2. A month-to-month residence lease

Page 1 of 5   (initials) _____   _____

* RESIDENCE MONTH-TO-MONTH LEASE *

This month-to-month lease, made and entered into this _____ day of
_____, by and between _____ of
_____, _____, hereinafter called the "landlord," and
_____, of _____,
_____, hereinafter called the "tenant."

The landlord owns the following described real estate and premises, situated in _____ County, _____:

_____

The landlord rents and leases to the tenant the described premises, from the
_____ day of _____, for each month thereafter, until thirty (30) days'
notice is properly served by either the landlord or tenant, onto the other.

The tenant promises and agrees to pay the landlord payments as follows:
_____ for the security/cleaning deposit paid to landlord at
the execution of this contract. The entire security/cleaning deposit will be
refunded to the tenant within ten (10) days after tenant's normal lease termination or move-out, whichever comes last, if the property is left in
move-in condition and will be escrowed in a safety bank account until
such time. The security/cleaning deposit's refundable amount will be prorated accordingly if the property is left in less than acceptable condition.
The sum of _____ is already paid for the first full month's rent
of occupancy (_____). The sum of _____ will be payable on
the first (1st) day of each and every month after this lease signing, until
notice is given by either the landlord or tenant to terminate this lease, by
serving thirty (30) days' notice to the other.

No part of said money shall be due and payable until the tenant has been
placed in the actual possession of said premises with the keys needed to
gain access. This has been done as of this contract's date.

FIGURE 4-2, cont. A month-to-month residence lease

Page 2 of 5   (initials) _____   _____

It is agreed that the tenant will keep and maintain all portions of the building let to him or her by the terms of this contract in as good a state of repair as the same are turned over to tenant. This means woodwork, walls, floors, ceilings, windows, screens, doors, carpet, shades, electric, grounds, plumbing, and outside storage, all of which may be inspected by the landlord on notice from the tenant of intent to vacate and in no event will this lease terminate unless the foregoing is acceptable to the landlord. Normal use without evident mars will not constitute violation.

The tenant agrees to be responsible to pay for the repair of any damage done to any of the buildings or grounds by any of tenant's family or guests. If the tenant notices any signs of property damage or signs of any negative physical attribute, including but not limited to water leaks, extreme floor or wall or ceiling cracks, insect infestation, appliance breakdown, or roof damage, the tenant will immediately notify landlord by phone or by written notice.

The tenant agrees to keep the property clean in and around the house and agrees to maintain proper sanitation of the area by preparing trash for pickup by the regular trash service of the surrounding neighborhood, unless other arrangements have been made and agreed to in writing by the owner.

The tenant agrees to keep the lawn, landscaping, trees, and shrubs neat, clean, mowed, trimmed, watered, and maintained as needed to ensure a healthy and visually appealing homestead, unless different arrangements have been agreed to in writing between landlord and tenant.

The tenant agrees to hold the landlord from any and all expense for lights, heat, water, or any other expense incident to the occupancy of said property, unless specifically agreed to in writing. The tenant agrees to keep these standard utilities connected and their corresponding bills paid in a timely manner as required by the utility companies:

FIGURE 4-2, cont. A month-to-month residence lease

Page 3 of 5   (initials) _____   _____

_____

If ANY utilities are not kept current, the tenant agrees to terminate this lease and give up the property's occupation at the landlord's discretion.

The tenant shall not engage in, or allow any other person, pet, or animal to engage in, any conduct that will disturb the quiet and peaceable enjoyment of the other tenants, neighbors, landlord, or use the property for any purpose whatsoever that violates the laws of the United States, the State of _____, or the City of _____.

The tenant will keep no pets of any kind, inside or outside the property, without a separate and written consent of the landlord.

Time is the essence of this contract, and should the tenant default in the payment of any installment herein named, the landlord shall be entitled to possession of the premises, at landlord's option in accordance with the _____ Landlord and Tenant Act, and the landlord shall have the right to store and/or dispose of such property in accordance with said Act, and thereafter the tenant shall be liable to the landlord for any amounts uncollected from such disposition, and the expenses therefor, including a reasonable attorney's fee.

The property herein leased will be used for residential purposes only and for no other object or purpose and this lease shall not be sublet without the written consent of the landlord.

In the event of assignment to creditors by the tenant, or the institution of bankruptcy proceedings against the tenant, such events shall cancel and hold for naught this lease, and all the rights thereunder, and possession of said property shall immediately, by such act or acts, pass to the landlord at landlord's option.

FIGURE 4-2, cont. A month-to-month residence lease

Page 4 of 5   (initials) _____   _____

The tenant shall pay a late fee of _____ in addition to each monthly payment that is paid after the _____ day of any month within the terms of this lease. Starting on the _____ day of the month, a late fee of _____ per day will be added to the existing late fee due.

The tenant will waive tenant's rights under the _____ Landlord and Tenant Act if the rent and all late charges are not paid in full by the _____ day of the month, immediately relinquishing possession of the property to the landlord at the landlord's request.

The tenant agrees to pay all rents and fees with a personal check, money order, cashier's check, or cash. If a personal check is ever not honored by the landlord's bank, for any reason whatsoever, the tenant agrees to pay a check charge of ten dollars ($10) then pay with cash until the expiration of this lease term.

The tenant shall check each and all smoke alarms weekly, replacing the battery as needed with an alkaline battery to ensure that adequate warning is provided. Also, the fire extinguisher's gauge will be checked monthly to make sure the extinguisher gauge indicates a full charge of pressure.

The tenant agrees to keep the window screens on the windows at all times, paying a twenty-dollar ($20) service charge plus parts, if a screen is removed or damaged in any way, for its replacement.

The tenant will let no more than _____ guest(s) stay overnight for a maximum period of seven (7) consecutive days in any two-month period without written consent from the landlord. This limitation _____ apply to immediate children of the tenant.

The tenant _____ keep any water-filled furniture at the property without the landlord's written consent.

FIGURE 4-2, cont. A month-to-month residence lease

The tenant agrees to keep no more than _____ vehicles, including but not limited to trucks, motorcycles, and cars, on the premises. These vehicles must be both operable and currently licensed. The tenant agrees not to repair any vehicles on the premises if the repairs will take more than twenty-four (24) hours, without prior written consent from the landlord. Tenant agrees not to keep off-road vehicles, including but not limited to boats and trailers, without prior written consent from the landlord.

Landlord has obtained insurance to cover the landlord's interest and liability, but does not insure tenant's belongings or negligence.

The tenant will return any and all property-related keys upon lease termination and will give up five dollars ($5) per nonreturned key out of the security and cleaning deposit.

The tenant further agrees that after the expiration of the time given in this lease, by thirty (30) days' proper service by either the landlord or tenant to the other, to give possession of property to landlord, and upon tenant's failure to do so shall become liable to the landlord for an additional one-month extension of this contract upon notice from the landlord. This month-to-month lease remains in effect each month, until a proper thirty (30) days' notice is given by either the landlord or tenant to the other.

Contact the landlord at _____
(phone: _____).

IN WITNESS THEREOF, the parties hereto have hereunto set their hands the day and year first above written.

_____   _____

_____   _____
          (Landlord or Agent)   (Tenant(s))

copies can be run off for you with a few keystrokes, saving you time and errors. You will appreciate this when you begin modifying leases. I have never written a lease that is identical to another; I find that each tenant situation demands different requirements. Although you can purchase legal lease forms from an office supply store, the forms rarely contain the wording I want to convey. I'm no attorney, however. The leases that you purchase have been checked for accuracy so the ones that you create with a word processor should also pass by your attorney just to make sure you're covering your bases. I do not pass every lease that I give to every tenant by my attorney, but when I make significant changes to my general lease document, I always get my attorney's advice.

If the house has flooded within the last five years, you must notify the tenants of that fact in the lease. You are not responsible for flood insurance, but you must tell the tenants about the flooding so they have fair warning that it could happen again. They can then weigh the risk of not insuring against the return of the flood. If you do not inform the tenants of the flood *in writing*, you are liable for flood damages that occur. Other kinds of disclosures, such as some kinds of past structural damage, may also be required. Check your local ordinances for more details.

> **TIP**
>
> You must notify the tenants if the home has flooded recently.

Filing the Lease

This is another little-known aid in the world of landlording. Your county clerk is the legal entity concerned with fair rental dwelling laws. In addition to being an upstanding citizen and landowner, everything you can do to show knowledge of the legal system will be in your favor if you ever have to go to court.

Filing a lease is easy. Just call your county courthouse and ask how much it costs to file a landlord–tenant lease agreement (the fee is nominal). While you have the court clerk on the phone, ask for the courthouse's full mailing address. Mail the lease with a check or money order for the filing fee, enclosed with a letter that says, "Please file this landlord–tenant lease agreement." The court clerks will take care of the rest. Enclose a self-addressed, stamped envelope if you want a copy of the filing.

Filing the lease gives you no more legal recourse than you already had. However, if you ever bring your tenant up before a judge, the more you do to prepare legally and the more you show that you take your job seriously, the more apt the judge will be to lean in your favor. It is no secret that the success of many legal proceedings is a direct result of preparation and commonsense tactics. Most of the time, a little bluffing is thrown in to help win cases as well.

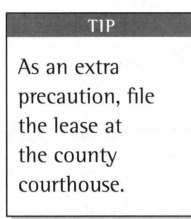

TIP

As an extra precaution, file the lease at the county courthouse.

Bluffing does not imply that the courts are corrupt. Put yourself in the judge's shoes. Two people, with good backgrounds, come before you with two different stories. Many times, both parties honestly believe they are telling the truth. The more prepared party, and the one who followed legal proceedings to the letter, is the one the judge is most likely to view with favor. By filing the signed lease, you show that you regard it as a legal document, and your tenants have less chance of denying that they signed it. The date of the lease is also better determined, especially when you file the lease immediately after signing. Be sure to file the lease within one week after the new tenant signs the lease.

Don't Let the Lease Terminate in the Winter

Consider structuring leases so they end sometime other than the harshest winter months. Landlords often find that winter is the most difficult time to find renters. More important, you don't want your pipes left unheated in the dead of winter unless you live in an area with mild winters. If I had a tenant who wanted a six-month lease that ended in winter, I would try to talk that tenant into a nine-month lease.

COLLECTING THE FIRST MONTH'S RENT

After signing both copies of the lease, collect the check for the first month's rent. Don't make it a big issue—just politely say, "Well, I need the first month's rent, and we're almost done here." Casually glance at the check as you put it into your wallet or purse to make sure the tenant filled in the proper amount, signed the check, and dated it correctly. Never accept a postdated check for the first month's rent. If you do, it could spell trouble for the rest of your tenant's stay.

Typically, the canceled check will be the tenants' receipt. But have on hand a pack of blank receipts from your local office supply warehouse in case tenants request a receipt. Even better, type some up on your computer's word processor and print them yourself to save money. When they pay, even if by check, they deserve a receipt if they want one, so be prepared.

HANDLING KEYS

Now that you've received the rent, give the tenant the keys to the home. If there are several different locks, provide at least one key for each. Always make sure you have copies of every key, since you won't always get them back, despite the key-return clause in the lease. Of course, you can deduct missing keys from the deposit when the tenant moves out, but the cost of new keys is a minor consideration; you need a copy of each key in case you must enter the home for repairs or in an emergency situation.

Keying every lock to the same key (including any locks on outside storage buildings or garages) will save you many hours over your landlording career. Keeping track of multiple keys is a nightmare, especially if you have more than one rental home. Your tenants will tire of so many keys, invariably losing one or more of them. After the tenant loses a key, guess who has to come up with an extra one? You, and it will be in the middle of the night, during a cold spell! I am surprised at the number of new tenants who seem surprised that their new house requires only a single key for the doorknobs, dead bolts, garage, and outside storage building. I suppose many landlords fail to key locks the same for their tenants, who have become used to tracking multiple keys. My tenants appreciate the single key.

> **TIP**
>
> Pay a one-time fee to get every lock keyed to the same key.

Explain your lost-key policy to tenants when you turn over the keys. Tell tenants that they will have to pay for extra keys. Inform them that you want all screens and doorjambs left intact, even when the tenants lock themselves out of the house. Tell them that although you do not want to come unlock their door every time they misplace a key, you also don't want them breaking a window or screen to get into the locked house.

Find a café near your own home where tenants can meet you to get a key if they lock themselves out. You can say that you'll meet them "halfway" to give them another key. They do not have to know that the café is halfway closer to you than to them. After all, they're the ones who lost the key.

Whatever your lost-key policy is, tell them about it. The appropriate time to do this is when you give them the first key. Ask how many copies they'll need, and if they want more than you're willing to provide, inform them that they'll have to pay your duplication fee for extra copies. I usually give my tenants two keys for their new house.

I have an easy time locating the house's key that I take to the tenant's welcome interview. I do not like carrying a bunch of keys when I visit my properties. I prefer one key for all locks keyed the same around the home, if possible. In addition, for my rental properties that are far apart from each other, I prefer to make the same key work for multiple houses. Carrying one key for your four rental homes is easier than carrying four keys, or more if some of the houses have two or more locks on a door and on the garage. Chapter 11, "Renovating Your Rental Properties," includes other handy key-related tips.

DESCRIBING YOUR RENT COLLECTION POLICY

The happiest day in the landlord's month is the rent due date. The tenant interview is a good time to explain how you collect the monthly rent. Most landlords either personally collect the rent or ask tenants to mail the rent. There are drawbacks and advantages to each method.

If you collect the rent, you must make trips to the house each month and find a time when you and your tenants are available. If your schedules coincide or if your own home is close to the rental, this is no problem. However, you could be out of town on the due date or simply unavailable—and the first time you put something else ahead of your own rent collection, you wave a red flag to tenants indicating that rent collection is not a high priority.

Every time you see your tenants, you run the risk that they will ask for something. They may want more storage shelves, more flowers in front, or a bedroom repainted (unneeded and never recommended if you properly maintain the properties between tenants; the only exception would be for long-term tenants). You must judge the validity of your tenants' requests—but be assured that they will ask for things when they see you. These will be minor requests that build up quickly the more you are there. Never hide from your tenants but making yourself too available can backfire.

The advantage to collecting your own rent is that you get the rent on time and you see the property and tenants more often than you otherwise would. You can spot potential problems before they become big problems (such as excess trash and unexpected pets). Although you want to decrease the time you spend landlording, you don't want to become an absentee landlord. Be a part of your tenants' lives so they'll remember you when the rent comes due.

> **TIP**
>
> Self-addressed stamped envelopes encourage prompt rent payments.

Because it is logistically difficult to collect the rent every month, more and more landlords ask tenants to mail it in. For years, utility companies have included self-addressed envelopes in their monthly bills. They want to make it as easy as possible for customers to get the payment to them on time. The customers have no problem getting the address right and it makes it easier for them to pay their bills. Go one step further and supply self-addressed stamped envelopes. Give tenants five or six of them at a time. This puts full responsibility on the tenants' shoulders to mail the rent. Consider stating that you are providing stamped envelopes in your lease and have the tenant initial that clause. If both of you should ever find yourselves before a judge, the tenant then has even less of an excuse for failing to pay the rent. Although you are out the stamps, you help ensure timely payment, a worthy trade-off.

The only drawback to mailing rent is the "check's-in-the-mail syndrome." When the rent is late, tenants can too easily say, "I mailed it, it must have gotten delayed. It should be there tomorrow since I mailed it last week." This is no excuse; on-time rent is the tenants' responsibility, not yours. No matter what the excuse is, explain that when the rent is due, it needs to be in your hands. Tell your tenants that you trust them, but you need the rent on the due date, regardless of delays in the mail. Tell tenants that if they're afraid of mail delays, they should mail you a postdated check a few days before the due date; you cannot deposit the check until the due date. Of course, the date on the check must be the due date and no later.

Most landlords offer a five-day grace period (such as the one that appears in the sample leases shown earlier). Five days is a large enough time window to receive mail that was delayed a day or two at the post office. Again, the mail service is not your problem. If tenants want to mail the rent to you, they must take steps to ensure that the rent arrives on time, even if it means mailing early. Despite occasional delays in the postal system, I always base my decisions on the stamp's cancellation date. Although a check might arrive late, if my tenant mailed the check in a reasonable time frame according to the cancellation date, and if the check should have arrived on time even if the mail was slow, I don't say anything. I could always tell my tenants to mail the check a day or two earlier in the future, but I believe this is petty and would only frustrate my tenants over something that is not in their control.

If you receive a late payment after the grace period that does not include the late fee, *immediately* send tenants a letter such as the one shown in Figure 4-3. This late payment reminder serves many purposes. It shows that you will never again tolerate a late payment without a late fee. It states your eviction policy for an extremely late payment. It shows you mean business. The next time you see your tenant, be as kind and courteous as you would be if you had not sent the letter. Don't mention it again, unless of course late payment occurs again. You will get your point across.

Late Payment Policy

As you wrap up the tenant interview, explain what happens if the tenant pays the rent late. Make sure there is no misunderstanding here. State your policy and ask if there are any questions. You are in business, and on-time rent is vital. One of the first things I explain to my late tenants is that the rental property is my business and I must be able to cover my expenses when they come due.

To be reasonable, offer a five-day grace period for rent payments. This means that the rent is due on the first of each month and considered late after the fifth. If your tenants move into the home in the middle of the month, the rent can start on that day. If you have more than one rental property, a uniform due date makes things easy; many landlords like to make the payment due on the first of each month. Prorate the rent for those tenants who move into the home mid-month so their next payment is due on the first. If they move in close to the first, you are reasonable in asking for both the remainder of the month and the next complete month as well.

If the grace period passes, but the rent hasn't arrived, things should heat up fast. An automatic $15 late fee on the sixth is being

FIGURE 4-3. Late payment reminder

October 10, 2001

Dear Diana:

Thank you for sending this month's rent. I appreciate the fact that you are a good tenant and that you take such responsible care of your home.

However, I want to remind you that I received this month's payment on the 6th of the month. I realize there are delays in the mail at times; I wish we could better control such things.

Nevertheless, your rent is due in my hands on the first (1st) and late after the fifth (5th). Because of mail delays, you might want to send it a few days early to ensure that I receive it before the late fee date.

I certainly understand that time slips by. Don't worry about the late fee this time. In the future, if you predict that the rent will arrive late, please include the late fee. (Our lease agreement states the terms of the late fee. After the fifth of the month, there is an automatic $15 late fee and an additional $5 a day after that. After the tenth, I have to start looking for another tenant.) I have to make a payment on the home, and my payment depends on your payment to me.

Again, this is just a reminder. I am very happy to have you as a tenant. I want to be the best landlord you ever have and that will be true only if I hold up my end of the bargain as well as I expect you to hold up your end. Let me know if there is ever anything I can do.

Sincerely,

Sam Garrett

kind; starting on the eighth late day, the charge is $5 a day for each day the rent is late. Do not make the late fee a percentage of the rent due but rather a fixed fee. If your late fee operates on a percentage of rent due and tenants are late with only half the rent, the late fee is less of an incentive to get the other half to you. Explain to new tenants that the full late fee goes into effect if *any* of the monthly rent is outstanding at the start of the late-fee period.

Tell tenants that your late fee is extremely high for being just six days late, and the cost skyrockets after that for a few days before eviction. Let them know that you do not want them to have to pay the late fee. Let them know that the high fee is to encourage them to pay on time. Remind them that you can meet your payments if they meet theirs and that a happy landlord means a happy tenant.

Inform your new tenants that you start eviction proceedings if any part of the rent is outstanding after the tenth of the month (or ten days after whatever the original due date was). Be dead serious when you say this. But also assure your tenants that you trust them and just want to make sure they understand the rules of payment, since that is their number one priority, just as a roof over their heads is yours.

Some landlords prefer a more positive approach to a late fee. They like to offer an "early-payment discount" if the rent is paid on or before the fifth of each month, instead of calling the higher charge a "late fee." If your state does not let you charge a late fee (again, check your state's Landlord and Tenant Act at the library), use whatever method you prefer. Paying after the fifth is bad, and negative connotations (calling the fee a "late fee") may be a more effective way to show tenants just how serious you are about being paid on time.

> **TIP**
>
> Some states no longer allow "late fees," so offer "early-payment incentives."

Sometimes, people ask me if I ever have tenants who routinely pay late. I have had such tenants, and every once in a while, I have not made their paying late an issue. You know the circumstances of the tenants you accept in many cases. Sometimes, a tenant's pay schedule changes; as long as that tenant pays routinely based on his or her new pay schedule, I don't say a word and I don't worry about modifying the lease due dates with an addendum to the lease. Sometimes I have that rare tenant who takes excellent care of my property, is always nice, the neighbors love the tenant, and the tenant simply forgets to pay on time on a routine basis. I have to remind them consistently, but they will always get around to it. Keep in mind, this is not my usual policy and the tenant must be a rare exceptional tenant, probably a long-term renter whom I've gotten to know well, for this to be acceptable. In virtually all cases, I offer no more grace than the grace period allows, even with excellent tenants. I have learned that if I am too nice, or if I believe words I hear more than I believe evidence I see, trouble results and the tenant becomes a short-term tenant.

THE WALK-THROUGH CHECKLIST

Give tenants a walk-through checklist (a sample appears in Figure 4-4) and give them the first month to fill it out. The checklist is a form they fill out early in the lease period that states the outside and room-by-room condition of the home in the tenants' eyes. If you prepared the home properly, tenants will find little to comment on. Most of the time, they will return the list with everything checked off as being "in good shape and clean."

The walk-through checklist is really for your protection. When tenants move out and say, "I didn't make that hole in the wall, it was there already," you can show them the checklist, which proves the condition of the home at the time they moved in.

The faster the tenants fill out the form, the better. You can make it easy by letting them return it with the next month's rent. This gives them a chance to get moved in and to discover any little details that you forgot to handle when you prepared the home. The checklist also allows tenants to bring up safety hazards. Since they live in the home, not you, they have a better eye for potential dangers than you do.

FIGURE 4-4. A walk-through checklist

Please return with rent payment
WALK-THROUGH CHECKLIST
(1013 S. Illinois)

Dear Diana:

Please take the time to go through each room to make sure everything works fine and is in good condition.

Outside of home:

☐ Siding, shutters, windows, ground, screens, and storage building are in good shape and clean.

I feel I should bring the following to your attention:

_____

_____

Living room:

☐ Carpet, walls, lights, outlets, ceilings, and miniblinds are in good shape and clean.

I feel I should bring the following to your attention:

_____

_____

Kitchen:

☐ Shelves, sink, stove, floor, refrigerator, dishwasher, pipes, ceiling, and fan are all in good shape and clean.

I feel I should bring the following to your attention:

_____

_____

Bedrooms:

☐ Carpet, walls, closets, miniblinds, ceilings, fans, and lights are all in good shape and clean.

I feel I should bring the following to your attention:

_____

_____

FIGURE 4-4, cont. A walk-through checklist

Bathrooms:

☐ Floors, walls, toilets, sinks, tubs, and plumbing are all in good shape and clean.

I feel I should bring the following to your attention:

_____

_____

Other possible problems:

_____

_____

_____

_____   _____
Tenant's signature   Date

I owned a two-story townhome for several years that had a stairway without a handrail. I never lived there, I never walked up and down the stairs several times a day, and I never thought about the missing handrail until a tenant returned the safety checklist and requested a handrail. I was embarrassed that I had not thought of the rail and I didn't enjoy putting it up, but I was thrilled that the tenant informed me that the rail was missing. If the tenant had slipped going down the stairs, I could have paid a lot for the oversight. A stairway without a railing may make it tough for elderly people to go up and down. You should be glad when tenants spot a problem like this. Safety problems are best handled *before* they cause trouble (it is cheaper then also).

ONE LAST TOUR

Take your tenants around the inside and outside of the house one last time. Let them know that you want to make sure everything is clean and that the appliances work. This helps ensure honesty on their walk-through checklist, because they know you saw the property with them during the new tenant interview. Also make sure the tenants know where to locate the smoke alarms, the fire extinguisher, the breaker or fuse box, and the gas and water shut-off valves. Keep the fire extinguisher in the kitchen since that is where most fires begin. If you have an upstairs bathroom, show tenants where the plunger is (leave one for them in there). Urge them to use it whenever necessary to keep overflowing water from ruining their things and the downstairs of your rental house.

As you walk through the house, call it their "home" as often as possible. Home is what it will be to them, so acclimate them to that fact as soon as possible. A little public relations never hurts, and your attitude toward the tenants helps set the tone from that point on. Whether the home is a house, duplex, or apartment, it is home to the tenants.

> **TIP**
>
> Being prepared for winter saves you and your tenants trouble.

Outside, show the tenants how to open the garage and gates. While outside, let them know how important it is that they get along with the neighbors. You might let them in on a little "secret"—the neighborhood is not a typical rental neighborhood (if it were, you probably would not have bought the house), and the people living around the rental own their own homes and take as much pride in them as you hope your tenants will. The tenants should monitor their noise and respect their neighbors. You also want them to let you know if a neighbor starts causing problems. (Chapter 6, "Neighborly Advice," discusses neighbor relations in more detail.)

Let tenants know how you maintain the house and how you respond to repair problems. Assure them that you take care of emergencies quickly and other maintenance items within three days, five days, or whatever period of time is your honest assessment. Don't fib here; give yourself ample time. Your tenants will magically remember these words every time a problem occurs (even though the monthly rent sometimes slips their minds for a few days).

Tell tenants what you will not do as well. Most landlords do not mow the lawn, unless the property is a duplex, fourplex, small apartment complex, or condo. Tell your tenants that you will not always grant them everything they ask for, but if their request is reasonable or if it is an emergency, they can count on you to take care of it in a timely manner.

Explain how winter weather conditions can affect your property. If the home is raised above a crawl space, the pipes can freeze easily. Even homes on concrete slabs can suffer

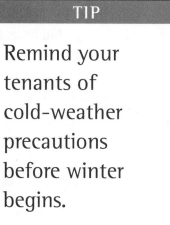

TIP

Remind your tenants of cold-weather precautions before winter begins.

pipe-freezing damage in sinks and tubs that are next to outside walls. The best way to ensure a smooth winter is to leave the cold water running slightly during freezing weather in all sinks and tubs placed against outside walls. The tenants can also help the situation by opening the cabinet doors under their sinks so the room's air can circulate around the pipes and warm them. Consider installing heat tape if you have severe winters (see Chapter 2 for details).

Just before the annual cold spells begin, send a letter to your tenants reviewing cold-weather conditions. Remind the tenants how expensive their water bills will be if their forgetfulness results in a broken pipe. In addition, remind them what the water can do to their furniture if they fail to leave a faucet dripping during an extra-cold night. You can also remind them that your insurance covers the dwelling but not their possessions. When the tenants learn that they share cold-weather risk with you, they are much more likely to help keep the cold weather from harming your property.

Before leaving the new tenant interview, let your tenants know how to dispose of the garbage. The neighborhood may have curbside service or another type of pickup. Tell tenants not to leave garbage around (inside or out) the home, garage, or storage building. Let tenants know the trash pickup days for the area and how to prepare the trash for pickup. Some cities supply garbage cans while others supply trash bags. Some cities charge for refuse collection along with water bills while others charge separately, and your tenants may have to sign up for the service.

SAYING "GOOD LUCK!"

Now your job is done for a while, perhaps for many months. Your only responsibility is to deposit the rent check each month—a job no one tires of. Leave your tenants the keys, a copy of the lease, a walk-through checklist, and your blessings. Tell them that they can rely on you to be a good landlord and that you know you can expect them to be good tenants.

> **TIP**
>
> Provide your e-mail address if both you and your tenants use computers.

Consider giving them one last piece of paper: a new tenant information sheet such as the one shown in Figure 4-5. This sheet lists phone numbers for fire, police, and emergency assistance, and gives the location of the closest post office, shopping center, and gas station. You should also include your name, phone number, and address. Include your e-mail address if you have one. If there is a problem, you will want to hear about it earlier rather than later.

During the walk-through, discuss important details of the home, such as the location of the extinguisher, smoke alarms, and breaker or fuse box. (Give them extra fuses if the home has a fuse box.) Make sure all the lightbulbs still work and have spares with you in case you find one that has burned out.

The walk-through gives you one last opportunity to leave tenants with a few of your requirements, such as how to handle plumbing and appliance problems. Tell them that you do not want them to call a plumber except in extreme cases when water damage is imminent. (Tenants might think a Jacuzzi is necessary for occupancy if they have free rein with plumbing "repairs"!) List the plumber's emergency number, but be sure to emphasize that you are to be called first if at all possible.

Unless you are available 24 hours a day, 7 days a week, 365 days a year, you must let your tenants know who to contact if you cannot be reached. Although the tenants need to know that you are always the first contact in case of emergency or any other trouble, they deserve help if they cannot reach you. Supply an approved maintenance person's name and phone number for emergency service when you are unavailable. Be sure to warn the service person that he or she may get calls from your tenants, and set the boundaries as to what the tenant can order. For example, you'll probably want to approve plumbing and electrical repairs but not necessarily painting and wallpapering!

TIP

Give your backup service information.

Show tenants the water shutoff valves under sinks and toilets. What first appears to be a water emergency turns into a momentary inconvenience if a shutoff valve is close by. I dread water leaks more than any other problem, except fire. Water can de-

FIGURE 4-5. An information sheet for new tenants

NEW TENANT INFORMATION

Landlord: Sam Garrett, 913 East Oak Road, Miami, FL 41156, 555-4321
Fire: 911 or 555-3234 **Police or Ambulance:** 911 or 555-2982
Post Office: 13 Sycamore Drive, 2 blocks north of home
Closest Shopping Center: 943 Oak Street, 1 block east

Please check the smoke/fire alarms WEEKLY. There is a button to press that will test them. One alarm is located in the upstairs hall close to the ceiling; the other is downstairs to the right of the bathroom. For your safety, please use a replacement 9-volt alkaline battery if yours fails. The batteries are easy to replace if you stand on a ladder or step stool.

Please do NOT store any items in the air-conditioner and heater closet. The air is to circulate throughout the closet and it is so important that you will be damaging the unit and will be responsible for ALL REPAIRS including replacement of the entire unit if needed. I trust you, and I only put it this bluntly to show you how important it is to me that you understand.

If you see a leak, turn off the shutoff valve to the tub, toilet, or faucet. Call me as soon as you get the water turned off.

Obviously, if you see a water leak, shut it off if you can and call me. IF it is an emergency and it is about to cause major water damage because of its size, call a plumber. For most "average" problems, I would like to be called first. In an extreme emergency, call Donald's Plumbing at 555-1109.

* * * I have provided you with a plunger in the upstairs bathroom under the sink. It is VITAL that you help keep water off the floor in the upstairs bathroom, otherwise it will damage the ceiling and your furnishings downstairs if it comes through.

The electric breaker box to your home is located in the air-conditioner and heater closet.

Please keep in mind that your lease extends to the outside storage building in back. Its floor, walls, and outside should be kept as clean and in the same good condition as your house. If you leave oil drippings on the floor, I will have to keep part or all of the deposit. (Please use a pan if you store anything with an engine in there.)

FIGURE 4-5, cont. An information sheet for new tenants

Your fire extinguisher is under your kitchen sink. If you have to use it, pull the safety pin first. Check the gauge MONTHLY to make sure it is charged. If it is not charged, please let me know immediately. Usually, they hold their charge at least 2 years, so you should not have a problem. Please do NOT "test" it by shooting it to try it out. This WILL discharge the unit and make it unusable.

Please treat this home with the care that it deserves. Please be aware of noise that may disturb your neighborhood. If your neighbors cause you trouble, please call me and I'll take care of it immediately. Conversely, they will call me if there is something you are doing that bothers them. I will let a house sit empty for several months rather than let someone move in who bothers the neighbors or who does damage to the rental property.

In return, I will be the nicest landlord you have EVER had, and if there is an emergency, I'll get it taken care of faster than you have ever seen. I care about you and want you to be as happy as possible.

---

stroy a fine home and cause expensive damage. I want my pipes dry and my furnace free of condensation, and my service people know that.

Unless tenants brought their furniture to the interview, you will probably leave the home together after the walk-through— you to relax and the tenant to begin the arduous job of moving. Sneak back, if you can, to leave a basket of fruit, or at least a thank-you note on the counter to welcome the new tenants when they walk into their home for the first time. This is another little expense that pays great dividends in your tenants' appreciation.

Finally, consider contacting small moving services to see if they would be willing to enter into an informal relationship with you. Ask if they will offer your tenants a discount if you routinely tell your new tenants about their service. Tell your tenants about that moving discount. If the moving company says they will pay you a finder's fee every time they move one of your tenants into one of your properties, consider giving the new tenant this finder's fee after the move and explain to the tenant what you did. This goes a long way toward building trust early in the landlord–tenant relationship. Moving gets expensive and you want your tenants to spend as little money as possible in the process so they have more money later to pay the rent.

SUMMARY

The new tenant interview is the most important step in hands-off property management. This chapter highlights the best way to present the lease, collect the first month's rent, turn over the keys, explain your late payment and eviction policies, and prepare the tenants for a happy and confident stay in their new home.

Congratulations! You can never guarantee tenant success 100 percent, but you have taken all the steps necessary to select and prepare your tenants for occupancy in your prized rental home. Other landlords would like to be in your position. Despite all the work these first few chapters have required, you will now see how little you have to do to own rental property. Up to this point, the work has been an investment of your time. The dividends should now start rolling in. Your tenants should be happy and, more important, you should be happy, especially with the extra time you have to pursue other interests.

The next chapter deals with day-to-day tenant maintenance. Good tenants rarely bother you, especially after they get settled into their new home. Chapter 5, "Tenant Management," shows you how to perform top-notch duties as a landlord with minimum effort; you can be absent most of the time without being an absentee landlord.

CHAPTER FIVE

Tenant Management

IF YOUR RENTAL keeps you busy you will not have time to pursue other interests and find additional properties. The day-to-day management of your property should not actually require you to pay attention to it every single day. Now that you've prepared the rental and filled it with one or more good tenants, your real work is done. Most landlord–tenant problems occur because the landlord did not prepare the home properly or take the time to find good renters. With house payments staring them in the face each month, some landlords feel they must rent to the first tenants who want the home. But too many problems result from choosing tenants this way. You might get tenants who cannot, or will not, pay the rent. Even worse, you run the risk of renting to tenants who will damage the home.

Very few landlords want to be actively involved in their rentals. You would probably like to retire temporarily from your landlording duties once you've rented your property. The good news is that you can practically do just that. One of the philosophies in this book is that you can be an absent landlord without being an absentee landlord; that is, you do not have to be in the middle of things all the time. You can put your rentals on autopilot and still be responsive to your tenants.

BE SELECTIVE BUT RESPONSIVE

You are in the rental property business and your tenants are your customers. Once your tenants move in, the most important thing you can do is show that you care. Never put the tenants second. If you make an appointment with them, keep it. If you promise to spray for bugs, do so.

You cannot respond favorably to every request. Do not feel obliged to do so. Better tenants will not bother you with petty requests anyway. That is another reason to select good tenants in the first place.

When you need to contact your tenants, remember the U.S. mail. Even if the rental house is in your own neighborhood, a quick note usually best tells tenants what you want to say. For instance, if your tenants run out of rent payment envelopes, send more. Taking them in person wastes gas and puts you in the home, where your tenants will invariably ask you to repair, replace, or paint something. The cost of postage is made up in the time you save by not meeting with the tenants, and yet you still show that you are thinking of them and that you are part of their lives.

TIP

Write, call, or e-mail your tenants. Only go in person when absolutely necessary.

Suppose you are going out of town for a two-week vacation. Don't leave without letting your tenants know. Otherwise, a small problem could turn into a bigger one before you get back from your trip. Find someone who can manage the property for you and mail your tenants the name and number of that person. You can also call—but again, you want to minimize minor requests.

If you and your tenants use the Internet, be sure to give them your e-mail address and ask for theirs. When you travel out of town and bring a laptop computer, you can usually check e-mail in your hotel room without having to make a long-distance call home to retrieve messages. Keep in mind, however, that as a rental property owner you do have some responsibilities that require you to check in by phone. Calling home once a day to see if a tenant has left you a message is in your and the tenant's best interest. Knowing about problems early is the best way to keep them small. Exchanging e-mail addresses with your tenants is still a good idea, of course. That way, tenants can use e-mail to get your advice about something minor happening with the property, which means you don't waste time or money on the phone unless it's absolutely necessary.

Only visit the house in person if the mail and the telephone are inappropriate for the message you must deliver. Making extra trips wastes time and money and usually is less productive than if you had written or called.

Writing and calling do not imply that you wish to stay away from the home—quite the opposite. It's just that you want to avoid seeing your tenants too often. It seems to be human nature for tenants to ask for petty things when you are there in person. Maximize your efficiency and the pleasantness of your own life by eliminating unneeded trips to see renters.

DRIVE BY YOUR RENTAL

Every time you are in the neighborhood, drive by your rental. Even though I encourage you to see your renters as little as possible once they move in, you still need to check on your property.

By driving by, you can eliminate many problems before they balloon.

It is amazing that some landlords do not drive by, even when close, out of fear that the tenants will think their landlords are checking on them. You *are* checking on them! This is your property. You want to make sure it is not blighted by unmowed grass, trash on the porch, and broken-down cars. The care your tenant takes now will reflect on you in the future. You don't want the condition of the property to become bad enough for others to notice it. Rather, you want your neighbors to be glad you own it—and possibly even to call you when they have relatives who are looking for a rental.

> ## TIP
> Call your tenants when you see problems on drive-bys.

Feel free to stop and knock on the door if you see problems around the house when you drive by. However, even in this situation, there are advantages to telephoning instead. First of all, you may catch the tenants at a bad time if you drop in. It is always more polite to call first before visiting anybody. You, however, are the owner of the property, and a truly bad situation warrants an immediate knock on the door, rude or not. Usually, though, you will see nothing that warrants immediate, in-person attention.

When the circumstances allow, phoning distances you a little from the situation and from the tenant. Some tenants will feel less threatened if you call. Start the conversation on an up note by asking if everything is okay and whether there is anything you can do for them. After the preliminaries, tell them you want to bring something to their attention. Small problems, such as an unmowed yard, stay small when you *remind* tenants that the grass is getting long. At the same time that you remind them pleasantly of this, they are also getting the word that you drive by every so often.

RENT

Nothing frustrates a landlord or tenant more than a change in the rent. Although some tenants balk at an increase, others will understand. You'll need to prepare yourself with some solutions before increasing the rent to ward off undesirable effects such as late payments and early move-outs.

Rent Adjustments

When the lease expires, anything can happen. You can raise the rent, ask the tenants to leave, or renew the current lease as is. The sample multi-month lease shown in Chapter 4 automatically converts to a month-to-month lease at its expiration. If you prefer, you can change the closing clauses to state that another multi-month lease agreement must be executed and signed by both you and the tenant upon termination. With a month-to-month lease, you (or the tenant) can change the terms at the end of any month.

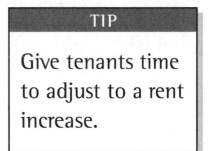

TIP

Give tenants time to adjust to a rent increase.

If your rent return is not adequate, you must increase it. There is very little you can do but that. Over time, insurance and repair costs rise and you can only survive your landlording experience if you cover costs with rental income. Few landlords can afford to, much less desire to, operate their rentals at a loss.

Approach the unpleasant task of raising rents the same way you approach other rental tasks. Be businesslike but understanding of your tenants' viewpoint. Don't tell tenants that the rents will increase in five days. Give them a few months at their current rate to get acclimated to the idea of paying more. (Of course, you cannot raise rates if a long-term lease is still in effect.) Raise the rents in small increments. Unlike the post office, which only raises rates every few years but does so in large percentages, be gentle with rent increases. A 10 percent increase is about as much as most tenants will bear. If you must raise the rent higher than 10 percent, consider offering your tenants a bonus plan: If they stay for ten months, you'll refund them $100 of the increase. This lets the tenants recoup some of the higher rent and it helps ensure that your tenants will stay a while longer.

This means you must think seriously about the rates you charge before you ever place the ad for a home. Try to predict the costs so that the rent is adequate and you can minimize rent increases. Tenants realize that rents are not guaranteed for their entire stay, but they would prefer to avoid increases. They will be willing to pay more if the increase is not dramatic and if your attitude is understanding. Let them know that your costs have increased and that you have no choice but to raise their rent as well.

> **TIP**
>
> Tell tenants in person about a rent increase.

One of the few times a phone call or letter is inappropriate is when you raise the rent. Call first to arrange to meet the tenants at the rental home. When you arrive, sit down with them and explain that you have kept the rent as low as possible but that you must raise it to meet current costs. Explain that you want to give them a little time to adjust and that the new rent takes effect in a few months. If the lease has expired, let them know that you need to agree to a new lease, but that you will go month to month for two or three months to give them a chance to adjust to the new rent. The odds are on your side; most people hate to move. Your tenants are likely to stay if the increase is reasonable, still competitive, and you have done your job as a caring landlord.

Be warned that you may lose tenants when you raise the rent. Like you, they have only so much coming in each month. If they feel they cannot meet the increase, be kind by giving them a good recommendation to their next landlord (assuming they paid on time and were good tenants). Being kind at this point encourages tenants to leave the home in good shape, and they may want you as their landlord again someday.

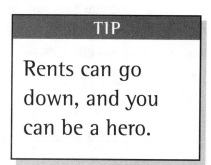

TIP

Rents can go down, and you can be a hero.

Instead of raising rents, you can try to lower costs, but this is rarely feasible. Once you've prepared and rented the home, there is very little you can do to lower your costs. The interest rate on your home loan is probably at a fixed rate, so that will not decrease. (You may want to consider refinancing the loan; Chapter 8, "Handling Money," discusses this.) If you are paying the utilities, you may have to be less generous and cut that out of your rental package.

Are you making *too much* money? Your answer is probably "no," and that answer is understandable. To determine whether you are competitive, you should research competing rentals to see how they compare with yours. Find homes listed for rent that are in comparable condition to your own and are located in similar neighborhoods. Then, perform some rental comparisons. You will certainly lose tenants if you offer similar housing at a higher rent than others.

Attempt to beat your competition. You will have better tenants and fewer complaints. If you make a profit but your rents are higher than others, lower them. In the long run, the fewer move-outs you have will make up for the decreased income. One of the most important tenant benefits I've ever given is an unexpected rent decrease after a tenant of mine has rented for a year or more. I have lowered rent *numerous times.* No tenant has ever refused a rent decrease! In every case, my tenants stayed in the home at least one year after I lowered their rent, and I attribute the unexpected lower rent to the tenant's longevity. Although you may not be able to afford a rent decrease, I find that even $5 a month may keep a tenant several months longer than they might otherwise stay.

Late Fees or Early-Payment Discounts?

The leases shown in Chapter 4 included a late-payment clause. The tenants' rent is due on the first of each month and is late after the fifth of each month. From there, a late fee escalates rapidly until the tenth, when you begin eviction proceedings. Unlike other elements of landlording suggested in this book, paying rent late deserves no understanding, except in extreme circumstances. Only if the tenant has been the epitome of "good" by paying on time for many months should you consider letting that tenant think a late payment, with late fee or not, is okay.

TIP

Early-payment plans can be confusing to tenants.

To encourage on-time rent, some landlords call on-time payments "early" payments. Instead of a late fee, they allow for an early-payment discount.

Use whichever makes you feel most comfortable, but be aware that most tenants are confused by the idea of an early-payment discount. After all, the rent is due or it isn't on a specified date. They realize that the early payment is really an incentive to pay on time. If that works, so much the better. Some states may not allow a late fee tied to the length of time the renter is late. Such laws make little sense because they seem to encourage bad citizenship and broken contracts. However, if your state has such laws, an early-payment discount may be your only alternative to recoup some of your losses when a tenant pays late.

To implement this approach, the early-payment amount actually must be enough to cover your expenses and make the return you require. In other words, the early payment must be high enough so that if your tenants always pay early, you will be comfortable with the income. The "regular" rent, which comes due after the early-payment period, must be severe enough to inspire the tenant to pay on time. And to deal with tenants who pay very late, you still must incorporate a late-fee structure into your payment plan. This simply increases the confusion without adding to the incentive. To eliminate unneeded confusion, avoid the early-discount approach; instead, charge a fair regular rent (a little lower than competing houses) and add a late fee for late payments.

I know of several landlords who use the early-payment plan and love it. I'm not sure that their tenants do, however. The tenants can see that an early-payment discount is really a late fee in disguise if the rent is paid late.

Rent Odds and Ends

Throughout your tenants' stay, they will have requests that you should consider, such as moving the rent due date. As mentioned in Chapter 4, if tenants change jobs, their payroll date could change, too. This may mean that they need a new rent due date. Don't be too strict about things like this. The large apartment complexes are the ones that will not bend. You are smaller and have more flexibility than the big-time players—and that is yet another reason why you are more competitive and have a greater choice of renters.

Suppose a tenant tells you that he or she now gets paid on the fifteenth of each month instead of the first. The tenant will want the lease changed to reflect the new pay period. Changing the due date should pose no problem to you, but the tenant must realize that the first month of the change he or she must bear the extra fifteen days of rent. In other words, the tenant must pay forty-five days' rent on the first to cover the rent until the fifteenth of the following month. You should not be the one to wait the extra fifteen days for the rent. If you did, your tenant would constantly be behind by fifteen days.

> **TIP**
>
> Tenants must pay for a change of rent due date.

Someday, you will invariably get a call from a tenant who cannot pay the full rent. Should you accept partial rent? The answer is a resounding "yes," but the tenant has not helped his or her cause by paying only some of the rent. Until the entire rent is paid in full, consider the rent outstanding. The full late fee must apply or your tenant will not have as much incentive to pay what he or she owes you. The rent should be the tenant's highest priority, just as the home is yours. In extreme cases, all legal eviction proceedings are warranted if your tenant is still past due any part of the rent by a specified date.

You will have to be the judge of what to do in partial rent-payment situations. Extremely good tenants have unexpected expenses they cannot control, just as bad ones do. If a family has prized your home for the three years they've lived there and can only pay half the rent some month, you may be prudent to accept it and let them extend the deadline for the remaining past-due rent. Be firm about the next month, however. If you decide to let them pay late, inform them that you expect another rent amount in full on the first day of the next month.

KNOW YOUR TENANTS

Keep a list by your telephone with all your tenants' names, phone numbers, full mailing addresses, places of work, children's names, and their ages. Leave room for little notes about them. For instance, if you lease a home with a fenced backyard, jot down the name of the tenants' dog (if they have one). Then, whenever you speak to them, you can ask about their children and pets by name. Write down each tenant's monthly rent, too, so you will know that when they call.

The list will give your own family a better idea to whom they are talking when they answer a phone call from your tenants. If you have more than one rental unit, the list becomes even more important.

This list is not just a ploy to make your tenants think your memory is better than it is. You *should* take an interest in your tenants. As long as you realize they are human beings and not just "the renters," they will view you as a real person, too, instead of that "rich Mercedes-driving rich high-class rich mean rich landlord," an image that the media (and other less intelligent landlords) promote.

MORE TENANT MANAGEMENT ADVICE

Landlording does not require you to hold your tenants' hands to keep them happy. Most of your tenants will want you to stay away unless there's a problem, and you will want to do the same as long as the tenant is taking care of your property. Nevertheless, tenant maintenance is important.

Don't Be Ostentatious

After much success with landlording, you and your family will be swimming in money (we can dream, can't we?). Seriously, though, you *can* make your fortune in the rental property business, but it only happens over time and with lots of skill. If you do succeed beyond your wildest dreams, take care not to flaunt your success, especially to your tenants.

> **TIP**
>
> Rarely do expensive clothes favorably impress your tenants when you drop by to change an air filter or to collect the rent.

When you see your tenants, consider their impression of you and don't try to be someone you are not. If you have a very nice car as well as a moderately nice car, consider driving the more modest one when you visit your tenants. Don't wear your best suit or dress. Again, you do not want to pretend to be poor, but you do not want to put on airs either. Be humble with your tenants. Show them that you care about them, their needs, and their home.

Lower Your Tenants' Utility Bills

There is a lot you can do to prepare the home for efficiency. Chapter 11 describes ways you can remodel your rental houses. It mentions several things you can do to lower utility costs for your tenants during remodeling. The more your tenants save, the more they have for the rent each month.

There are two easy, quick, and inexpensive things you can do to the rental home's water heater to lower your tenants' costs right now. A water heater costs only a few dollars a month—and a gas heater costs less to run than an electric one. But over many months the bill adds up to a costly sum, which you can help shave. Whether gas or electric, check the temperature control on the water heater's tank. The control will be located toward the bottom and is usually red or blue. If it is as high as it goes (pointing to the side marked "Off"), turn it down a few degrees. Your tenants will probably be glad they no longer get scalded each morning when they first enter the shower. Most water heaters are turned too high for comfort and the extra degrees of heat gobble up money each month.

Your local hardware store can sell you an insulating blanket for the water heater. Buy one and wrap it around the heater, securing it with tape. The cost of the blanket is deductible to you as an expense, and the money saved by the blanket pays for it within a few months. These cost savers help your pocketbook (when your home is between occupants) as well as your tenants'.

By the way, if your tenants complain that there is not enough hot water, try turning up the temperature control. Often, a low temperature forces your tenant to use a greater volume of hot water. If the hot water still does not last and you use an electric water heater, the heating element may not be heating uniformly and probably needs to be replaced.

Remember the Holidays and Special Events

If at all possible, budget enough of your rental income to offer a December discount. Figure 5-1 shows a holiday present that any renter would love to see. Landlords rarely offer these kinds of extras, yet it is another way to show your tenants that you think of them.

FIGURE 5-1. A holiday present for your tenants

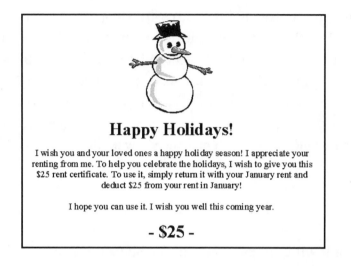

Happy Holidays!

I wish you and your loved ones a happy holiday season! I appreciate your renting from me. To help you celebrate the holidays, I wish to give you this $25 rent certificate. To use it, simply return it with your January rent and deduct $25 from your rent in January!

I hope you can use it. I wish you well this coming year.

- $25 -

Why is it that some landlords never think of their tenants during the holidays? Businesses offer sales throughout the year to attract and keep good customers, and so should you. If this holiday extra helps keep a good tenant, the discount is worth it. Your tenants are good people, but realistically, they usually have less to spend on holidays than you do. Your discount will help them enjoy that special time much better.

There are landlords who like to give their renters a turkey, ham, or some other treat during the holidays. These are nice gifts, too, and they add a more personal touch than a rent discount. Nevertheless, no matter how good the turkey is, the money will be needed more and therefore appreciated more. Either way, the thought is what counts.

Be happy for tenants with a new baby. Send flowers loaded with baby's breath. In most cities a modest sum (deductible as a valid rental property expense) buys an attractive, delivered floral arrangement. While it's still fresh in your mind, add the baby's name to your records.

Don't Let Maintenance Slip

Once your tenants move in, continue to maintain the rental. The tenants' faces will glow if you freshen up the outside paint job after they've lived in your rental for several years. Each spring, consider refreshing your rental in some way. You extend the life of the home, improve its drive-by appearance, decrease your fix-up costs, and most important, make your tenants glad they rent from you.

TIP

It is easier and cheaper to keep good tenants than to find new ones.

PEST CONTROL

Some landlords consider their tenants to be pests, but this book is not for those types of landlords! The pests you need to control are those six- and eight-legged critters that every house gets at one time or another. If your tenants consistently dispose of the trash, wipe up after meals, and keep clutter to a minimum, bugs will find another place to thrive. Nevertheless, no matter how clean your tenants are, pests can still enter the home.

You cannot police your tenants' every move, and there is a fine line between ensuring tenant responsibility and overmonitoring their home. There will be occasions when you may catch tenants at a bad time—you'll ring the bell and find a mess in progress. Spills happen, clutter occurs, and trash piles up. Unless you see a continuing sanitation problem, keep quiet about minor problems such as these. Bugs will show up in a clean home as well as a dirty one. Accept pest control as a regular part of your landlording responsibilities.

Regular pest control is not too difficult to learn. The biggest expense is the sprayer, but it will cost less than one service call from an exterminator. You may cringe at the cost of the chemicals, but their price is misleading. Many pesticides must be greatly diluted, so that often you use only 2 to 5 tablespoons per gallon of water.

Even common household pesticides are *highly dangerous* if used improperly. Respect their use and storage instructions. Better yet, check out your local college to see whether it has an agriculture extension center that offers pest control advice.

Despite the danger, you can spray the home if you learn about the chemicals and how to apply them. This will keep your costs way down. When you call a pest control service, you pay proportionately more for people's time, knowledge, and trucks than you do for the chemicals. As with any do-it-yourself project, though, you must realize that your own time carries a price, too. Always consider the fact that every legitimate expense related to your property is tax-deductible against the rental income. If you take the after-tax cost of a pest control service, you end up paying much less than at first glance. The advantages of spending your own time quickly lessen.

> **TIP**
>
> Being your own pest controller doesn't always pay off.

Use only licensed and bonded pest control services, because their exposure to liability is much lower than yours is if you spray the house yourself. If you spray improperly and make your tenants sick, you run a risk that you could have easily avoided by calling professionals. Learn before you spray, or call an expert.

How Often Should You Spray?

Weekly, monthly, yearly—how often should you spray? It depends, but if you have good tenants, you will have fewer pests. A pest control service certainly will be conservative in its recommendations, suggesting that you spray every one to three months. In many cases, this is probably more often than you need.

Some landlords, especially those with pride in their homes, rarely need pest control services. If you choose your tenants well, you can probably ignore pest control until your tenants see signs of activity and let you know about it. This would make many pest control services cringe, but the simple fact is that if you learn to inspect the home yourself for pests, and if you tell your tenants to let you know if they ever see problems, you can save money.

The Hard Ones: Termites and Roaches

Many homeowners fear the dreaded termite. They envision their home evaporating into dust in a matter of moments. In reality, termites damage houses very slowly. It takes time to notice visible termite damage, and you can usually get rid of the bugs with few problems.

Because of the time needed to do extensive damage, catching termite activity early is the key to minimizing its destruction. Most professional pest control services offer free termite inspections. The next time you call for a regular pest control appointment, ask the technician to show you how to check for termite activity. If you routinely do business with the service, the technician will probably oblige.

The cautious can pay a pest control service to do an initial termite job. Because termites come into your home from the ground, the service will attempt to put a barrier between the ground and the home. Most pest control services guarantee that you'll never have termite activity after this initial service, if you pay them to inspect your house every year thereafter.

You can now control termites fairly well with new devices that stake into the ground around your property and keep the bugs at bay. Some of the higher-strength termite stakes are available through pest control services in some areas. These stakes help keep the critters away and work as a fairly good deterrent. Consider pricing these devices and using them on a regular basis. They can be costly, so ask a pest control technician what time of year is best to use such devices in your area. Termites may not be a problem during all seasons in your part of the country and you'll want to use the stakes at the proper time.

I've never been too worried about termites. They are easy to spot as long as you are not an absentee landlord. If you regularly use a pest control service, the technician will monitor the home for termite signs and warn you before problems get too severe. Even so, learn to spot the signs yourself so you'll know what to look for. Learn what attracts the termites, as well as carpenter ants. You want to take preventive measures when possible so that small problems remain small.

To locate potential termite trouble, you must check the outside and inside of your home. On the outside, inspect all wood fencing for small, pencil-sized tubes of dirt running from the ground upwards on the fence. Termites must return to the ground throughout the day for water and they do so in these dirt tunnels that they build. Actually, the tunnels consist of part of your fence as well as dirt from the ground so these tunnels are taking away your fence as they expand upward. Fortunately, if you routinely inspect your house annually in the mid-spring months, the termites will not have time to do much damage before you take care of them.

In addition to any wood fencing, inspect every part of your home where wood touches the ground. Look carefully at beams that hold porches as well as wood siding and doorjambs that may be buried in the earth. As you can see, ground-to-wood contact is vital for the successful infestation of termites. Although most builders use treated wood to slow down the termite problem, infestation is still possible.

If you see the dirt runs, immediately scrape them off the wood surface. The termites will require a few days to build the tunnels back, and by then, you'll have the termites taken care of. A professional exterminator will apply a barrier of pesticide so termites stay away. If you can sink posts in concrete, or raise fencing off the ground just an inch or so, you will greatly decrease the likelihood of termite problems.

On the inside of your home, look for the same tunnels on all walls made of sheetrock. The termites will use your wall's sheetrock as they use dirt to move from the ground up through your walls. Obviously, if you find the raised tunnels on your walls, the termites' first point of entry is under your home or on an outside wall and you'll have to take care of that entry point to solve the problem. Unless the termites have been working on your walls for some time, you should be able to prevent significant damage once you have discovered their existence. If you have wallpaper, the tunnels will form under the paper so check carefully.

Less damaging than termites, but more disgusting to most people, are roaches. Nothing bothers tenants more than these critters, and your tolerance for them should be equal to that of your tenants'—none. If your rental gets roaches, get rid of them immediately. The sooner they are exterminated, the sooner your tenants will sleep. If a tenant's mess causes a roach problem more than once, get rid of the tenant as quickly as you would the roaches.

Roaches can be one of the hardest pests to control. Even termites have a more difficult time getting back into a house after an extermination job than roaches do. Although there are more than two hundred kinds of roaches, fewer than ten nest naturally indoors. Most are brought in from the outside. Grocery sacks are notorious for hiding the creatures.

> **TIP**
>
> Spray every unit of a multi-unit property.

If you have a duplex, fourplex, or apartment, spray *every* unit for roaches if you spray at all. Roaches are persistent and smart, although a professional can get rid of them if given the freedom. To eliminate them, each room in the entire building should be sprayed. Otherwise, the roaches will find the one room that was left alone. For bad infestations, empty all drawers, especially in the kitchen, before spraying.

SUMMARY

Your day-to-day landlord activities do not have to be difficult—or day to day. Most landlords put their properties on autopilot and spend time doing other things. Once you select good tenants, your job becomes a pleasure and you'll wonder why you do not have twice as many rental properties.

You can handle most of your duties with a letter or phone call. Don't drive to the tenants' house every time you want to tell them something. You'll waste time and money, and get a lot of trivial requests. Stay in the tenants' lives in other ways: Send them a card and discount coupon during the holidays. Lower their rent when you can. Freshen up their home each spring by caulking the doors and windows, painting, and doing other similar chores.

If you prepared your rental home properly, your routine fix-up chores will be minimal. The only recurring problem may be pest control, and even that is minimal if your tenants keep the home clean and tell you about infestation problems early. You can choose to spray for pests yourself, but first consider the advantages of using a licensed and bonded service.

Now that you've made your tenants happy as well as yourself, you must consider one other party: your neighbors. Most landlords do not concern themselves with the neighbors around their rentals. But those neighbors can be your best friends. The next chapter, "Neighborly Advice," describes their importance.

CHAPTER SIX

Neighborly Advice

GET TO KNOW your rental property's neighbors. The most often ignored aspect of landlording is the relationship between the surrounding neighbors, the tenants, and the landlord. The people who live around your rental house know the property's goings-on much better than you ever will. They see your property night and day. They see the good and the bad sides of your tenants.

As an efficient and effective landlord, you see your tenants only every so often. The more properties you have, the less time you should spend at each. There comes a point when you can spend only so much time on your rentals before the job takes over all your free time. This book emphasizes streamlining your property management. But if you succeed in streamlining, you will be around your property very seldom. If you trust your neighbors and approach them properly, they can be your round-the-clock house watchers and the best friends a landlord can have.

This chapter offers neighborly advice. "Getting in good" with the neighbors pays dividends you can reap for the rest of your landlording career. The best rental homes are the ones not found in typical rental neighborhoods. You'll find the best rental homes in neighborhoods with owner-occupied housing. The neighbors will naturally be suspicious of "that rental house" of yours until you knock on their door and greet them with your caring landlord attitude.

GET TO KNOW THE NEIGHBORS

If you have yet to meet the neighbors on either side of and across the street from your rental home, *run*, don't walk, to their houses right now to meet them. As soon as you close the deal on any future rental house you buy, be sure you've met the neighbors before lifting one paintbrush.

The neighbors around your rental will be there much longer than any tenant ever will. They have much more at stake in your tenants than you do. Good or bad neighboring tenants directly affect their home life. Their children play with your tenants' children. Your tenants' loud parties interrupt their sleep. Your rental properties should be an asset and not a liability to any neighborhood. Make yourself a one-person crusade against a negative attitude toward rental houses on the block! Help improve the neighborhood by being a good citizen, keeping up your property, getting to know the neighbors, helping neighbors if you have the chance, and, above all else, getting tenants that are an asset to the neighborhood.

TIP

Good neighbors are better assets than good tenants.

If you think about it, you will realize that the neighbors want good tenants in your home *more* than you do. If the neighbors like your tenants, you can bet that you will like them, too. If the neighbors do not like the tenants, they probably have good reason. Your bad tenants may jeopardize their peaceful neighborhood. If so, those are tenants you do not want.

Introduce Yourself

Make it easy for your neighbors to get to know you. Before going to the neighbors, write down your name and phone number on a slip of paper, include your rental home's address, and write "owner" by it. You will give this paper to the neighbors once you introduce yourself to them.

When you first introduce yourself, greet the neighbors with a smile and tell them your name. Inform them that you are the owner of the house next door (or across the street). If you have yet to remodel the home, tell them of your plans to make the house something to be proud of. If you are a smart shopper, the rental house is probably a little shabby looking but is structurally sound. Anything you do to improve its appearance will make you a hero to the neighbors. The value of their homes is affected somewhat by the homes that surround theirs.

What they don't know is that you plan to make your home even better-looking than theirs. They will be the ones playing catch-up once they see the white shutters, fresh paint job, and flowers in front.

> **TIP**
>
> Earn the neighbors' trust immediately.

Tell the neighbors this: You value their neighborhood or you would not have bought the house. You will turn your house into something they will be proud to live near. You want them to enjoy having your tenants for long-term neighbors instead of wondering who the next occupants will be and what they will be like. Say these things sincerely; if you cannot, you will not have success in this business and you should try something else.

While you're remodeling the home, be aware of the neighbor's activities. If you can help with something, offer your assistance. Be as much of a good neighbor in your rental home's neighborhood as you are in your own. After all, it is your house, and the success of your rental home depends partly on the neighbors around the home.

Hand the neighbors the slip of paper with your information written on it. Then drop the bombshell: Tell them that you want them to call you if they see *anything* about the house or tenants that they do not like. Tell them that if there are loud parties or too much trash or whatever you will handle the situation *immediately*. Let them know that your tenants will never know who told you about the problem. Reassure the neighbors that you mean to respect their privacy—and make sure that you honor your promise.

TIP

Respect the neighbors' privacy.

Tell the neighbors that if they ever see any illegal activity around your property or if something as simple as a party gets out of hand, they should call you immediately. If you do not answer the phone, they can call the police and you will take full responsibility for the phone call.

Implore them to help you keep good tenants in the home. Tell them that you want tenants they will be proud to have as neighbors. Believe me, this is not a job they will dislike; rather, they will be *very glad* they have a say in who moves in (or better yet, who stays). Tell them you will let the home sit empty for three months rather than let someone move in who might bring down the neighborhood.

Think how powerful this approach is! Can you imagine the respect the neighbors will feel for you? These people, who have a much larger stake in your rental house than you, now feel a part of it, and they know they can trust you. To them, the house is no longer a ghost property with people coming and going every six months, but a home occupied by people you chose with care. It will be a home monitored by you, but more important, by your neighbors, for many years. Your neighbors will get along better with your tenants and you will have fewer problems down the road. If a tenant gets out of hand, you are going to know about it much faster from the neighbors than you would have otherwise.

Introduce the Tenants

When you lease the home to new tenants, give your neighbors the tenants' names so they know who will be living there. Tell your tenants who the neighbors are as well. After learning each other's names, neighbors and tenants are more apt to say, "Good morning," and a neighborly relationship can begin between them.

> **TIP**
>
> Make your tenants and the neighbors feel special.

Better yet, after the initial tenant interview, take your tenants around to all the neighbors and introduce everyone. Be upbeat about the entire situation. After all, you may be building a relationship that could grow into a friendship that keeps the tenants renting your place longer than they would have otherwise. At the very worst, you will know about problems faster and will be able to solve them before they grow too big to handle.

NEIGHBORHOOD PUBLIC RELATIONS

Good relations with the neighbors is yet another way you separate yourself from the cliché of the uncaring landlord. Gaining the trust of the neighbors helps prove with deeds that you care about your rental home, its occupants, and the surrounding neighborhood.

The benefits you reap from good neighbor relations are plenty, but your aim should always be a peaceful and happy rental house. When your tenants and their neighbors are happy, you will be too.

The neighbors are great resources for finding future tenants. If a neighbor recommends people to live in your home, you can bet they will be quality tenants. Still, perform the typical credit checks on them. But all you need for a character reference is the neighbor's recommendation.

> **TIP**
>
> Neighbors often recommend the best tenants.

Would neighbors be honest in their recommendation, or would they recommend someone just because they are friends? Think about it. Don't you have friends who you love, and yet you would *never* want to live next door to them? They might be loud, have too many children, have too many pets, be messy, or whatever. Most people would consider their own situation before recommending anyone, even a best friend, to live next door to them.

The next time your rental home becomes vacant, tell the neighbors that you would like their advice about renting it. They may suggest sprucing up the home in a way that had not occurred to you. Better yet, they might know someone who would make a good tenant and be an asset to the neighborhood. If you rent to the person they suggest, remember to send a thank-you card and a $20 gift. This acknowledgment goes a long way toward ensuring future help as well.

If you eventually sell the home, be sure to tell the neighbors ahead of time. The neighbors very well might have relatives or friends who would love to live there.

Advertise with the Neighbors in Mind

If your neighborhood is decent—and it is if you bought wisely—let the neighborhood help rent your home. When you place an ad for new tenants, consider advertising the neighborhood. If you were a tenant, consider your reactions to an ad headed with the following:

```
GOOD and QUIET Neighborhood!
```

All other ads will pale in comparison. Families and retired people will be drawn to such a heading.

Knowing the lifestyle of the elderly neighbor next to his property, one enterprising landlord used the following headline:

```
Elderly Lady Prefers Same as Neighbor
```

The landlord got calls from more interested senior tenants than from anyone else. Is this age discrimination? The landlord did not make older age a requirement for hiring, but the ad did produce *only* elderly applicants. The landlord knew that older people often make quieter and longer-term tenants than college-age people. The pool of tenants to choose from was skewed toward an older group, and the landlord found that the most qualified tenant happened to be the oldest applicant. Several years later, the tenant was still happily living in the house.

Although I mentioned this in Chapter 1, the advice is worth repeating here: Be careful about opening yourself up to liability by stating in your ad that the neighborhood is safe. You cannot control crime, even in good neighborhoods, and the litigious tendency in today's society means that you should not suggest that your tenants will always be safe living in your home.

Tenant–Neighbor Problems

Although you've done everything you can to promote good relations between your tenants and the neighbors, you cannot control other people's lives. Personalities sometimes clash between the best of people. If you do your job—you are a caring landlord to your tenants and a good neighbor to the rest—you will probably be pulled into the middle of the feud, and you must decide the next step.

The first part of this chapter emphasized how important your house's neighbors are. You saw how the neighbors' view of your tenants is usually better than your own. However, this does not necessarily extend to everyday feuds between the two. If your neighbor calls you about a specific negative behavior repeated by your tenants, step in and handle the problem; evict the tenants if the problem is severe enough. However, if the neighbors call you to complain that the tenants do not get along with them (however they may phrase this), you will need to distinguish the difference between a problem concerning rights and responsibilities, which may need your attention, and a problem of personality or difference of opinion, which usually you should not have to solve.

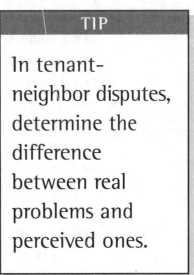

TIP

In tenant-neighbor disputes, determine the difference between real problems and perceived ones.

Here is where you must employ tact and good timing. You cannot, and should not, always jump into the middle of such a feud, at least at the beginning. You cannot police every little detail. Many neighborly feuds fizzle into quiet acquiescence after a while.

I had one situation where the perfect tenants caused problems with some of the home's neighbors. The neighbors own their home and have a bigger stake than my tenants. The neighbors called me about the rift, so I called the tenants. My tenants paid on time, never complained, and kept my place clean, so I gave them an initial benefit of the doubt. My tenants told me that the neighbors had been yelling at them and throwing trash in their yard. I made the decision to do nothing at that point, but I was in a dilemma: Despite the fact that the tenants were great, my neighbors were also.

About two weeks later I received a call from the neighbors again stating that the feud was growing and that they were about to call the police. I decided to side with the neighbors for this reason: Although I was in the middle of what seemed to be petty arguments, both my tenants and the neighbors seemed reasonable and not the kind to blow up at something small. I knew that I could get different tenants but not different neighbors. I was fortunate in that my tenants' six-month lease had expired and converted to a month-to-month lease, so I could give my tenants their notice. I called them up and told them that I appreciated their living in my home but that I could not afford to have problems with the neighbors. I was pleasant but firm and my tenants gave me no trouble.

I've never had problems with those neighbors again. Although I truly believe that neither party was doing a major wrong, and that it was just petty friction, I knew that my long-term obligation was ultimately to the neighbors. I showed my neighbors that I respected their opinion, I solved their problem, and I know that the neighbors are happy with the tenants I've had ever since.

SUMMARY

I cannot overemphasize the importance of your rental home's neighbors. The neighbors' view of your house and its tenants is probably more accurate than your own, since they see the home day in and day out.

Get to know as many neighbors around the home as possible. They can be a valuable resource for finding new tenants and policing current ones. You could very easily encourage a friendship between the tenants and the neighbors as well. If that happens, the tenants may stay in the home longer than they otherwise would.

If a problem arises between your tenants and the neighbors, you must sort it out and decide what to do—not always a simple task. The benefit of the doubt should fall with your neighbors, however, because they will be around much longer than your tenants will be.

CHAPTER SEVEN

Handling Tenant Problems and Problem Tenants

PROBLEMS CAN OCCUR between the best of people. Problems *always* occur between bad tenants and good landlords. Despite the fact that this book stresses carefree tenant management, you will sometimes have problems with your tenants. You cannot manage rental properties for many years without running into a hassle now and then. If landlording was easy and took no time whatsoever, everybody would be doing it! Your aim should be trouble-free management, in as far as that is possible. From reading this book so far, you already know how to improve your odds of getting good tenants. You also know that honey catches more flies than vinegar does, and the more friendly, honest, and sincere you are to your tenants and would-be tenants, the more they will respect your wishes during their stay.

Not all problems are major. Actually, unless you get deadbeat tenants or tenants who destroy your property, you can avoid most major problems if you deal with them early. This might mean an amicable parting of the ways. It might even mean releasing tenants from their lease early, giving them a full refund of their deposit, or actually paying them to move somewhere else (it's been known to happen and in some situations may be cheaper than letting problems fester). Despite good people and best intentions, personality clashes and difficulties can occur.

This chapter describes how to deal with tenant problems and problem tenants. When annoyances occur, you must decide if they are worth the tenants' stay or if they could turn into something more serious and costly. Whether a discussion or eviction is warranted, you must be armed with a friendly but businesslike attitude and be ready to take stern action. As the last chapter explained, your tenants and neighbors can clash and your neighbors are almost always right. Dealing with the problem tenants, however, is not usually an easy job.

Tenants do not always believe in a landlord's "conviction of eviction." Your tenants will probably assume you are not the type of landlord who would want to evict anyone. They are correct: You do not want to, but you know that you might have to at a moment's notice, and you must be prepared. Some landlords will let problems continue as long as possible as long as the rent comes in, but let me assure you that the rent is secondary to problem tenants, and you'll be worse off financially if you put rent before the problem.

> **TIP**
>
> Do you stand firm with a "conviction of eviction"? You should!

TENANT COMPLAINTS

Tenants want to be happy, get value for their money, and have a safe place to live. They deserve all these things. Help them achieve this goal by treating them as you would want to be treated. Before refusing any tenant request, put yourself in the tenants' shoes. Remember that from where tenants sit, you are their caring landlord who showed them so much attention when they first looked at your house and when they moved in.

Not all tenants are honest, but neither are all landlords. However, many tenants and landlords are honest. If a tenant calls to tell you about a problem with the house, assume it really is a problem and check it out. The worst disasters are not always true disasters. Each situation is different, but after a while, you will be able to read your tenants and their problems and know how to cope best.

> **TIP**
>
> Assume that your tenants are honest until you have reason to believe otherwise.

Suppose a tenant calls in the middle of a blizzard to inform you the central heating unit stopped working and the family is freezing. The first thoughts that flash through your mind are the cost of a new unit, the cost of putting up the tenants in a hotel until the unit arrives, and the difficulty you will face trying to find the cheapest and best deal on a new unit. After your split-second of agony, calmly assure the tenant that you'll be right over to see what needs to be done. When you get there, you discover a tripped circuit breaker; in one minute, the heat is working again. Show the tenants how to correct this problem themselves for future reference and wish them a warm winter. (Warn them that if the breaker trips repeatedly, more than once or twice a week during heavy usage, to call you. Another problem probably exists in the circuit, and you should have a licensed electrician check it out.)

TENANT REQUESTS

Tenants must understand that you do not have to honor all requests. If they request something that is unreasonable, tell them so. Every time your tenants ask you for something, you must perform a quick cost analysis to see whether you can afford to make the change (assuming it is not safety related, which is always warranted). The cost is more than just money: The tenants' happiness is also a worthy asset, depending on the quality of the tenants and how long they have rented from you.

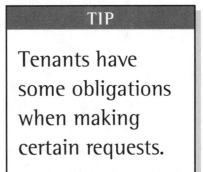

TIP

Tenants have some obligations when making certain requests.

If you feel that a tenant's request is unjustified, you might consider other alternatives before denying the request altogether. Suggest that you go halfway. If tenants want a garbage disposal, tell them that you will pay for half (including installation costs if you don't do it yourself), but the disposal must remain with the building when the tenant leaves.

If the tenant balks at paying half and you balk at paying all, the stand-off might not be worth the hard feelings. An easy way to deal with such a request is to tell the tenants that the house at this moment is the house they originally rented. If they want an extra such as a garbage disposal, they must pay more rent or help pay some of the disposal's cost to you. If the tenant does not like this, you can draw up an agreement stating that one of you will buy out the other's half upon the tenants' move-out. Approach such small "partnerships" with caution: Buying the other's half is a lot of trouble, especially if you do not agree on a price at the beginning; and if the tenant removes the disposal, you must make sure no damage was done to the surrounding structure.

Give the Tenant a Deductible

Your insurance company asks you to pay for the first few dollars of any damage. This is the deductible that you must cover before the insurance begins to pay. The deductible keeps you from bothering the insurance company for minor complaints. Why not do the same for tenant complaints? Put a deductible in your lease that requires the tenants to pay for the first $25 of each expense. Your tenants will ask for much less than they might otherwise ask for.

You run a risk in requiring the repair deductible, however. The tenant may let a needed repair go undone, causing greater damage. In addition, the tenant might try to fix the problem to save the $25 and end up making things worse. I do not require such a deductible, because I can tell my tenants no when their complaints are unjustified, and I certainly do not want the tenants fixing things around the house to save $25. Some landlords let their tenants fix whatever they want to fix. Generally these landlords are lazy and do not want to properly maintain properties themselves. If your tenants are by nature or profession handy in one or more key areas of rental property maintenance, such as plumbing or electricity, then you may want to give them permission to make certain kinds of repairs. Be sure to pay the tenant as you would pay someone who does not rent from you for making the repair.

A deductible makes sense for some. However, I would let the prospective tenants know about the deductible when they fill out the application at the open house or else it could catch them by surprise and anger them when it's time to sign the lease. In addition, if your rent is below market value, you have more reason to use the deductible to keep expenses down.

Don't Be Blackmailed

Tenants cannot "hold out" rent just because you do not honor their requests. Just as you cannot shut off the utilities, remove important items from the house they rented (such as the front door), change the locks, or sell their furniture if they do not pay; they cannot refuse to pay just because they don't like the way you handle things. (Of course, this excludes safety measures you've neglected and serious maintenance items you've left unfixed.)

If tenants hold out payment as ransom until you bow to their whims, deal a swift and *strong* hand with a notice of eviction (6 A.M. is always a good time for a deputy to serve notice; it gets tenants' attention). Rent is not a tenant's bargaining tool. As long as a lease is in effect, even a month-to-month lease, the tenant cannot refuse to pay without defaulting on the lease.

Suppose that when you rented to your tenants, you specified that they could not have a waterbed in the house. There are many reasons for not allowing waterbeds: For one, they are heavy. Before letting your tenants have them, you should make sure the second floor can hold the weight (a structural engineer can tell you). Another danger is leaks; a leak on the second floor wreaks havoc on the first-floor ceilings. Since leaks are common, you should make the waterbed/no waterbed decision before leasing your property. Let's say you've decided not to allow waterbeds at the risk of losing some good tenants who might use a waterbed. You even included a clause in the tenants' lease that clearly states your waterbed policy. Nevertheless, your tenants call you one afternoon to tell you they just bought a king-size waterbed and traded in their old bed. They ask whether it's okay to put it in the bedroom directly over that new dining room ceiling you painted last week.

At this point, you will feel like the bad guy when you politely state your objection and remind the tenants of the no-waterbed policy in the lease. Obviously, if you did not want a waterbed when you rented to the tenants, you certainly do not want one now. Here is what you can say:

I enjoy having you as a tenant, and I hope the waterbed is not so important that it forces you to find another place to live. However, whether it is justified or not, I sleep better knowing that only regular and lighter beds are in the home. My insurance agent sleeps better also. Therefore, I hope there is another place you can store the bed while you stay in the home you rent from me.

You can adjust this statement for other problems that come along. Waterbeds are not the only change a tenant may want to make. Adding pets where none or only one was allowed is common. Most of the time, you find out about new pets only after the tenants have had them awhile. The really bad thing about a pet is that once tenants have owned one for more than a week or two, the family will be very attached—probably more so than to your house. Such tenants will probably move quickly rather than give up the family pet. This is one of the problems with being a landlord: Tenants never like you as much as they like their own dogs and cats.

Obviously, guide dogs and other disabled-support dogs play an important role in many people's lives. In most states, you cannot prohibit guide dogs except in rental agreements entered into before November 1, 1985. Some local ordinances actually let you stand firm against renting to people with animals of *any* kind, but if you do not rent to people who require guide dogs, the odds are great that you're depriving yourself of the best tenants you'll ever have. By the way, dogs are now trained to help people with disabilities other than impaired vision.

In addition, some people may need a waterbed for back problems. If you are unsure if your structure can handle the weight, you'll have to deny this tenant requirement on those grounds. To protect yourself, you might want to ask a structural engineer about the weight before turning down such applicants. Get a written suggestion that you should not allow waterbeds from the engineer to protect you from lawsuits based on Americans with Disabilities Act discrimination charges. At the same time, you can protect yourself from fraud by asking to see a prescription for the bed if you suspect that a tenant might be exaggerating the need for a waterbed. Tell the tenant that you normally do not allow waterbeds, but if they show a legitimate need, you will consider it as long as your structure can take the weight.

Most multilevel residences built in the last twenty years can handle waterbeds just fine. The older units may require some structural inspection, however. Look in your yellow pages under "Engineer" and you'll find listings for the ones who inspect structures.

A NOTE ABOUT UTILITIES

Once tenants let a utility get shut off, even those who stay current with their rent, you can bet that they will either move out or get behind on the rent almost immediately afterward. There is rarely an exception to this rule. Some tenants have their phone removed because they never use it enough to justify the expense. But that can be a hassle for you as the landlord since you cannot reach them very easily. You can feel justified in requiring that all utilities, including the phone, remain on and paid up. (The lease contracts in Chapter 4 contain utility bill clauses.)

The utility clause in the lease gives you added protection to get the tenant out before the rent invariably becomes past due. You cannot evict tenants just because they do not pay their utilities, despite what the lease says, but the agreement does give you a little more control in a court battle if one ensues. The clause is as good as gold if the house is in danger of freezing pipes because the tenant did not keep the heat on.

THE OFFENDERS

Although you have done everything in your power to get good tenants, showing them that you care about them and the home they live in, some will still take advantage of your good nature and test your "conviction of eviction." There are not many different possibilities. Evictions usually occur because of lack of payment (including bounced checks), disturbing noise from loud parties (the last chapter made it clear what to do if a trusted neighbor complains about parties), destruction of your property, extreme uncleanliness, and, probably the worst of all, illegal activity on your property. You can handle many of the minor tenant problems without the strong arm of eviction.

> **TIP**
>
> Utility shutoffs indicate that rent shutoffs are imminent.

Sometimes, bluffing about an eviction is enough to take care of the problem. Nevertheless, do not use this bluff too often. A tenant will call you on it and force you to take eviction steps, or the bluff becomes a cry of wolf that falls on deaf ears.

If a tenant deserves an eviction threat, the tenant deserves an actual eviction. Since you clearly explained what activities could cause an eviction during the new tenant interview (an important process described in Chapter 4), your tenants have no excuse. When you lay down your rules at the beginning, you make it clear that those rules are not to be broken. You have informed the tenants that they are renting in a peaceful neighborhood—and you want it kept that way.

Problems Collecting the Rent

Sometimes tenants make requests that really test your mettle as a landlord. Say a new tenant calls you the second month of tenancy to say that an unexpected doctor's bill took this month's rent money. You have two options: Let the tenant pay later or evict the tenant.

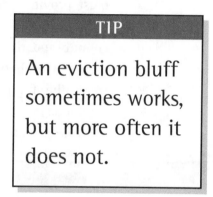

TIP

An eviction bluff sometimes works, but more often it does not.

The problem with the first option is you may be too trusting. The tenant's background checked out or you would not have rented the house. At the time, the tenant seemed able to pay. The biggest problem with the news is its timing. Tenants who have paid on time for two years but need a break one month are much different from tenants who are only into their second month's rent. You thought you could relax for six months to a year, but it looks as if you must go through the open house and tenant-selection process all over again. With that staring at you, you will want to be lenient, but whether you should be is a judgment call that only you can make.

In such a situation, you would be more than justified to ask to see the doctor's bill. The tenant can cover up the treatment information if the cause is private, but you have the right to know why your rent is being pushed to the end of the line. Remind the tenant that you trusted the tenant enough to rent to him or her originally. Also tell the tenant that you both just recently signed an important legal document, the lease, stating that the tenant would pay you in full every month. Your tenant signed that lease knowing the risks involved, and so did you. You do not take that type of thing lightly and neither should the tenant.

Most landlords would evict these tenants, and such landlords would not be wrong in doing so. Heartless? Not at all. You can start your own charity if you like, but rental properties are not charities. Your first priority is to your own family, for whom you must provide adequate stewardship support. But what will the tenants do and where will they live? If they want to stay badly enough and their backgrounds checked out when they applied, they can probably get the rent money from somewhere, either from other family members or from a bank.

Nobody wins with eviction. You lose tenants (albeit usually bad ones), your tenants lose a nice place to stay, the courts stay full, and the economy stays down. Before evicting tenants, consider offering them a *temporary* option. If they pay monthly, as most do, see whether they can pay weekly or every two weeks until they catch up with their other bills. You can draw up a very informal agreement stating that from a certain day of this month until a specific day in the future, a weekly payment overrides the monthly payment section in the tenants' original lease agreement. A certain amount is due and payable on a specific day of the week. Add a clause to state that there is no late fee in this temporary lease amendment as *no late payment will be accepted*. Figure 7-1 shows a sample lease-change agreement that you and your tenants can sign for this special case.

Be sure such a lease-change agreement is very short term and ends on a specific date. It takes just as long to evict tenants who pay weekly as it does those who pay monthly, and giving tenants

> **TIP**
>
> Consider changing the payment plan only as a last resort.

FIGURE 7–1. A sample lease-change agreement

---

* TEMPORARY LEASE-CHANGE AGREEMENT *

From June 1, 2001, until June 30, 2001, Sam Garrett, "Landlord," and Diana Haynes, "Tenant" (both signed below), agree to modify temporarily, within the date limits just described, their lease agreement.

The tenant agrees to pay the full monthly required rent in four weekly installments of one hundred fifty dollars ($150) due in the Landlord's possession on Friday of each week of the temporary time period.

There is no late statute or fee in this temporary lease amendment as no late payment will be accepted from the Tenant. If any installment is not paid on or before the due day of each week, the original lease agreement will take effect again, with the full past-due portion payable and due, and full eviction proceedings will begin.

Signed on May 29, 2001, by:

_____   _____
(Landlord)   (Tenant)

---

an easy payment plan makes you that much more vulnerable later. The easier you are, the more you can be taken advantage of, so be sure your leniency is limited.

Will this same scenario happen with your tenants? It may not, but there are a million other problems that occur without easy solutions. You must consider your peace of mind, your income, and your property's well-being to reach the right decision for each situation.

Whatever problems come up, attempt to resolve them without going through the legal hassles of eviction (a later section describes how to evict tenants). Use eviction only as a last resort.

Alternative payment plans may help your tenants in a pinch and also keep them faithful to you for a long time. Don't feel like an ogre if you offer an alternative payment plan that adds up to a higher monthly rent than what your tenants normally pay. After all, it is the *tenants'* fault that the situation occurred, and dealing with it in this way requires more of *your* time and effort—for which you could justifiably require reimbursement.

> **TIP**
>
> If possible, it's best to resolve problems without resorting to eviction.

Good Tenants, Bad Circumstances

Tenants with good intentions and bad circumstances are the difficult ones to evict. Suppose tenants just cannot pay because of bad luck or the loss of a job. Perhaps they rented above their means but neither you nor they realized this early enough. You can evict them, but there is something that might work better and be quicker and easier for both of you—as long as the tenants are responsible in other ways (they are quiet and take care of your property).

Set up a meeting with the tenants at the home. When you get there, sit down with them and say:

You have not been able to pay me for this month's rent. I think that you and I both know that this place is just a little more than you can afford at this time. I would be willing to let you out of your lease and give you your full deposit back, if you leave the home just as good as or better than you found it. Also, if you want to rent a place that is less expensive, something you know you could afford, I would be willing to tell your next landlord that you took care of my place, were good tenants, and that my price was just too high for your current needs and payment abilities.

After this conversation, the odds are good that your tenants will be *relieved* to hear this. First of all, they assumed when you made your appointment that you were going to read them a three-day notice for eviction or something equally bad. Instead, they heard an understanding landlord who wants to help them in an amicable way.

Tenants Who Break the Law

Some of the worst tenants are those who break laws on your property. Drug offenses are common, but other illegal commercial activities could be going on at your property as well. But even these severe situations do not always require an eviction.

You must handle tenants' criminal activity carefully. You cannot walk into their home while they're gone and snoop for evidence of crime. This is illegal, and in a free country your tenants have a protected right to privacy. However, if you fix their water heater and smell marijuana, or if a neighbor complains about comings and goings throughout the night, you have a responsibility as a citizen to do something about it. No matter how promptly these

TIP

Show no tolerance for law-breaking tenants.

tenants pay, you do not want them in your rental or your rental neighborhood. You want to make it as difficult as possible for these people to continue their wrongful business; you do not want to provide them shelter.

If you have strong reason to believe that illegal activity is taking place, call the police immediately. You can meet the police at the property or just report the incident and request that your name not be mentioned. If the police find a problem, you will not have to worry about eviction. Whether or not the tenants go to jail, their police record will be the only eviction defense you need. Again, a full legal eviction may not even be necessary. If the tenants are convicted, you have only to find designated family members who can remove the tenants' belongings.

Even if the tenants are not sent to jail, you can go to your property with an off-duty police officer to discuss the situation with the tenants. The officer can back up the fact that an illegal offense is enough to warrant and win an eviction. Tell the tenants (or any innocent family members left behind) that they must leave or you will have to evict them. Do not say you are sorry at any point in the conversation. This is one time when you are not bluffing about the eviction and when you should be forceful in every regard. I personally have no tolerance for landlords who tolerate illegal activities. Although our judicial system often offers second chances, I do not.

My position is upheld by the law. In 1995, the U.S. Housing Secretary signed a "one strike and you're out" law that orders eviction for anyone committing a violent or drug-related crime in public housing. Before the law went into effect, notification and hearings would have to take place before the eviction could occur, and such hearings can often extend indefinitely. I would not hesitate to extend that to my own housing, although public housing standards have been known to differ from those that apply to private homes. The law states that even if the rest of the family is left homeless by the eviction, the eviction can take place without recourse. The American Civil Liberties Union has challenged this law. At the time of this writing, the ACLU's challenge has been ignored and the government's position of "one strike and you're out" still holds for renters who commit a violent or drug-related crime.

Tenants Who Write Bad Checks

Not as serious as drugs, but still a big problem, is a bad check. If tenants write you a bad check, make sure your bank runs it through twice. Most banks do this, but call your bank to verify the process used to return the check. A call to the tenants' bank will verify whether you can now cash their check.

Even the richest of the rich sometimes write bad checks. Math errors and spousal spending sometimes lead to bad checks. If you get a bad check, the tenants' bank has probably already mailed them a notice. However, they may not have received the notice yet. With luck, the tenants only made a mistake, and they have the cash to correct it. If tenants do write a bad check, for whatever reason, require cash or a money order or cashier's check from that point forward. This is a hassle for your tenants—but it is not your fault they wrote the bad check.

TIP

Mistakes do happen. Ask tenants about a bad check before you take any further steps.

Some landlords go to the tenants' bank and ask how much they can cash the check for. Suppose your tenant wrote you a check for $500 but only has $350 in the account. You can request the $350 in payment of the check. Banks do not like to do this (it messes up their ledgers and their accountants do not like unbalanced transactions), but they will if you insist. The risk you run is timing. The longer you wait, the less the tenant may have in the account. But if you go too soon, you might beat a deposit that would have given you the full amount. When you request a lower withdrawal on a check, you usually give up your rights to the remaining balance on that particular check because the bank will consider the check paid in full.

Another relatively unknown tactic is called "submitting a collection item." This is rarely done, and many tellers may not even know it is possible, so ask a bank officer to help you. Submitting an item for collection requires a small fee, so you won't collect the full amount, but the fee is typically $15 or less per item. When you hold a check for collection, you put yourself next in line for the account's funds. Suppose your tenant writes a check to a doctor and deposits just enough money to cover the doctor's check but not yours as well. If your check is being held for collection, the bank waits until there is enough money in the account to cover the check, no matter what is next in line, and pays the money to you. Even if the tenant deposits a paycheck and wants cash back, your check will take precedence (that is, unless the teller is not paying attention).

The drawback to collecting a check in this manner is that the bank often notifies the tenant that the check is being held for collection. Evasive tenants will know not to make a deposit if they do not want to pay you. Many times, however, the tenant will make a deposit before being notified and your collection item gets top priority. By the way, some people who are caught off guard bounce many other checks before they learn that yours was at the top of the list for collection. Although they wrote you the bad check, the collection item can sometimes allow you to be paid by a deadbeat whose problems instantly multiply when checks he or she thought would go through begin to bounce.

Figure 7-2 shows an example of a collection item letter you can mail to the bank along with the bad check if you want to handle the problem by mail. You could mail the collection item to the bank if your tenant vacated the premises and you're busy

FIGURE 7-2. A sample collection item letter

February 3, 2001

Head Cashier
c/o: LaSalle Bank
Chicago, IL 60629

Dear Head Cashier:

Enclosed is a check I received back due to insufficient funds.

I'm placing this check in your hands as a collection item for 60 days. If there is a charge, please deduct the charge from my remittance regardless of how much of the $20 the charge consumes.

I've enclosed a self-addressed, stamped envelope for your convenience.

Thank you very much for your time. I realize this is a small matter for you, but I appreciate your cooperation.

Sincerely,

Sam Garrett
913 East Oak Road
Miami, Florida 41156

getting the property fixed up for another tenant, or if the bank is located far from your town.

If the tenant says, "The check should be good now. Run it through and it should clear," be wary. You have every right in the world to expect and require cash or its equivalent when a tenant writes you a bad check. Inspect each bad check written to you. If the check says "insufficient funds," the tenant does not have enough money in the account to cover the check. If the check was written on a "closed account," you have a much more interesting situation on your hands. The tenant may now be a felon.

Writing a check on a closed account is a much more serious offense than writing a bad check from an active account. Call the tenant's bank to find out the date the account was closed. If that date falls before the date on the check, the tenant probably knowingly wrote a check on a closed account. But again, a simple phone call is in order first. Maybe the tenant's spouse closed the account because he or she found a better interest rate elsewhere and the tenant forgot and wrote you a check on the old account. This is a long shot but worth checking out.

If the closed account is not easily explained and corrected with cash, your town's local district attorney may be interested in the problem of checks written knowingly on a closed account. Even if the D.A. does not seem interested, report it. A hot check deserves immediate cash payment, although an eviction is probably more appropriate in most cases. Nothing should be more important on your list of tenants' priorities than paying you in full and on time. If something else gets in the way of that, eviction will at least ensure that they don't do it to you twice.

TIP
Bad-check writing may be felonious.

Even if your district attorney ignores the problem, the D.A.'s office will record the bad check in the city's records, and it will be added to the tenants' credit report. Subsequent credit checks done on your tenant will see the D.A.'s entry, which will make it harder for your tenant to take advantage of someone else.

GETTING RID OF BAD TENANTS

If your tenants deserve eviction, you must act swiftly. Illegal activities and lack of payment deserve nothing less in most cases.

Of course, each situation requires your attention and not every situation warrants eviction. Try eviction last; attempt to work with your tenants, especially ones that have been good up until the problem began.

Your state's Landlord and Tenant Act (a copy of which is available at your county library) describes your rights to evict as a landlord. The sad news is that most landlords rarely read this important governing document. The good news is that most tenants fail to read it also. The odds are on your side if you follow the act's rules regarding landlording and eviction allowances.

Most counties' small-claims courts handle evictions. Normally, you do not need a lawyer, especially if you do your homework. Take with you to court all records (including the details of payment or lack of payment) that pertain to the current tenants' occupancy. Show proof that you properly escrowed the deposit. If you filed the lease at the courthouse when the tenants moved in, bring a certified copy of the filing to the initial hearing. If you did your part (especially escrowing the deposit, which most landlords fail to do), there is little chance the tenants will win.

> **TIP**
>
> Show up at the eviction hearing and hope the tenant does not.

When tenants are sued in court (eviction is a type of lawsuit), they must show up to the hearing or they will automatically receive a guilty verdict. Tenants do not always show up for eviction hearings. Most of them know they will lose, especially if you have been a first-rate landlord in every way. What tenants may not realize is that today's court system works around bargaining. You may want your $750 in unpaid rent plus court costs, but tenants might be able to get the judge to lower the judgment amount. Such judgments are not always fair (many courts are too liberal in most landlords' eyes), but tenants give up all bargaining power by not showing up. No defense means guilt by default.

Although I rarely have to take renters to court, all but one have failed to appear and I got default judgments in every case but that one. The one who did show had to pay full damages. In court, I have received a large majority of what was due me. I hope you are as fortunate. Judging by my history, I would strongly urge you to take your case to small-claims court every time a tenant does you wrong.

Just because a judge rules in your favor, awarding bargained or full damages, it does not mean you will get your money. But that is not your primary goal: Throughout the entire eviction, stay focused on getting the bad tenants out of your rental and good ones into it. Be aware that even if the judge rules in your favor, not all tenants will pay you. You can garnish their wages and even their income tax refunds for past-due rent, but you will have to pay added court costs—and you still may not get the rent if a tenant later quits or loses his or her job.

> **TIP**
>
> Some states let you garnish tax refunds for past-due rent.

If all else fails, you can request a body attachment: A deputy will pick up the tenant and jail him or her. Again, you shoulder the cost of this, but the tenant will not be doing the same thing to another landlord down the road. Cost, trouble, guilt, and even fear keep many landlords from going this far. Your role is not district attorney or likable landlord. Make sure that getting the old tenant out and a new one in is your primary concern.

The only time I had to request a body attachment was when a tenant failed to appear at every hearing. The police first called her to see if she was home and warned her they were picking her up. Before the police knocked on her door to take her to jail, she had called me and put cash in my hands within the hour. She stayed out of jail and I got my money including *all* court fees and late charges (it was either that or jail). I called the courthouse to cancel the attachment and filed a cancellation order as soon as I got the money. Although I didn't think the police were prudent to warn her by phone that they were coming, things could not have turned out better.

The Steps to Eviction

To make an eviction, you must follow several steps. Check with your state's most recent Landlord and Tenant Act to make sure what these steps are in your state. Eviction means a court appearance, and to get someone in court means that you must inform that person of your intent to sue. This is called "giving proper service." The eviction steps described in these pages are merely guidelines. The actual process varies from state to state. The county court clerk will help you with the details and verify that your eviction notice is being handled properly for your state.

You must do the following to evict a tenant:

1. Formally ask the tenant to leave with a delivered notice similar to the example in Figure 7-3 (get proof of delivery or use a process server). The notice gives your tenant fair notice of your eviction intent.

2. File an action for eviction with your county's small-claims court. The clerk will set a date for your court appearance, of which the tenant must be notified. The clerk will ask how you want the notice served to the defendant (you are the *plaintiff* and the tenant is the *defendant*). You and the clerk must ensure that proper time is given between the serving of the eviction paper and the court appearance.

FIGURE 7-3. A sample eviction warning

EVICTION NOTICE

To: Tammy Medlin

November 1, 2001

Please consider this letter a 30-day notice from the above date to vacate premises at 205 N. Monroe, Braggs, Oklahoma. If, after inspection, the unit is found clean, free of damages, and in move-in condition, your deposit of $195.00 will be returned to you upon the return of the unit's keys to the owner/landlord.

Glen Harrison, Owner/Landlord

cc: Muskogee County Court Clerk

Although an attorney's recommendation is always safer than going without one, you have little need for an attorney in an eviction proceeding. Small-claims court costs are minimal, and your damages rarely justify the expense of an attorney. One of the only exceptions is if your tenant has done severe damage to your property and you are suing for an extremely large repair amount. If the suit is too large (the amount varies state by state), the small-claims court will refuse to hear the case and you will have to move it (with the help of an attorney) to a higher court.

3. You must serve, or have served, a proper eviction notice informing tenants of the court appearance and the reason for the suit. State the tenants' names as they appear on the lease (be sure to include every name on the lease if you rent to more than one person), the property's address, the total amount of rent and late fees due as of the date of the serving, the reason for eviction (a

one-sentence general description is better than details), and the date of the court appearance. Sign the notice. Figure 7-4 shows a sample eviction notice that you can modify to meet your own needs. The notice differs from Figure 7-3's warning in that the tenant has fair notice of the court appearance, and the tenant's refusal to adhere to the court summons is serious business. It is most important that you properly serve the tenants. You can call your local sheriff's office for a brochure outlining proper serving requirements.

Better than serving notice yourself, although a little more expensive, is hiring it out. The sheriff's office will serve your notice, usually within three days, for a moderate fee. The sheriff's office will ensure that the notice is properly served. In addition, a sheriff's car and uniform is a little more intimidating than a landlord's suit. The drawback to using the sheriff is that there may be a backlog of notices that must be served before yours. When you evict a tenant you want the wheels of justice to turn as quickly as possible. Three days is a long time before the tenant gets the notice; from there, your county's ordinances will dictate how many days the tenant has before being required to appear in court.

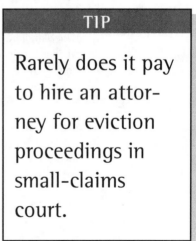

TIP

Rarely does it pay to hire an attorney for eviction proceedings in small-claims court.

More timely, and a little more personal, is hiring an off-duty police officer to serve the notice. Find an officer who is interested in serving an eviction notice during off-duty time for a fair fee—usually the same amount the sheriff's office charges. The officer will appear at the property to serve notice, at a time agreed on by both of you. The officer will be familiar with proper serving requirements and will get the notice served

FIGURE 7-4. A sample eviction notice

Date: _____

This Warrant for Eviction, being filed in the _____ County Courthouse and Sheriff's Office in _____ County, is the immediate application for _____ to vacate the premises of _____, within 5 (five) days, on or before _____, or face physical eviction by the Sheriff of _____ County.

The violations of the contract for rent, with continued late payments despite a written warning from the landlord about such, as well as multiple neighborhood complaints, immediately and adequately warrants the owner of the property to re-establish vacancy.

Upon the _____ day of _____, should the former tenant, _____, still hold vacancy, of any kind, all possessions in the household will immediately be confiscated, stored, and sold according to the laws of the State of _____.

The vacancy of the property in no way concludes the moneys owed to the owner/landlord, _____, and the owner/landlord can make full use of the _____ court system to claim the moneys owed him as well as any damage to the property after the tenant's vacancy.

This notice is intended for the purpose of terminating the rental agreement by which the tenant now abides, and should the tenant fail to comply, legal proceedings will be instituted against immediately to recover possession, to declare said rental agreement forfeited, and to recover rents and/or damages for the period of unlawful and unpaid detention.

Dated this _____ day of _____, _____.

_____
        Owner/Landlord

Filed: _____ County Courthouse

- -

On _____, _____ properly served this eviction notice.

quicker than the sheriff's office usually can. He or she will also appreciate the extra income. Pay the officer in cash. The off-duty officer will appreciate the extra income more and you will waste less of your money on red tape.

Whether the sheriff's office or an off-duty officer serves the notice, get the server to sign a statement at the bottom of the notice (and on your copy) that says something similar to "Officer Marlin Underwood properly served this eviction notice on this 8th day of November, 2001." You will then have a record that the server properly served the notice, and it will be difficult for the tenant to maintain that he or she never received it.

4. Appear in court. In small-claims court, you will represent yourself, so take all your records, including the bank account statement showing that you properly escrowed the tenants' security and cleaning deposit. State the facts, but do not speak until the judge asks you to. You are holding all the cards in this case, so don't lose your cool. The tenants are the ones who must defend your allegations. Even though defendants are innocent until proved guilty, eviction laws are clear and you must be prepared to justify your side of the case.

5. Upon awarding you damages, the court will require that the tenants make all payments, including past-due rents and late fees, to you. Inform the judge of the original deposit's amount and ask if you can apply it to the judgment. Although the deposit is not meant to be used for past-due rent, the judge will almost invariably rule that you can use it in this case.

If the judge lets you use the deposit for part of the past-due rent, you may still have a problem. If the tenants are still in residence, you haven't been able to inspect the home's move-out condition, so you don't know how much of the deposit will be left. Ask the judge what you can do in this case. He or she will probably allow you to use your own judgment when the time comes and to keep however much of the deposit is left, once you clean up and make necessary repairs.

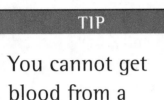

TIP

You cannot get blood from a turnip or money from a tenant who simply will not pay.

If the tenants do not have the money, the judge will dictate a payment schedule or ask you and your tenants to determine one. The judge has the right to delve into the tenants' financial status to determine exactly how long they have to pay you full restitution.

The judge will also specify the date that the tenants must vacate the premises if they have not already done so (most tenants will already be out by this time). Giving them three to five days to move is fair. If the judge is a little more lenient with tenants and allows them one or two weeks, *politely* state that you need to rent the property as soon as possible. Ask if there is any way the judge can shorten the tenants' occupancy. Rarely will a judge change an initial declaration, but you have a chance if you are humble and polite.

6. If the judge has set up a payment schedule, you must wait for the tenant to pay you. While waiting, begin the process of getting good tenants into the home. An empty house invites trouble (some insurance policies require your rental property to be rented before the policy is valid), so do not let the negative aspects of the eviction outweigh your positive attitude toward the house. Again, if landlording were extremely easy, everybody would have rental properties, and your competition would be fierce.

If tenants fail to pay you according to the schedule agreed to in or dictated by the court, you can garnish their wages. But garnishment requires you to appear in court again, and costs more money. At this point, you may have to drop the eviction case if the additional costs do not seem to justify the possible income. Getting the tenants out of the house is more important than squeezing past-due rent from tenants who refuse to pay.

If you decide to continue with the garnishment, you must be able to find out where the tenant works. Not all employers support wage garnishment, but they will respond if the court requires it. If the tenant does not have a job, or if you cannot find out where the tenant works, you can get a body attachment, as described earlier, which allows the sheriff to arrest and jail the tenant until he or she pays you the money.

Of course, jailed tenants cannot get your money to you if they do not have it, so make the body attachment procedure your last resort. Nevertheless, if a tenant is simply not going to pay you, do not feel guilty about the body attachment; the tenant might stiff the next landlord.

If the tenants have not vacated the premises by the court's determined date, a sheriff will help move them out for you. This can get messy, so ask the sheriff's office about its procedures. Despite the court order, no sheriff will help you move furniture to the curb (I know this from personal experience). When you get possession of a home that is still illegally occupied by tenants, the sheriff will accompany you to the home to help turn the home over to you. The sheriff will help reduce problems and can provide some protection if your tenants decide to stay at any cost. (This worst-case scenario rarely and usually never happens.) The sheriff can make sure that you get the tenants out while you change the locks and begin getting a moving company to haul off the possessions.

Most moving companies will itemize the possessions and store them for you. This record is helpful if you later sell the possessions to reimburse yourself for lost rent and damages. In addition, the record will show that you did not remove some-thing the tenants might accuse you of stealing later.

In all my landlording years, I've been left with a house full of possessions only once. The sheriff and I went in and the place was a mess but not torn up. All the tenant's possessions were there. With the court ordering me to take possession, I began moving the items out to the curb. Perhaps I should have itemized things and hired a moving company but prudence doesn't always come easy to a landlord who's been stolen from. I didn't think it was my responsibility to worry about her things since I had legal possession of the home. The sheriff told me that the stuff that was left, although it included furniture, looked like junk and that most people (including himself he confided) would consider the belongings refuse.

I changed the locks and left things at the curb overnight. The next morning, most of the stuff was gone, and I believe people driving by during the night, not the former tenant, took the things. I never heard from that tenant again. She let an entire household of goods and furniture get taken because she did not want to face the courts. Later, the district attorney called me and wanted to know if I'd heard from her. It seems that she had writ-ten bad checks all over the county.

If your tenant leaves you with a similar house full of belong-ings, and those belongings are in fairly good shape and could not be considered abandoned refuse, you must notify the tenant and give him or her at least fifteen days' notice that you will sell the property after that time. If you must store the property, the tenant must pay the storage costs. If you sell the property, you must apply the proceeds to your tenant's unpaid rent and bills and return the rest to the courts for the tenant's return. (I cannot imagine the courts tracking down your tenants to give them this money, but that is the law.)

How Much Deposit to Keep?

Once tenants vacate the premises, you must determine the cost of the damages to take out of the security/cleaning deposit. Remember that the escrowed deposit is not yours but the tenants' unless they leave the house dirty or damaged. Once the tenants are out, compare their walk-through checklist with the present condition of the home (the checklist, which describes the condition of the home when the tenants moved in, is discussed in Chapter 4).

If you must use some or all of the deposit for cleaning and damages, detail exactly how much you will deduct and keep all receipts as proof. Do not list "$25 cleaning costs" because this does not provide enough justification. Be very specific. Remember, you cannot charge for your own labor; but you can hire others to clean the house and deduct their fees, if reasonable, from the deposit.

Some states require you to send the remaining deposit, if any, plus a detailed schedule of deposit deductions, to the tenants by registered mail. Your state's Landlord and Tenant Act describes how to return the deposit and the description of charges against the deposit. Of course, if during the eviction hearing the judge said that you can use whatever is left of the deposit for past-due rents and fees, list the remaining amount you used to offset these rents and fees with the other charges against the deposit. Mail the tenant this description if the state requires you to do so.

HIT THEM AT TAX TIME

If all else fails and you do not collect the money owed to you, why not make it more difficult for the deadbeat tenants at tax time? When you cannot collect the rent despite victories in court, you have no recourse except to forgive the debt even though you were technically awarded the debt in the courts. The IRS treats uncollected rent as *debt forgiveness* and you can send a 1099-MISC form to the renter for the amount of the uncollected rent.

Send the form before January 31 to the renter's last known address. Sometimes, the address is that of your own property and you hope that the tenant left a forwarding address. Also send the notice to the IRS and let it take things from there. I never mind if the tenant fails to receive the notice despite my best efforts. I know that on April 15, the IRS will match up the 1099-MISC statement to the tenant's taxes and ask for more tax money. One of the few times I cheer for the IRS is when it goes after this unreported money, and I wish the IRS luck in collecting.

Keep in mind that once you send the 1099-MISC to the IRS, you no longer have recourse to collect the rent. In some circumstances, the tenant may not want the IRS to know about the situation (especially if the tenant collects public assistance), and you have a slight chance that the tenant will want to pay what is owed to you if you drop the 1099-MISC. Therefore, be sure to let the tenant know when you send the 1099-MISC that you will send the form to the IRS in ten days if you do not hear from him or her about payment.

SUMMARY

You don't want bad tenants. There are many ways to get rid of bad tenants, but the end result is the only thing that matters: getting them out *as soon as possible.* You may have heard that it is difficult to evict certain people, but you won't have a problem if you follow proper small-claims proceedings and keep proper records. Sometimes the eviction notice is the only thing needed to get rid of tenants (although getting past-due rents may be tougher).

Eviction should be swift, firm, and businesslike. Eviction is tough, but having bad tenants is much worse than having no tenants. The courts will eventually attempt to equalize your situation if you have the patience. Even if you do not get your past-due rent, and even if your home sits empty while you look for good tenants, you are better off without bad tenants than with them.

You may have heard about messy eviction proceedings, and this chapter described a few such scenarios. Don't let such possibilities scare you away from leasing your home. Many landlords never have major eviction problems unless they let problems go too long.

After an eviction, can you find good tenants? Of course you can! After several months with good tenants, you'll forget you ever saw a bad one. There are millions of people out there who want to rent from a good landlord like you. And with the precautions described in the earlier chapters, you will be able to find the right tenants for your rental.

CHAPTER EIGHT

Handling Money

PEOPLE OBTAIN rental houses for different reasons. You may have gotten into the rental property business by accident, which happens to many people. You may have inherited an extra house or gotten stuck with one you can't sell because of a housing slump. If you are an "accidental" landlord—thrown into the job involuntarily—this book has so far given you advice on making your day-to-day management easier. But you also need advice on how to handle your rental property finances. (If you have yet to acquire rental property but are interested in doing so, read the next chapter, "Thinking About Landlording?" It will give you an idea of some of the things you can expect as a new rental property owner.)

By following the guidelines in this book (and some shortcuts you'll develop on your own), you will rent your properties to good people who stay a long time. This not only translates into fewer headaches for you but more money as well. Less maintenance, less advertising, and fewer turnovers all combine to release you from the financial burdens that problem tenants can cause. From the early chapters of this book, you now know that a little money and effort up front make more money for you in the long run. Landlords who are chintzy on spending for upkeep and tenant recruiting are out more dollars in the long run and tend to have much worse tenants.

Once you begin to keep more of your rent money, you must find ways to manage it and increase it. This chapter discusses the important aspects of rental property finances that you should consider: profits, insurance, taxes, expenses, mortgages, appreciation, and depreciation.

YOUR PROFIT PICTURE

The rental property you own *must* make money. Because of taxes, insurance, vacancies, and repairs, you can't expect your property to make money every month. But over several months, it should produce more money than it consumes. If it doesn't, you're in trouble—and unfortunately, there are very few ways to decrease costs in the hope of improving your profit picture. Although this chapter discusses one common method of lowering costs (refinancing a high-interest mortgage), if your expenses are as low as possible and your rents are as high as the market will bear, yet your property still loses money, you have only one alternative: Sell it.

When Selling Is Not Easy

Even in economic slumps, rental properties can offer very attractive returns for their owners. Whether savings interest rates are high or low, the prudent landlord will almost always beat the interest rates of banks and certificates of deposit (CDs), often by a large amount. However, if you cannot make money with your property, you probably should sell it. If selling is difficult, find out whether your loan is *assumable.* If buyers can assume your loan, they'll find the purchase of your property more attractive.

If the interest rate on your mortgage is lower than that of current mortgage rates, an assumable loan offers buyers a better rate than they can get elsewhere. However, not every seller would feel comfortable letting a second party assume the loan. If the buyer defaults on the loan, the bank may be able to come back to you, perhaps years later, for the balance. By then, however, the "buyer" will have paid the loan down some, so this is not always a bad thing for you.

> **TIP**
>
> Some lenders will remove your name from an assumed mortgage after a period of time.

Before letting someone assume your loan, ask your mortgage lender for its policy on removing your name from the loan after the assumer maintains a good payment record for a while. Most lenders will let you off the hook in a year or two. But lenders do not have to do this. The more people responsible for a loan, the better the lender's chances of collecting the loan.

Not all loans can be assumed. Also, if your loan's interest rate is not competitive with current rates, an assumable loan would only be attractive to buyers with poor credit ratings; these people cannot get a loan of their own so they look for a nonqualifying loan to assume. These people are certainly not all crooked. Some of them just want a chance to improve their credit history, and they want to own their own home. To protect yourself, however, understand the buyers' financial situation before letting them assume your loan.

If you cannot find any buyers interested in assuming your loan, you have only one solution: Lower the selling price until the home sells. Only you can determine how low to go before you lose even more money on the sale than you would from continuing to rent it. A banker can help you with the computation (called "time value of money"). If you were losing $100 a month after all expenses, it wouldn't take you too long to make up a $1,000 reduction in price to sell the house quickly. When a house does not sell, and you've done your best to put that house in good condition, your price is too high. Do not let feelings get in the way of your understanding of the market. People often feel their houses are worth more than the market says they are. Never love something that cannot love you back.

In desperate situations, consider offering tenants a *lease-purchase* option. Under such an agreement, your tenants' rent will go toward the purchase of the home and you can often charge significantly higher rents than you could if the tenant were not, ultimately, buying the home. Your tenants can leave at any time (as long as they follow the terms of the lease-purchase agreement), but they have an incentive to stay and you have a fairly good chance of selling the home in a down market. Often, such lease-purchase agreements fail to materialize because the tenants decide to leave. If so, fine. You keep the rent and start another lease-purchase agreement with the next tenant.

> **TIP**
>
> A lease-purchase option might provide a quick sale.

The lease-purchase agreement is nice for tenants who may not be able to purchase a property with a standard mortgage. I've heard landlords who say that such an agreement helps the tenant but never the landlord. I must disagree. Although I've never offered a lease-purchase, if I did, I would make sure that the tenants (who are, until they change their minds, buying the home) pay for all repairs. After all, I have turned into a home seller and not a landlord. The primary reason I do not offer lease-purchase agreements is because I lose too much control over the property. Although I technically own the property under the agreement, the tenant has more freedom to "fix" things or do their own painting than they would have if we kept a strict landlord–tenant relationship.

Sell Despite Tax Profits

Probably the last advice you thought you would get in a landlording book is to sell the house. Nevertheless, prudent landlords know when to cut their losses. If you find that you are losing $100 each month, you know you could invest that money much better elsewhere.

Many people own a rental house that loses only $10 to $50 a month. They feel justified in keeping it because they are out so very little. They see the situation differently from me: They believe they are buying a house for only $10 to $50 a month. They are not being smart rental owners.

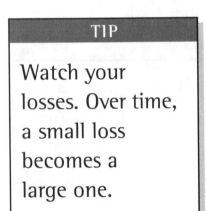

TIP

Watch your losses. Over time, a small loss becomes a large one.

As your banker will tell you, $10 to $50 a month over several years adds up to a tremendous sum. Compare a landlord who loses $25 a month to one who profits by that amount each month. How many properties can the first landlord own? One or two or even five may be possible, because $25 each is not a big loss. However, there comes a point when that landlord can no longer continue to lose money. Despite the tax advantages of rental property ownership, you cannot afford a lot of losses, even small ones. How many properties can the landlord who *makes* $25 each month on a property own? In theory, as many as he or she wants. You may think you do not want more properties than the one you have, but after implementing some of the money- and time-saving shortcuts in this book, and after putting your rental property on autopilot, you'll see that this job is not so difficult after all. You may then want to acquire more properties to further increase your income.

> ### TIP
>
> Tax breaks do not equal profits . . . at least not for long.

Can you have too many properties? Obviously the answer is yes, but people may not want to invest the time and energy to have more than one or two. You must decide how many is enough. Keep in mind that as long as each of the houses is profitable you can own as many as you want. If you end up with too many profitable houses than you can manage alone, you are ready to decide if it's time to hire help, rent a property-management company, or form your own management company.

If your rental property loses money, you may think the tax deductions will make up the difference. Although tax breaks play an important role in a landlord's decision making, you should never include taxes when determining the real income from a rental property. After you've computed your taxes, you may have a "profit" for the year, even if you started out with a loss—but because tax laws constantly change, this may not be the case next year.

Consider the following scenario: A landlord makes $500 a month in rent on a property that costs $600 a month in expenses. Annualized, that landlord's situation looks like this:

Annual rental income:	$6,000
Annual expenses:	7,200
Annual loss before taxes:	–$1,200

Suppose this landlord's deductible depreciation and mortgage interest add up to more than the loss. At tax time, the landlord finds the following profit picture:

Annual rental income:	$6,000
Annual expenses:	7,200
Annual loss before taxes:	−$1,200
Annual depreciation and interest:	2,000
Annual profit after taxes:	$800

It appears that this landlord is doing fine. All things being equal, he or she can have as many rental properties as desired, since each property makes money at the end of the year even though the properties lose money before all tax deductions are considered.

The only thing you know about the tax laws, however, is that *they will change.* Washington will continue to battle over raising and lowering taxes, and while it does so the laws that apply this year may not be in effect next year. It would not be prudent for a landlord to base an investment decision on taxes. Always look at your income and expenses *before taxes* when deciding to sell or keep a property. Just because you make a profit this year as a result of tax deductions does not mean that you will make a profit next year (after Congress changes the tax laws). The landlord whose balance sheet you see here is in a fragile situation. If the tax laws change to decrease deductions for depreciation and interest, which happens all the time, this landlord will lose money on the property.

If you are in a similar situation, seriously consider selling the property. When tax laws change against the landlord, as they will at some point, fewer people will go into landlording and more landlords will sell their properties. The more landlords sell, the lower selling prices go. You will be better off selling your home now (if you cannot decrease your expenses or increase your rent), before the tax laws change. Once you get rid of the property, you can search for one that *makes* you money for your hard work.

Appreciation Is Nice . . . If It Occurs

Do not justify a losing rental property by thinking that you can sell it for a profit later. As many people found out in the 1980s, there is no rule that guarantees a house will increase in value. Popular thought over the last thirty years was that buying a home was the best investment a person could make. But bank foreclosures and closings proved that people can lose a lot of money on properties that do not appreciate; many owners face properties worth much less today than the day they bought them.

Treat the possibility of appreciation as an added benefit, one that may or may not happen. Do not assume that a monthly loss will be made up the day you sell your house. Nobody knows the future, and the future of housing prices is an uncertainty that you cannot risk.

IMPROVING PROFITS BY LOWERING COSTS

Before selling your home, you can try other alternatives to improving your profit picture. As with a federal deficit, you can either lower spending or raise income to eliminate the loss. Although your renters will not appreciate you raising the rent, you may have to. But before you do, try to lower expenses.

Many landlords make raising rents an annual event. This book does not advocate that; its philosophy is *tenant driven*. If your tenants are happy, chances are vastly improved that you will be also. When you practice tenant-driven landlording, you spend time and money up front to provide a clean, attractive home and get good tenants. After that, your problems and expenses are minimal. Therefore, if you've taken the time to attract good tenants, the last thing in the world you want is to lose them.

Suppose your tenants pay a monthly rent of $650. If your profit picture shows a loss of $100 a month and you decide to raise the rent to make up for it, you'll find very few tenants willing to accept such an expensive increase, from $650 to $750. If you lose your tenants by raising the rent, it will take more than six months to make up the loss of a month's rent (the amount you will lose while finding the next tenant). Avoid this situation. Before tenants move into your rental, make sure that the rent you are asking is reasonable, from your point of view as well as the tenants'. Most people are fair-minded and realistic. Tenants who have rented from you for a long time will understand that you may have to raise rates a little. Costs do increase and they know it. However, do not spring a large increase on your tenants all at once.

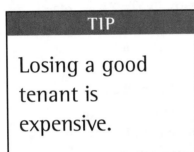

TIP

Losing a good tenant is expensive.

Shop around every so often to make sure other homes similar to yours rent for about the same amount. If they rent for more than yours, feel justified in aligning your prices with theirs. If you can beat your competition by renting just below their prices, lower the rent; you will benefit by having lots of happy, paying, long-staying tenants.

Refinancing

If you are like most property owners, your property has a loan. Very few landlords own their rental properties outright. Most have mortgages to pay each month. This is the most expensive cost of owning rental properties. If your mortgage's interest rates are much steeper than current rates, consider refinancing. When you refinance, you exchange your current high-interest loan for one of lower interest. Sometimes you can lower your monthly mortgage by more than $100.

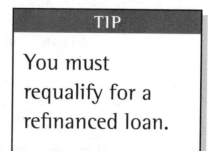

TIP

You must requalify for a refinanced loan.

Lenders know that you can go elsewhere for a loan, so your current lender generally will be glad to lower your interest rates. The process is not as easy as it should be, however. Even if your previous payment history at the higher rates is perfect, you must go through the qualification process again for the new loan. Your bank knows that you would have to go through the entire application process if you went elsewhere, so your current lender requires one, too, even if you are refinancing an existing loan.

The bank's watchword in refinancing is *protection*. Banks are in a riskier situation than you are, and they must think about security. When you obtain a fixed-rate loan, your bank cannot raise your rates. If the loan is at 8 percent and interest rates climb to 30 percent, your bank must still accept your payments at the lower rate. However, if rates fall to 5 percent, you can walk to another bank, get a new loan at the lower rate, and pay off the other one. Therefore, banks take a risk when they give you a fixed-rate loan. They have to do something to make up for this risk every time they loan you money.

When you apply for a new loan with the same lender, you pay a fee for its trouble (processing the application, legal filings, and so forth), and it deserves the fee. The bank also gets a chance to review your current financial situation. Suppose you recently lost your job and no longer qualify for the new loan, even though its payments will be lower than those of your existing one. Your bank will be forewarned.

In most cases, refinancing takes several months. If you've done business with the bank for a long time, it may be able to speed up the process. Do not expect to lower your monthly payments until you sign the final paperwork on your new loan.

When you apply for refinancing, you will have to pay the application fee *even if you later do not qualify for the loan.* The fee is fair: The mortgage company wants to discourage people from frivolously applying, which makes a lot of work for the lender with no reward. The fee also prevents borrowers from applying at lots of different places at the same time, causing needless work for multiple lenders.

By the time your loan is refinanced, you will have spent from $500 to $2,500. Do not let this frighten you; most lenders roll these fees into the loan itself. Because of the lower interest rate, your monthly payments will be lower than your current payments, even with the added fees. Nevertheless, you do pay the refinancing costs eventually, and they do add to your overall costs. Therefore, a general rule to follow is that refinancing makes sense only if you can get a mortgage that is *2 percent lower* than your current one, and only if you plan to keep the property for *longer than two years.* If your mortgage is now 12 percent and you can only refinance for 11 percent, the loan costs would make refinancing prohibitive.

But even if you can lower the interest rate by four to five percentage points, refinancing does not make sense unless you will keep the property for more than two years. After two years, the money you save in payments makes up for the refinancing fees.

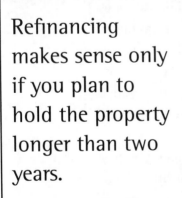

TIP

Refinancing makes sense only if you plan to hold the property longer than two years.

When you refinance your mortgage, do not feel that you have to get a thirty-year loan. Because interest rates are the main determinants of monthly payments, you can almost always lower your current payments by refinancing for only fifteen to twenty years. This knocks a few years off the loan, pays off the principal (the actual cost of the house) faster, and puts more money in your pocket and less in the bank's.

The shorter the loan's life (called the "term" of the loan), the more real money you get back when you sell your property. Since you will be paying off the principal sooner, you will own more *equity* (the amount of the home's real cost that you have paid). More of the selling dollars come back to you when you sell the house. Often, you can deduct all the costs of loan refinancing for rental properties, so check with your tax adviser on the ramifications of deducting the costs.

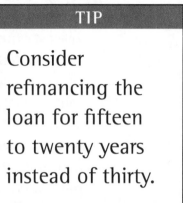

TIP

Consider refinancing the loan for fifteen to twenty years instead of thirty.

The ability to handle debt differs with each investor. If I were trying to build a rental empire, with fifty or more properties, I would take a different approach to debt than I would with only one to five properties. The larger-scale property owner wants to leverage debt to purchase numerous properties. In most cases, I would want to put each property on a long-term, thirty-year mortgage, maximizing the amount that I borrow to maximize my monthly profits. Such an investment would enable me to continue to purchase more properties because my monthly net cash flow is so much greater.

With only one to five properties, I would not want to leverage my properties with a lot of debt unless I had outside, reliable sources of income. Your risk is not spread as thin with a smaller number of units. If one or two units go vacant for a month, or if one of the properties sustains major and expensive damage, you may risk your ability to make the monthly payments on your properties. I'd like to see the smaller owner work on paying off at least one house to give that owner breathing room in case of unexpected expenses. By purchasing rental properties wisely, using the advice found in this book, you can pay off properties about every four-and-a-half years if you apply the entire net monthly profit to the loan principal. For your first property, I suggest adding even more each month from other sources of income to get that property's mortgage paid off sooner. Your paid-for property can then create even more cash flow to apply to your other property. When you apply the net profit from the second property, along with the larger net profit from the paid-off property, you'll pay off that second property even faster. If you continue to piggyback loan payments in this way, you will own a number of properties free and clear of any debt in ten years' time. At that point, you might want to consider expanding your property ownership even more and becoming a full-time rental property owner, which I think means getting the equity out of about half your properties and buying as many as you can afford to purchase. (Or you might just want to stop buying and ride the income wave from six or seven rental units each month.) By keeping four or five properties paid for, you help ensure that you can meet unexpected cash flow problems. Once you are successfully buying and managing fifty or more properties, give me a call because you can give me lots of advice!

Shop Around for Loans

Do not feel that you have to use the same bank when you refinance a mortgage. As in any other industry, different banks offer different prices for the services they provide. Money is a commodity and banks within the same city can offer vastly different interest rates. Most will quote you their current rates over the phone. But banks are not the only institutions that loan money on houses. Look under "Mortgage" in the yellow pages for a list of lenders who will be happy to tell you their rates.

The majority of mortgages are fixed-rate loans; that is, their rates cannot rise or fall (except through the refinancing process), no matter what happens to other prevailing rates during the life of the loan. Another popular loan, an adjustable-rate mortgage or ARM, offers some advantages over fixed-rate loans.

Adjustable-rate mortgages change over the life of the loan. You could get a mortgage for 10 percent, and two years later, you may be paying only 8 percent. Of course, the opposite is also true: If rates rise, you could pay as much as the lender feels is competitive with other interest rates at the time. Many view the ARM's changing interest rates as a disadvantage; yet, prices on everything tend to change with time. An adjustable-rate mortgage is one of the only loans that changes as the economy changes. You are truly paying market prices for the money you borrow when you borrow with an ARM.

> **TIP**
>
> A fixed-rate loan is not always the best choice.

Be sure to get an ARM that has a maximum cap on its rate changes. For example, you might find an ARM with a cap of 1 percent on interest per year and another with a 2 percent cap. The first one can only increase by a maximum of 1 percent in any given year; the second can increase as much as 2 percent. The first loan simplifies budgeting. Some ARMs offer a total rate cap; that is, they have a maximum limit on the interest rate over the life of the loan. For example, a 10 percent loan with a 20 percent ceiling will never rise higher than 20 percent no matter what other interest rates do. With a cap, your risk is lower than it would be with no limit.

Rate caps are not the only incentives that banks offer to ARM holders. Generally, ARM rates are 1 to 2 percent lower than fixed-rate loans. If your bank currently offers 12 percent mortgages, it probably offers ARMs at 10 or 11 percent. More people qualify for ARMs than for fixed-rate loans because the ARM's lower interest rates result in lower monthly payments.

If you still don't know whether to get a fixed-rate or an adjustable-rate loan, you must try to predict what interest rates will do in the future. If you think interest rates will rise (as a result of inflation), then you would prefer a fixed-rate loan, since the interest rate you pay will be locked in for the entire mortgage. If you think rates will drop or stay about the same, you would prefer an adjustable-rate mortgage, since its rate will be lower than that of a fixed-rate loan.

A much larger percentage of homebuyers use adjustable-rate mortgages during high-interest times. During the late 1970s and early 1980s, when inflation and interest rates were in the double digits (sometimes mortgage rates went as high as 21 percent), people rushed to get adjustable-rate mortgages. During the late 1980s and into the 1990s, fewer people wanted adjustable-rate loans since prevailing interest rates were low compared to the previous decade. No one can predict the future exactly, but your expectation of future rates should determine which type of mortgage you obtain.

Balloon Mortgages

Some special mortgages have a balloon payment provision. These are attractive to borrowers (and refinancers) whose current monthly rental income would not cover a regular loan's payments. Here is how balloon mortgages work: Suppose you want to borrow or refinance a home worth $150,000. You can get a loan (ten-year or twenty-year; some banks even offer thirty-year balloon mortgages) for the first $100,000 only. At the end of the loan, you will make a final payment of $50,000 (plus the accrued interest on the $50,000). Balloon loans have many variations, and your banker can help you decide whether one is right for you.

If the final balloon payment frightens you, most lenders let you roll it into an additional loan that you can pay off in time. Even better, if you can afford to pay a higher monthly payment than the actual payment amount, you will pay off the house quicker, and any balloon payment at the end will be much smaller.

Balloon mortgages are useful if you believe your rental income will rise from its current rate. With balloon mortgages, you should do your best to pay any additional money each month on the loan to get the final payment lower. Any time you pay the additional money, be sure the lender credits the extra to the principal and not to escrow. If the lender puts the extra payment in escrow, the extra money you paid does not go to pay off the loan, but is put in a safety fund in case you miss a payment down the road. Although you would eventually get the money back if the bank did not have to use it, you would still have been paying interest on the mortgage amount that the extra money could have been applied to. If you make sure your lender applies the extra money to the principal, you will be paying as little interest as possible throughout the life of the loan.

Should You Pay Points?

When you obtain or refinance a mortgage, your lender will ask you whether you want to pay *points* on the loan. Points are nothing more than a percentage of your mortgage amount. For example, if you get a mortgage for $175,000, one point would be $1,750 (one percentage point of the full loan).

The idea is this: If you pay one or more points when applying for the loan, you can get a lower interest rate than those who choose not to pay points. For example, here is a typical interest-rate schedule:

Rate	Points
10%	0
8%	1.5
7.5%	3

Given this schedule, if you wanted to borrow $100,000, the interest rate you would pay would automatically be 10 percent. However, if you paid up front a fee of 1.5 percent of the loan ($1,500), you would get the loan for only 8 percent. You could pay three percentage points ($3,000) and get an even lower interest rate (of 7.5 percent). Since the interest rate is such an important determinant of your monthly payment, points can greatly reduce it and thereby increase your monthly cash flow.

Although you should check with a competent tax adviser, the points you pay on a mortgage may be deductible as a business expense. It is best if you can deduct them in the first year of the loan, but you may have to amortize them (spread the cost) over the life of the loan. Either way, if points are deductible, it is generally best to pay as many as you can to reduce the interest rate you pay over the life of the loan. Some lenders will also let you roll the points into the loan itself, although in this case, you can rarely deduct them in the first year of the loan.

Rental Owners May Pay More

Do not be dismayed if the first lender you approach does not want to refinance your loan. Not all lenders offer loans on rental property. Many do; however, they sometimes require a higher interest rate or, more commonly, require more money down. For instance, one lender may offer a 10 percent loan rate with 5 percent paid down for owner-occupied homes. The same lender may require 10 to 20 percent down (money paid in advance) at an 11 percent rate for rental property loans.

Expect this discrimination and be happily surprised if the lender does not charge extra in your case. Actually, lenders have good reason for requiring a little extra from landlords: People buying homes to live in are less likely to default on the loan than people who are buying property to rent. During recessions, landlords are more likely to ignore the mortgage payment on their rental properties than on their own homes. Despite the fact that you are refinancing an existing loan, the lender considers the loan to be brand-new and must protect its own interests.

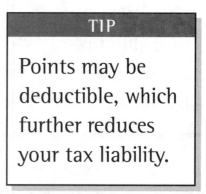

TIP

Points may be deductible, which further reduces your tax liability.

TAX ADVANTAGES FOR RENTAL PROPERTIES

Although many people dread the thought of owning rental properties (until they read this book!), almost everybody knows that rental properties offer many tax advantages. The advantages are not as great as they once were, but tax savings play a very important role in your financial decisions as a landlord.

The government wants to encourage the demand for housing. When people buy houses, more money is filtered into the community, builders and suppliers maintain their jobs, and it contributes to the health of the economy. To encourage landlords to own properties, the government offers tax incentives that reduce the tax burden on landlords while spurring the rest of the economy.

As a rental property owner, tax laws give you more deductions than you get on the home you live in.

Depreciation

Most expenses you incur while owning rental property are deductible business expenses. Even the cost of the home is deductible. However, the IRS does not let you write off the cost of your home in one year (the same holds true for some other items, such as refrigerators). You can only write off a fraction of the house each year, for several years, until you have written it off entirely. This is called *depreciation*.

The faster the IRS lets you write off an expenditure, the more money you have in the long run. Since you have to pay fewer up-front taxes because you were able to write things off in the early years, you have more money to invest in other things. A few years ago, the IRS changed the rules so that you now must take longer to write off investment property (twenty-seven-and-a-half years in most cases). The faster depreciation schedules of old (called *accelerated depreciation*) are no longer allowed. Therefore, depreciation is not a big advantage for the rental property owner who bought property after 1986.

Depreciation does, however, play an important role when you sell your house. You must recapture depreciation when selling the home. Let's say you're losing money on a rental property you bought eight years ago for $100,000, so you sell the house for $100,000. How much profit did you make? You might think you made no profit and therefore owe no taxes, but the IRS knows that you depreciated that property for the eight years you owned it. If you have so far depreciated $25,000, the IRS thinks that you made a $25,000 profit and wants you to pay taxes on it.

We can hope that the IRS will change the tax laws again to favor faster depreciation. There is talk in Washington that this will happen. Senators and congressional representatives are finding out that taking tax incentives away from people hampers the economy—something landlords could have told them long ago. Until new rules go into effect, however, depreciation is a nice additional deduction each year, albeit a small one. I would also suggest that landlords contact their U.S. representatives to strengthen landlord positions in the landlord and tenant legal relationships.

After-Tax Expenses

When you pay for a repair, a lightbulb, or a utility bill, the price you pay is less than appears at first glance. You should learn to think in terms of after-tax dollars. Since each lightbulb you purchase is deductible, that lightbulb actually costs you less than you paid for it.

To find the after-tax cost of any item, you must determine your marginal tax rate: the rate (percentage) of taxes you must pay for every dollar you make. Your tax preparer—and as a landlord, you are wise to have one—can determine your marginal tax rate from last year's tax return.

For example, suppose you are in the 28 percent marginal tax bracket (sometimes just called your "tax bracket"); 28 cents out of every dollar of rent you earn goes to taxes. More important, 28 cents out of every dollar you *spend* is deductible from taxes as well. Therefore, if you know your marginal tax rate, you can compute the true cost of an item with this formula:

after-tax cost = cost × ($1.00 – marginal tax rate)

For example, if you are in the 28 percent tax bracket, the $30 sink repair costs you only $21.60 as computed here:

after-tax cost = $30.00 × ($1.00 − 0.28)
giving a result of after-tax cost = $21.60

The other $8.40 offsets some year-end tax liability. When considering a purchase, learn to think in after-tax dollars to get a true perspective on what the item actually will cost you. (Depending on your withholding, you may not realize the savings until tax time, when you pay fewer taxes, but the tax advantage is really there.)

To compute after-tax income (the amount of income you receive after taxes), you use a similar formula:

after-tax income = income × ($1.00 − marginal tax rate)

Therefore, if a renter pays you $500 in rent, you only realize $360 of it ($500.00 × 0.72).

At a glance, it may seem that the after-tax cost and after-tax income cancel each other out. After all, if your true income is actually less than you receive and the money you pay for expenses is less than the money you hand the clerk, is there any reason to ever take after-tax costs into consideration? The answer, as you may have guessed, is yes. Rarely do you have equal income and expenses. You should hope that you have more expenses than income at tax time.

As you saw earlier in this chapter, you cannot operate at a loss for very long. However, two tax deductions—interest and depreciation—can easily produce a loss for the year even though your monthly cash flow might still be positive. There is nothing wrong or illegal about these paper losses. The IRS gives you the interest and depreciation expenses, even though depreciation is a smaller benefit than it used to be, to encourage you to buy more rental properties.

Until you get close to paying off your mortgage, your interest payments alone will probably offset much of your property's income. When you consider insurance and depreciation as well as the other incidental expenses you incur throughout the year (which should be small if you fixed up the home properly), you will almost certainly have a tax loss, even if you made a small "profit" each month when you collected rent. Therefore, you really do pay an after-tax amount for property-related expenses. Your rental income is offset long before you run out of expenses over your many years of property ownership. You pay an after-tax cost on each one of those expenses that exceeds income.

The bigger this paper loss is the fewer taxes you pay and the more money you have. As long as you are not incorporated, the loss will offset your other income (from your job, interest on savings, or whatever), and you will have much more money to invest elsewhere throughout your landlording career.

CAN YOU BENEFIT FROM WEEKLY OR BIWEEKLY PAYMENTS?

How would you like to collect rent every week or two instead of every month? Sounds like an increased workload, doesn't it? But such a payment plan might be better for your tenants, especially for those tenants who get paid once a week or on the same day every two weeks.

Here's the best part of weekly or biweekly payments: Every year has twelve months, so you'll get twelve monthly payments if you collect rent monthly. Every month, however, has *4.3 weeks*! If you divide your monthly rent by four and get paid weekly, you will receive an extra *two weeks'* rent by the end of the year! Each year has fifty-two weeks, so if you collect rent on the same day every week or two instead of on the first of every month, you'll automatically get an extra half-month's rent payment each year.

PAYING THE BILLS

There are several things a landlord can do to expedite bill paying. One of the newest and easiest is automatic payment of your common monthly bills. For example, your monthly mortgage payment can automatically be deducted from your checking or savings account. Most utility companies now offer this method as well.

Do not fear losing control of these kinds of payments. Several days before the company deducts from your account, you will get a bill that looks just like the bill you always get. Simply write the transaction in your checking account, and on a certain day (always specified on the statement) the company will deduct the amount from your account. If the bill is wrong, you have plenty of time to correct it. If a company deducts more than it said it would on the statement, they will always correct it (this situation occurs rarely, if ever). Not only do you save the time writing the check, but you save the cost of the check (some carbon copy checks cost as much as 15 to 20 cents each) and the stamp. Plus, you know the bill will never be past due, and you are free to do something else with your time. Consider automating all your personal bills as well. You can save a few dollars a month in checks and stamps and a lot of time in a year.

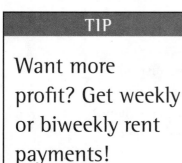

TIP

Want more profit? Get weekly or biweekly rent payments!

You would be surprised at how much a checking account dedicated to your rental business simplifies your work at tax time. Every expense related to the property is recorded, and the checking account ledger makes a good backup record if you are ever audited. A separate checking account keeps you from mixing up business and personal income and expenses. You can still withdraw as much as you want for your own use, since the money is yours (write yourself a check). However, by separating the funds into two accounts you show that you're trying to maintain accurate rental records.

There is nothing to keep dishonest landlords from mixing money between the two funds. For instance, a dishonest landlord might buy a box of lightbulbs for his own home but use a check from the rental property's account. Doing this is, of course, illegal unless the landlord clearly states on the check register that the funds were for personal use and he does not deduct the lightbulbs at tax time. A much better approach is to write a check to yourself, deposit it into your personal account, and write a personal check for the purchase. The IRS knows that separate accounts do not ensure integrity. Nevertheless, maintaining separate checking accounts indicates that you are doing all you can to keep accurate records.

Smart landlords write checks from their property's checking account for every transaction they make. Even if you need a single battery for a rental's smoke alarm, write a check for it.

But sometimes you don't want to bother writing a check. Your landlording life would be more difficult if you had to write a check for every small purchase, especially during property renovation. Small cash purchases are known as "petty cash expenses." These purchases are too small to bother with check writing. (You can also pay for large purchases with cash as well, but keep very good records and receipts if you do, because larger cash purchases appear more suspicious to IRS auditors.) Go ahead and pay cash when necessary and keep all receipts (whether you pay with cash or check). Either keep a log of the cash receipts or keep all the receipts together. Once you have several dollars' worth, do a perfectly legal little trick that accountants have known about for years: Write yourself a check for the amount of the items purchased and write "petty cash" in the memo area. Keep a separate record of the items you bought with cash. Then, deposit the check *back into the property's checking account*. This may seem as though you have done nothing: You wrote a check to yourself and deposited it into the same account it was drawn on. However, you now have a checking account record *for every purchase*, even those you paid for with cash. This way you can safely find a transaction in the checking account for every single outlay you make on your property.

>
> **TIP**
>
> A separate checking account makes tax time much easier.

Be aware that some banks charge extra for a "business" checking account, even though you may write only one or two checks a month on it. Stay away from these added fees. There are many banks that want your business, so find one that offers a no-fee checking account (and preferably one that pays interest on your daily balance as well). Even if you don't use a business checking account but choose a second personal account for your rental expenses, shop around for the lowest fees possible. Consider how you will use the account and locate the best checking account for your needs. For example, some checking accounts are free if you write fewer than ten checks a month. If you regularly write more for your rentals, search for a checking account that offers free checking if you keep a certain minimum balance.

UTILITIES

You or your renters might pay utilities, but you have to determine your own involvement in the utility bills. Decide what you'll do during and between occupancies.

> **TIP**
>
> Use the rental property's checking account for all business purchases, even cash purchases.

Leave-on Policy

Having to turn utilities on and off frustrates most landlords. You already know the routine. When your tenant moves out, you must call the utility companies to have the electricity and gas turned on so you can clean and show the home. Not only do you pay for the energy, but you pay the connection fee as well. This can be especially frustrating if a tenant leaves in the winter unexpectedly and the pipes freeze because the heat was turned off.

As you learned in Chapter 2, you can solve some landlording problems by signing up for your utility companies' leave-on policies: When a tenant moves out and has the utilities shut off, the utility company automatically transfers the service to your name at a greatly reduced rate (typically about one-fifth the cost of turning on the utility without the leave-on policy). The utility company then informs you that the utility is in your name. You must register for the policy with the utility company and pay a small one-time fee.

All you have to do when a new tenant moves in is call the utility company. The company will contact the tenant if the tenant has not yet called, transfer the billing to the new tenant, and send you your final bill.

It is nice to know that all future utility turn-ons will be cheaper. It is even nicer to know that your utilities will never be turned off again.

All-Bills-Paid Policy

You may have to decide whether to offer your renters an all-bills-paid policy, especially if your competition does. Generally, you are better off when tenants pay their own utilities. Even people with the best intentions tend to overuse services they do not pay for, which makes your costs extremely unpredictable.

A lot of landlords pay water only, leaving the gas and electricity to the tenant. This is more common in multifamily dwellings (duplexes, fourplexes, and apartment buildings), because the refuse collection is usually included in the water bill. If a tenant defaults on the water payment, no one's trash gets picked up.

Even more likely is that a multifamily dwelling has only one water meter per property instead of per rental unit. If this is the situation, check with your water company to see how much it costs to put the rental units on separate meters. The cost may be worth the savings in a year or two because each of your tenants can then pay their own water bill.

APPLIANCES

Rarely can you rent a property that has no appliances as quickly as one that does. Despite the initial expense, stoves, ovens, and refrigerators last for many years when purchased new. Also, their after-tax cost is not as great as it would be if you could not deduct the cost from your taxes. (Most appliances require depreciation; you can deduct only part of their cost each year for three to five years.)

Unless your rental is on the expensive side, a stove, oven, and refrigerator are all you need to offer. Tenants seem to clog garbage disposals so often that the repair bills will not justify their benefit in rental appeal. Supplying a washer and dryer is an extremely good rental incentive, but their costs are high and most tenants either buy or rent their own or go to the commercial laundry once a week. Install a dishwasher only if competitors do the same. If you want trouble-free landlording, the fewer appliances you have (besides the standard refrigerator, oven, and stove), the fewer trouble calls you will get.

Although each situation is different, most financial experts agree that buying extended warranties on appliances are almost always losing propositions. Your stove may break the day after the original warranty runs out, but the odds are extremely great that it will not. If a stove or range does break, a new heating element usually fixes the problem, and it is inexpensive to replace.

Large appliances are made to last many years with or without extended warranties. If appliances broke a lot, stores could not offer such attractive extended warranty deals, so the odds are in your favor if you refuse the extended warranty. Some stores make you initial a legal-looking clause stating that you refused the extended warranty. Don't let this tactic frighten you into purchasing an extended warranty at the last minute.

In an attempt to humble eager employees who get extra commissions for selling extended warranties, I always ask why my new appliance will break down so soon after they sell it to me. I ask them if perhaps I should go to a more reliable company that offers better equipment that does not require the extended warranties. Although I'm being a little mean, and asking such a question sometimes flusters them, they are not as eager to sell me the warranty's bad deal.

When buying appliances, buy sizes adequate for the rooms they will occupy. More important, always buy white, no-frills appliances. No matter what color you paint the walls later, the appliances will fit right in.

TIP

Do not buy extended warranties on appliances.

Look for ads in your local newspaper from discount appliance/stereo dealers offering rock-bottom prices on refrigerators and ranges. (Be sure the refrigerator is frost-free. People sometimes damage freezers by scraping and hammering frost off the freezer walls.) Discount stores generally get people into their stores by advertising the low-priced models, then they attempt to move the customer up to a higher-priced model with more features. You want the no-frills, inexpensive model; other than a few extra dials, these are probably the same on the inside as the more expensive ones. As long as the refrigerator cools and the oven heats, you and your tenants will be happy.

INSURANCE

Insurance is a very individual thing. Each landlord needs different coverage. There is certainly a plentiful supply of agents around the country who will be more than willing to tell you what you need. Consult several before deciding on a policy and choose the one that fits your situation best. The best insurance agents are those who take the time to find out your specific landlording environment and personal needs before telling you which insurance is right for you.

No landlord should be in business who does not have liability insurance, and $1 million worth is okay for a start. In today's litigious society, tenants can sue you for lots of things, many of which may not even seem (and may not be) your fault. Protect your own assets by obtaining liability insurance to cover any negligence or liability suit that you may face. You can often get a rate quote without ever leaving your home and without making a phone call by searching the Internet for quote worksheets. Chapter 12, "Record Keeping and Computerizing Your Rental Properties," explains more about this method of comparing insurance rates.

Umbrella Policies

Umbrella policies are popular today and offer an inexpensive way to get higher liability coverage. Instead of buying a $1 million insurance policy, you buy a standard policy (it may include property damage, medical coverage, and $100,000 or so of liability) and extend its liability coverage (the umbrella that protects you when bad things happen) to $1 million or more. In most cases, the total you pay will be less than for a full $1 million policy.

I cannot overemphasize the need for liability coverage. People rarely have enough, so shop around for the best deal and make sure you are amply covered. The loss of a life is difficult to put a price on (but whatever it is, you can bet it will be huge), and your peaceful rest at night is worth the price of liability protection.

If you own bare land on which you may someday build rental units, buy liability insurance for it as well. Children playing on your land can hurt themselves. Even if they should not have been on the property in the first place, you can still be charged with negligence.

You might have the best insurance agent in the world, but you should still shop around every year or so to see whether another company offers better values. Don't spend a lot of time looking (you don't have to call every company in the phone book), but call four or five to see what is out there. Insurance policies are just contracts, and most of them are very similar. Remember that your agent is completely out of the picture if you ever have a claim (an adjuster steps in to handle the proceedings), so don't base your patronage of a company solely on a nice agent.

How Much Is Enough Property Insurance?

Once you have enough liability to cover disastrous situations, you must decide how much property coverage you need. That is, if your home burned down, how much would you need to replace it?

There is no easy answer to this question, but your insurance agent should be able to help. However, make sure you get *full replacement coverage.* Without it, you will get only the depreciated value of your losses. In other words, the insurance will pay only a few dollars for the $500 refrigerator you bought five years ago, if you lost it in a fire. But if you have full replacement, the insurance will cover the full cost of a new, comparable model at today's prices.

Ask your insurance agent for the cost of insurance at each deductible level. A policy with a $250 deductible is typically much more expensive than one with a $1,000 deductible. As a review, suppose a small fire ruined $3,000 worth of your home. If you had a $250 deductible, your insurance company would pay you $2,750, since the first $250 is on

TIP

Shop around for insurance without leaving home by surfing the Internet for the best rates.

you. If you had a $1,000 deductible, insurance would pay you only $2,000.

Obviously, the smaller deductible means you get more if you have a claim. However, in most cases the price of lower deductibles is relatively high. Your insurance company does not want to bother with small claims; a higher deductible means you will not turn to them for petty damages, since you will have to foot so much of the total claim. Don't sweat the small losses. The money you save in premiums is almost always worth large deductibles. Besides, the more small losses you claim, the higher the company will raise your rates; the small losses are simply not worth the insurance expenditure.

TIP

Periodically review insurance policies, agents, and companies.

One person's small loss or large deductible is different from another's. Ask your agent to show you the price of your property coverage at each deductible level and then decide whether the marginal differences are worth the added costs. Since your losses are tax-deductible, large deductibles make even more sense; you can subtract the amount of the deductible from your taxable income.

Feel free to second-guess your agent when buying property coverage. You will probably need less than the agent first suggests, if he or she suggests that you insure the property for its current selling price. The cost of replacing damaged or even "totaled" property is never as high as the selling price of the property. If your home is brick, or partially brick, remember that bricks don't burn, and they will not need replacing after a fire. You also cannot lose the land the home sits on (the land is part of the cost of the home).

If you have done your job—installed smoke alarms and a fire extinguisher—chances are much improved that a small fire stays small. There is nothing you can do to avoid every catastrophe, but if you objectively look at the odds against a total loss, you will see that you need less coverage than it first appeared.

Some landlords have no property coverage. Rental property coverage is generally higher than that on owner-occupied homes. Some landlords feel that a complete loss is rare and not even worth the premium for property coverage. You have to do your own math and take your own chances in this situation. Consider how many years of premiums it takes to buy a replacement home (or fix yours if it is destroyed) and then decide. Whatever you do, have adequate liability protection. Also, make sure to recommend, in writing if possible, that your tenants get renter's insurance. Tenants should understand that your insurance does not cover their possessions in the event of a loss. Renter's insurance is cheap, but most renters fail to buy it even when advised to do so.

> **TIP**
>
> Generally, you save much more money if you maintain high deductibles.

I state in the lease that I only insure my own property, *not* renters' possessions. The lease gives them a reminder that they should look into renter's insurance to cover their possessions.

Paying the Premiums

A surprising number of landlords get yearlong insurance policies and pay for them in monthly installments. They use part of their monthly rent to pay for that month's premium. Although this seems easiest at first (and the insurance companies prefer this), there is almost always a small service charge added to each payment. If you pay the full annual premium at once, you do not get hit with the service charges. If you add up how much you pay in service charges over the year, you will find that it's a hefty percentage of the annual premium.

If you have a difficult time paying your full year's premium in advance, get a small loan from your bank. Generally, the interest rate on a small, short-term loan will be less than the service charge on your monthly premium. During the year, put a portion of your rent in a savings account so that the next year you can pay the policy in full and have some money

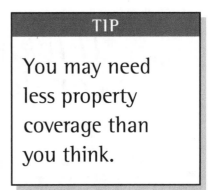

TIP

You may need less property coverage than you think.

left over. If you have difficulty covering the insurance, however, you might reconsider the rental property's investment risk. You may not be getting enough rent to justify the expenses, and you may need to sell the property.

SUMMARY

You must make money or you cannot own rental properties for long. No landlord can stay in business if he or she is losing money on the property. Rental properties make money if owned and managed the right way.

This chapter showed you how to maximize the profits and minimize the losses. With very few exceptions, a losing property should make money or else be sold. There are too many good rental houses waiting for a caring landlord such as you to waste time and money on a losing house. Consider all costs when analyzing your property's income potential including the mortgage interest and insurance costs.

CHAPTER NINE

Thinking About Landlording?

THE POSITIVE SIDE of landlording shines throughout this book, especially as you learn how to streamline your efforts. You've read how to save time and money as well as how to attract and keep good tenants. Most of you are landlords already. But some of you, although interested in rental properties, may not have taken the plunge yet because of doubts or fears.

This chapter attempts to answer the questions of would-be landlords. Even though most of your questions have probably been addressed in earlier chapters, there are many other things you should know before leaping into the landlording business. This chapter gives you an overview of some of the things you can expect.

THE PROBLEMS

Problems arise for the best of landlords. If you own rental property long enough, you are bound to encounter problems: You will get tenants who do some (or maybe a lot) of damage to your home. You will get tenants who move out in the middle of the night, leaving you nothing but a bad check. At times, you will curse your landlording responsibilities and want to bail out.

People have many reasons for not becoming landlords. But remember: If you have heard someone's landlording nightmares, chances are excellent that the landlord did not take the time to prepare the home correctly and to attract good tenants. Also remember that bad news travels much faster than good. The horror stories you hear rarely happen. Bad tenants will come and go, but you will have more good than bad. Although you cannot guarantee this, you can stack the odds in your favor (as you've already seen). Nevertheless, even the best landlords sometimes experience rental property grief.

TIP

It takes landlording savvy to minimize problems. If it didn't, the competition would be fierce and rents would be much lower.

So if you are doomed from the start, why bother to become a landlord? If caring landlords were to list the benefits they derive from their properties, in most cases the advantages would outweigh the drawbacks. Of course, if landlording were easy and trouble-free, everybody would do it. The simple truth is that landlording really is easier than most people think, which is why you should consider it. Your tenants will not view you as the big, bad landlord if you treat them with respect. Many tenants and landlords become very good friends.

If you prepare the home well and find good tenants, you'll rarely even see your rental house. The rent comes promptly in the mail each month and most of the tenants' calls are easy to handle. But suppose trouble does break out, say a heater fails in the middle of winter. Which tenant is going to be the most patient and appreciative of a landlord's promptness, and which is going to threaten to move out—the tenant living in a run-down home who never got a good look at the landlord, or the tenant who knows that the landlord cares about the tenant and the tenant's family? The answer is obvious.

Do not sweat the small problems. Learn to stack the odds in your favor. Enter your landlording career with a positive attitude. And be determined that you'll let the home sit empty for three months before you'll rent to someone with an inadequate income or a poor rental history. Landlords with this attitude often have lots of qualified people wanting the home; their biggest "problem" is having to choose among the many hopefuls.

> **TIP**
>
> You cannot predict every problem, but you certainly can learn from each one.

You are going to face situations that you never would have imagined before becoming a landlord. Tenants will try to use the furnace in the sweltering heat of summer (after you turned off the pilot light in the spring). They will remove dirty air-conditioner filters without replacing them with clean ones. They will miss appointments with you or send you an extra $5 in the rent check for no apparent reason (tell them about their mistake). Tenants will lock themselves out, lose their key, move their relatives in, and mow only half the yard.

Your problems will not only come from tenants. Seeing your success, your friends or relatives might want to go into the rental property business. They will want all your advice free of charge. They'll also want you to "show" them how to fix up their house (you do the work, all the while adding to the competition).

Since you cannot predict every disaster, annoyance, or happy event, do not try. When something goes wrong, analyze the situation during and after it passes. Decide the best way to keep that problem from recurring.

Landlording does not have to take much of your time. Expect to invest the most time and money at the beginning of your landlording career, when you spruce up the property and get good tenants. You can usually find tenants you want in only a few hours, at the open house. (And remember to beat your competitor's price so would-be tenants come in droves.) The new tenant interview takes another hour.

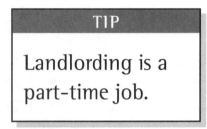

TIP

Landlording is a part-time job.

Obviously, if you grow your rental property business into ownership of more than fifteen or twenty houses, the time requirement will grow considerably. This is when you should consider hiring management help so that you can maintain quality while still maintaining your positive attitude. Be sure that your hired hand (or team) approaches the rental experience with the same positive attitude that you use (give them each a copy of this book!). You want your properties to run smoothly and positively as if you were there handling the business details yourself. Remember, too, that your hired help are your representatives. If they mess something up, you are just as responsible as if you did it yourself.

Be realistic. There is no way you can be an absentee landlord and still expect your home to remain in good condition. Day-to-day landlording does take some time—but much of it is on the phone with tenants rather than visiting them personally. You'll spend the rest of your time on routine tasks such as utility turn-on calls, depositing rent checks, and the like. Expect landlording to be a part-time job, because that is what it is. You can stream-line the job, however, to be the most rewarding and the most "part-time" job of your life.

YOU CAN RENT TO CORPORATIONS AND CHURCHES

If you are reluctant to hunt for renters, despite the invaluable advice in this book, you might consider a special kind of tenancy. Believe it or not, many landlords rent to corporations and churches. Generally, your property has to be in prime condition to get such tenants, but if you follow the advice in this book that should be no problem.

Corporations rent homes because they have short-term employees transfer to your town to work on a temporary job. The tenant may or may not move with a family, but the corporation knows that renting a home for six months or a year gives the tenant much more privacy and costs much less than renting a hotel room for that time period. You might contact companies that have corporate offices in your town and find out if they have any interest in working with you.

Many churches need housing such as yours for missionaries, long-term visitors, and guest pastors. A church often rents a home for a year and then moves people in and out several times a year.

If you find a company or church that is interested in renting from you, you might also find that they are willing to pay a premium for a furnished place. A couch, chairs, table, and bed are not too expensive at many discount furniture stores, especially when you buy all at once and strike a deal.

I have never rented to companies or churches, but churches have approached me in the past to see if I had vacancies (I did not). If I needed a good tenant I would not hesitate to rent to a church or corporation. I believe the odds are great that I'd be paid on time, that my place would be better cared for, and that the organization would have deeper pockets for repairs in case a bad tenant caused problems or destroyed something.

THE MONEY

Rental properties can make you money—a lot of money. As you saw in the last chapter, you can improve your profit picture a lot by following a few simple procedures and by regularly checking out the competition. Most landlords rarely do the latter, but they should.

Most new landlords are thrown into landlording without wanting the job. They inherit a home or get stuck with an extra house that will not sell. (This is especially true in depressed housing markets, when homes may sit for months without being sold.) Some of these reluctant landlords learn to cope with their newfound investment properties. And once they see the positive side of landlording, they start searching for more houses to buy. I have suggested in this book that the time may come for you to grow your rental property business. I suspect that you will want to do this if you are successful at your first one or two. Nothing comes close to owning rental properties if you get good at it. You deal with folks you appreciate, the feeling is mutual, and your equity and wealth grow surely although slowly over time. You are almost your own boss—your tenants are the closest thing you have to a boss because you must keep your good tenants happy or you don't get paid.

TIP

Know your competing landlords and you will trump their every move.

The amount of money you can make varies from situation to situation. Returns of 30 percent and higher are very reasonable, and unlike many fixed-rate investments, your profits should increase over time. When that fateful day arrives—you pay off the mortgage and have the rental income all to yourself—you will wonder why everybody is not a landlord.

Buying the Right Property

The primary factor that determines your rental profit is the amount of your mortgage payment. The best way to lower monthly payments is to buy a home at a good price. Once you do, find the best interest rate available and then refinance (described in the last chapter) whenever rates fall by 2 percent or more. Lowering the payment always increases your profit picture. (Those of you who inherit a mortgage-free house are way ahead in the income game!)

> **TIP**
>
> Many good landlords buy additional properties the longer they are in the business.

Do not go overboard with the purchase. Too many hopeful landlords make the following dramatic mistake: They buy a nice home in a nice area for a good price. There doesn't seem to be anything wrong with that so far. A nice home needs very little fixing up or money and should rent quickly. But the problem is that the owner made the mistake of getting a "good buy" as if he or she were going to live in the house instead of buying it to rent to others. Read on to find out why this is a mistake.

Search for a structurally sound house that is in good physical shape outside but looks terrible inside and out and is located in a clean, safe, owner-occupied neighborhood. Buy the worst-looking house on the block and turn it into the best-looking one. (Chapter 10 gives you more insight on buying rental properties, and Chapter 11 explains some ways to fix them up inexpensively.)

Bad-looking houses in good neighborhoods sell *far* below their actual value, in most cases. For some strange reason, owners and landlords alike rarely want to consider buying such a house. But smart landlords know that a bad-looking house can be made to look good and that as long as the structure is sound, the cosmetics are easy to fix. If you are wondering how to find these kinds of properties, select the five lowest priced houses in your newspaper's "For Sale" section, find the one with the best location, and you've probably found an ideal rental property.

Keep in mind that it's always better to own four inexpensive properties than one expensive one. Suppose you live in a part of the country where $120,000 buys a nice two- or three-bedroom house. That house will bring in around $850 a month in rent. Adjust these numbers upward or downward to fit your area. But if you buy four houses for $30,000 (you would buy them one at a time, of course) and fix them up, you could expect about $450 a month from each of them. That comes to $1,800 in rent. Compare that with the $850 for the one house, and you'll see that you've more than *doubled* your rental income. By buying cheaper houses and fixing them up you can make considerably more money than if you take the easy route, buying one "nice" house that demands higher rent.

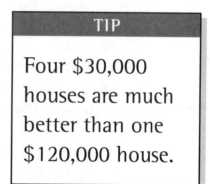

TIP

Four $30,000 houses are much better than one $120,000 house.

In theory (and one of the rules of thumb in real estate), a rental house should rent for 1 to 2 percent of its total purchase price. Therefore, if you buy a house for $50,000, it should rent for $500 to $1,000—quite a wide range, but the location and market determine which extreme is closest. The problem with this theory is that the more expensive a rental house is, the less rent it generates in proportion to its price.

It is very difficult to convince people that cheaper rentals are the way to make a lot of money. They don't see that the time they spend fixing up a run-down house pays for itself over and over. Even if they hired out all the renovation work, in the vast majority of cases they would still come out ahead. Please remember this important fact:

No matter how nice a home is, there comes a point when you cannot ask for more rent. Those who can afford the higher rent would much rather buy their own home.

The more you ask in rent, the fewer renters you will have. The reverse is also true: Cheaper rent broadens your rental base and provides a lot more qualified renters. In addition, the math is on your side. A cheaper home generates *much* more rent in proportion to its purchase price than an expensive home. That is why four $30,000 houses generate tremendously more rental income than one $120,000 home. Seldom can a $120,000 house generate $1,200 a month in rent (1 percent of its purchase price). If your local housing and rental prices are higher or lower, adjust the numbers and you will reach the same conclusion.

During the months that a property is vacant, you can much more easily afford the mortgage payment on a $30,000 house than on a $120,000 house. Landlords should estimate that their properties will be occupied eleven months out of the year. (Generally, for caring landlords, this is too conservative because their tenants tend to stay longer than eleven months.) During the vacant months, you will have to pay the mortgage as always, tenant or no tenant, and you will wish you owned a cheaper home when that payment comes out of your own pocket. Also, when you own four $30,000 houses, the income from the other three makes up for the loss of rent on one.

This scenario illustrates the point that cheaper houses bring in a much greater percentage of rent than more expensive ones. Do not even think about starting off with four houses at once, but do consider the advantages of cheaper homes and look for them when you search for properties; you can turn a diamond in the rough into a desirable and profitable rental.

> **TIP**
>
> Vacancies hurt much less when you own inexpensive houses.

Financing

Most of the information in Chapter 8 about refinancing applies to funding new loans as well. Search around for the best rate because different institutions offer vastly different interest rates.

Although there are times when a standard mortgage is not the best way to go, in most cases it usually is (unless you can pay cash). The midnight cable television channels are filled with real estate get-rich-quick schemes and fancy financing tricks that require you to buy their notebooks and videos before you can share in the wealth. Most of these schemes work in theory but are very difficult to execute in practice. They require equity sharing (making the tenant a part owner) or heavy, multilayered debt, which you do not need.

Not all of these purchase schemes are bad, but remember that there is no free lunch in this world. By far the best "scheme" for becoming a successful landlord is to do as this book suggests: Buy a house cheaply, fix it up well, and rent it for a healthy return.

That said, there is one financing trick that can work. It not only pays for the house and its renovation but also puts money in the landlord's pocket. (Before putting this plan into action, talk with a tax adviser and banker; in most cases, they will see nothing wrong with the idea.) Assuming you find a great buy on a house (you should not buy otherwise), take out a nonmortgage loan, at a higher interest rate if necessary, for the rental house's purchase price and fix-up costs. You can sometimes get a home equity loan on the house you live in to cover the rental's purchase and renovation.

> **TIP**
>
> Be wary of financing schemes that use mirrors (and fine print) to hide their subtleties.

For example, suppose you find an incredible deal: a house that nobody wants (except you) for $25,000. The house paint is peeling, the trash in the yard needs shoveling, the weeds reach the roof's loose shingles, and the inside walls and floors haven't seen paint and carpet for three generations. Because they take pride in their neighborhood, the neighbors have begun condemnation proceedings. Your knowledgeable eye looks past the peeling paint to see that the floors are solid and the structure sound. You know that in about two months you will be those neighbors' best friend and hero.

If you can, find a way other than a mortgage to get the $25,000 purchase price and an additional $2,000 to $4,000 for fixing up the house. It really does not matter how you borrow the funds as long as you do not get a mortgage. Mortgages take several months to obtain and require hefty fees up front. You can better use that time and money to fix up the house. To get such a loan, you may have to pay a higher interest rate. Do not worry about that—you will pay off this loan in two or three months anyway, and the interest for such a short time is negligible.

Some people get a single-pay note for three months. This is a short-term loan whose interest and full principal are due at the end of the three months (or whatever the term of the loan happens to be). If you have to use a credit card, do so. The price of the house should be small enough that you can get the funds.

Once you buy the house, spend the next two months renovating it. Improving the appearance improves the value of a home tremendously. Installing shutters, new shingles, new electrical outlets and circuits if needed, refurbishing the plumbing if needed, painting, carpeting, and installing miniblinds can easily turn a $25,000 house into one worth $60,000 to $75,000.

Once you finish the renovation, get a mortgage on the property. This mortgage does two things: It lowers the interest rate you pay (crucial to getting the rental income to exceed your loan payment) and it pays off that short-term loan.

The key to this financing method is determining how much the mortgage amount should be. You might think that the mortgage should equal the balance of the short-term loan, but you can get much more than that now. Remember that over the previous two to three months you created lots of equity by renovating the home. Most lenders will mortgage as much as 60 to 80 percent of a home's market value. If your rental house is now worth $65,000 after renovation, you can get a mortgage for $39,000 to $52,000. When you pay off the $30,000 or so of the short-term loan plus interest, you are left with $9,000 to $24,000 in your pocket!

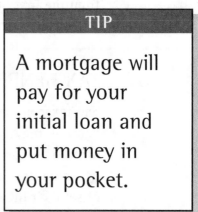

TIP

A mortgage will pay for your initial loan and put money in your pocket.

This financing method may appear to be just another one of those fancy schemes paraded on television and at real estate investment seminars. But the only "catch" is acquiring that first short-term loan. This should be easy, however, because you do not care how much the interest rate for that loan will be. The higher the rate you are willing to pay, the more lenders there are willing to loan you the money. Also, you can use your own cars and current home as collateral for the short-term loan if you have faith in your abilities to be a caring landlord. You will be successful at landlording if you want to be; and even if you hire professionals to help you with the renovation of your first rental home, you will soon have the rent rolling in, making those payments for you, in less than five months from the first day you began.

The money you put in your pocket from the mortgage makes the monthly payment higher than if you had gotten a smaller amount. The rent money should cover, or almost cover, the mortgage each month. If you need to use some of the extra money to make a few mortgage payments, do so. After several months, you can decide whether you want to roll the extra money into another rental or apply it to the loan to pay it off faster. Either course of action gives you the capital to invest in a second home even though you have only one mortgage. If you decide to buy a second home, you can pay for most of it with the extra money from the first home's loan. The two houses' incomes will let you pay off the mortgage very quickly.

TAX BENEFITS

The tax benefits of landlording are very good—although not as good as they once were. Landlords who actively manage their own homes (as opposed to passive real estate trust investors who never see the homes they invest in) enjoy tax deductions that offset their income from other sources.

You do not have to wait until tax time to enjoy rental tax savings. Once you buy rental property, go to a trustworthy tax adviser to find out how to maximize your income by minimizing your taxes. If you are employed, the tax adviser can perform a quick analysis of your records to see how many exemptions you can now claim on your job. By raising the number of exemptions (you must fill out a W4 form; the tax adviser will tell you exactly what to do), you can increase your take-home pay each paycheck instead of having to wait until year's end to enjoy the tax advantages.

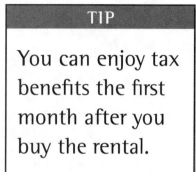

TIP

You can enjoy tax benefits the first month after you buy the rental.

KINDS OF OWNERSHIP

When going into any business, you have the right to form one of three kinds of ownerships: a single proprietorship, a partnership, or a corporation. (There are a few other possible legal entities, but these three are the most common.) Their differences lie primarily in their tax advantages and also in the way expenses and income are divided between the investors.

The single proprietorship is the most common method small landlords use to buy rental property. You are a single proprietor if you buy your own rental house, fix it up yourself (and hire help if needed, of course), and receive the income from the house. The house will be taxed at your personal tax rate. Although you must fill out an extra page or two on your tax form each year (Schedule C), the IRS treats rental income as ordinary income. The disadvantage to the sole proprietorship is its liability: You are fully responsible and liable for any and all decisions made regarding the property. If you are sued for negligence, your personal assets are at risk.

Partnerships are simply proprietorships between two or more people. No special tax consideration is given (although a lot more tax work is necessary, as described in the next section). The biggest advantage to partnerships over sole proprietorships is that your liability is limited to half that of sole proprietorships. If you are sued, you are responsible for only half the damages.

Corporations receive special tax treatment and liability protection. The corporate owners of a property are not personally responsible for damages. In most cases, only the corporation is responsible for damages. Therefore, in the case of a large lawsuit, the assets of the corporation may be lost (the house and any funds the corporation owns), but the owner's personal assets remain untouched. Here is a summary of the three types of business ownership:

Type of Ownership	Liability
Sole proprietorship	Owner is fully responsible.
Partnership	Owners are partially responsible.
Corporation	Liability is limited to the corporation's assets only.

Do not let this discussion of lawsuits frighten you. If you are a caring landlord who follows the landlording laws of your state, you will probably never face a lawsuit. In more than a decade of landlording, I've never once been sued. The types of ownership, however, warrant discussion, since something other than a sole proprietorship may be best for your specific situation.

Partnerships

Many landlords, especially first-time ones, fear going it alone. They prefer to have a partner. There is nothing inherently wrong with getting a partner. The two of you can share the expenses, get loans more easily, and work only half as hard. Despite the benefits, consider the disadvantages of a partnership before jumping into one.

To keep things legal and clean, the first step partners must take is recording their partnership at the county clerk's office. The state then considers the partnership a legal entity, entitled to own property and to receive income. You should then consult an attorney to write a partnership agreement. This explains how the two of you will share in the investment (typically fifty-fifty, although the division can be whatever you agree to). The partnership agreement also dictates the divisions of labor and contains clauses that specify how you will divide the assets if one or both of you ever want out of the partnership.

Tax time is much more difficult for partnerships than for sole proprietorships. In addition to your regular personal tax forms, the partnership itself must file tax forms, including a balance sheet and an income statement. Your tax preparer can do the extra paperwork, but you must pay for the preparer's time.

Not only do you divide the expenses between you and a partner, but you divide your income and tax benefits as well. Depreciation, deductions, and rent have to be shared according to the terms of the partners' original agreement. As you have seen throughout this book, rental property can be easy to manage. There is simply no reason to get a partner for one rental house. If you owned fifty houses, a partnership might make more sense (although incorporation would probably offer more advantages, as the next section explains). But even then, a good deal for a partnership is an even better deal for a single person, since that person enjoys all the benefits.

> **TIP**
>
> A good deal for two is usually a better deal for one. Rarely does a good rental property require a partnership.

As many partners have found out, including me, owning the property yourself is actually *easier* at times than owning with a partner. Invariably, one partner's heart is not into the job as much as the other's. Instead of risking hard feelings between friends, it makes much more sense to venture out on your own, keeping your properties separate and your friendships intact.

Incorporation

A corporation is simply a legal entity that can own income-producing businesses. To create this legal entity, you must file corporation papers with your state. Because of some legal advantages, many people prefer to file in the state of Delaware. You can do this by mail. An attorney can help you incorporate your rental property. Because there are several ways to incorporate, you might want to check the methods available so you can decide which is right for your specific situation and for the state in which you want to incorporate.

Although not necessarily a substitute for up-to-the-minute legal advice, your local library has books that describe how anyone can incorporate. Incorporation requires nothing more than filing some forms and paying a fee. If you are a do-it-yourselfer, you can save a lot of attorney fees by incorporating yourself.

Although people tend to link the word *corporation* with large businesses, anybody can incorporate any business. A corporation may consist of only a single owner, a group of two or three people, or more. The corporation simply acts as a legal protective blanket, so that your liability is limited only to the assets inside the corporation. In most cases, if a problem arises for the business, your personal assets cannot be touched.

Although the tax laws do not favor corporations as much as they once did (slowing down the economy and the housing market as well), corporations still enjoy some tax benefits over the other forms of ownership. As an officer of the corporation, however, you are actually taxed twice. Not only does the corporation pay taxes on its income, but you must pay additional taxes on any money you receive from the corporation (called "dividends"). This drawback limits some of the tax advantages you receive as a single owner in a corporation.

The other drawback to incorporation is the paperwork. At tax time you must file many papers; and you may need to file additional paperwork throughout the year. Again, a tax preparer can help you with all this, but you must pay for the preparer's time. Limiting your liability by incorporating generates less income, fewer tax deductions, and more paperwork.

Despite its drawbacks, incorporation makes a lot of sense. One lawsuit can devastate you. The more properties you own, the greater your liability risk. Incorporation significantly limits your risk. Because of the limited risk, you may

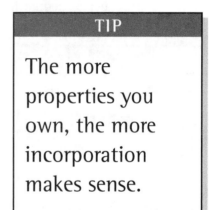

TIP

The more properties you own, the more incorporation makes sense.

be able to get by with less liability insurance than you would otherwise. If this makes you uncomfortable, talk with an attorney before changing your insurance policy after incorporating.

KINDS OF RENTAL PROPERTIES

Single-family houses make attractive rental units for a lot of landlording investors. The tenants take care of the yard in most cases, and you can be proud of renovating a run-down home. Single-family homes offer renter advantages as well. The tenants can have pets (depending on your regulations and the size of your yard), a garage, and privacy—three things not always available in multi-unit housing (like apartments).

If you buy the right properties—*cheap* properties in good areas—the rent you charge for your house can be competitive with apartments in the area (another reason not to buy an expensive home that is already fixed up). With competitive rent and the other physical advantages to single-family housing, you should never worry about a shortage of tenants. I happen to live in a town with an extraordinary number of apartments for the number of people here. I don't see the apartments as competition; in fact, I welcome them because I often beat their price but offer a fenced backyard, privacy, and a garage.

However, never rule out a chance to buy an inexpensive duplex, fourplex, or small apartment building. The advantages of rental properties increase the more units there are on the property. Leave the large apartment complexes to the big shots, because these kinds of properties pose problems beyond the scope of most beginning investors. They require on-site maintenance and management, and in certain areas of the country, rent control is more likely.

Tenants do not always want to care for a lawn. Typically, you the landlord are responsible for a lawn when you own a duplex or any multifamily housing (although you may be able to require tenants to take care of their part of the lawn). Find a trusty neighborhood kid to mow the lawn weekly if you do not want to do it. Although single-family housing offers a lot of tenant advantages, demand for multifamily units still remains high, so the advantages to you are tremendous.

> **TIP**
>
> Multifamily housing is generally easier to manage and produces higher returns than several single-family houses. That is why there are so many apartment buildings.

Suppose you own a little building consisting of four rental units. One trip takes care of four houses! When renovating the place, it is much easier and cheaper to renovate the one property than it would be to fix up four separate houses. The building only has one roof. The outside walls need less paint than the walls of four separate houses. Insurance costs less. The heating and air conditioning units are the same and take the same size filters. The shutters, miniblinds, and so forth are the same size for each unit. Any type of repair or replacement is automatically easier because the units are identical.

The biggest advantage to multifamily housing is its cost. A duplex *rarely* costs twice as much as two houses of the same size. In most instances, a duplex is only slightly more expensive than one house. You can buy a duplex, renovate one of its units, get a rent-paying tenant in, and take your time (and the tenant's money) to fix up the other unit. The more units per building (from duplex, to threeplex, to fourplex, and so on), the lower the individual cost of each unit.

In some areas of the country, mobile homes make attractive rental units as well. They are generally much less expensive than houses, especially used mobile homes (the best kind), and their renovation generally costs much less. The best thing about them is that they demand almost as much rent as a comparable apartment. A two-bedroom mobile home should bring you almost as much rent as a two-bedroom apartment.

Landlords lucky enough to have taken the mobile home plunge have been rewarded with higher returns than they otherwise would have received. There are drawbacks, however. Mobile homes do not appreciate as much as regular homes. When you buy one and renovate it, the renovation is worth less than it would have been had you fixed up a run-down house. Banks are not as apt to loan money for mobile homes, and insurance is generally higher for them, although their significantly lower taxes might offset insurance costs.

Not only do financing and insurance cost more, a mobile home does not last as long as a house, and you must find a space, with utility hookups, for the mobile home to stay. Generally, you must rent a mobile home pad in a mobile home park. However, if you have a vacant lot that is zoned for mobile homes, you can often get utility attachments installed on the property.

> **TIP**
>
> Mobile homes are cheaper than houses but their rent is not always lower.

My father has met extraordinary success with his rental mobile homes. He does not keep them in a mobile home park, but on a lot he purchased that supports mobile housing zones. He keeps the homes in good shape, and the condition they are in today is as good as it was twenty years ago (some people will tell you the life of a mobile home is ten years, which is simply not true). He bought them used but rents them for as much as comparable houses.

ORGANIZATION IS THE KEY

Once you become a landlord, you must keep accurate records of all your expenses and all your income. Keep all receipts as a backup and be able to justify any expense you make. Landlords are no more suspect for audit than anyone else, but there is always a chance the IRS will want to review your records.

If you are the kind of person who dislikes detailed record keeping, get organized quickly. Actually, record keeping is relatively easy. Keep a journal in your car; every time you make a purchase, enter it in the journal. Remember also that you can deduct mileage that is directly related to all rental property activities, so write the beginning and ending mileage for each trip as well.

Chapter 12 describes such record keeping in more detail. You don't need a computer for your first time as a landlord; all you really have to do is keep an up-to-date journal of your expenses. However, consider that today's laptop computers are small, powerful, and relatively inexpensive. They even make pocket-sized computing devices you can use to store expenses and maintain schedules and contacts. By the way, the IRS is fairly strict about recording expenses. Unless you own a commercial vehicle and use the vehicle solely for business purposes, you must record each trip you make related to your properties to deduct the mileage. The IRS does not like estimates, but it does respect journals you keep every time you make a trip.

SUMMARY

Many first-time landlords go through the following stages: fear during the purchase, regret in the middle of renovation, pride at the end of renovation, and joy when depositing their first rent check. After that, they wonder why they did not buy a rental property earlier (well, the caring ones do). It is a nice feeling to know that someone else (your tenant) is buying a house for you.

Return on a smart landlord's investment usually outpaces that of other investments by a large margin. The tax advantages are significant, too. Owning rental property will not make you an instant millionaire, but it will offer you a steady income and will outpace inflation by a large margin, in most cases.

If you are considering landlording, make sure you buy the right properties. Keep your sights low. Buying several cheaper

> **TIP**
>
> You can get rich in landlording, but it happens slowly and steadily—not overnight.

properties makes you a lot more money than one expensive one (and they are easier to keep rented as well). Cosmetically bad but structurally sound houses in good neighborhoods are gold to the smart investor. The buy-low-for-a-high-return rule multiplies if you consider multi-unit housing such as duplexes and fourplexes.

The kind of house you buy and the type of business entity you become are important decisions you must make, but not the most important for success. This book consistently emphasizes the most important aspects of landlording: Be courteous to your tenants, treat them like good customers as long as they fulfill their part of the agreement, offer them a clean, attractive home in a safe neighborhood, and you will be more successful than you ever thought you could be in this business.

CHAPTER TEN

Finding and Buying More Properties

HOW MUCH INCOME is enough? Once you become a successful landlord, you should duplicate that success. After putting one property with good tenants on autopilot, start looking for another to increase your return even more. Finding new properties to buy is fairly easy, but you must maintain control. The price you pay has got to be as low as possible to offer fair and competitive rent and still reap a large return on your investment.

This chapter explores ways to find and buy rental properties. There are always good deals out there, but you have to look for them. Instead of offering immediate hands-on advice, this chapter aims to teach you how to approach the business of home buying from an investor's point of view. In different parts of the country, buying a house, even an investment house, requires different strategies—and this chapter does not attempt to cover them all. But by the time you finish this chapter, you will feel more confident about your buying approach and you will be able to strike a better bargain than may have otherwise been possible.

Buying rental properties means finding more than good deals, it means finding *great* deals. Set your buying sights lower and do not be afraid to walk away from a deal you wanted. There is always another one right around the corner.

FILTER THROUGH THE HYPE

Rarely should you look for an investment property in your Sunday newspaper's "Homes on Parade" color supplement. The more money spent on advertising a house, the more money it must bring to pay for that advertising. Investors find good rental properties by reading the small hidden ads that read like this one, for example:

> For sale: 3-bedroom, 1 bath, garage. 12 West Pine Road. $40,000 or best offer. Call Bill at 555-9382.

A home such as this probably looks terrible. It almost certainly needs painting and renovating. The price is low (and Bill obviously couldn't spend much money for the ad). Investors like the fact that Bill announces he is taking offers. Although you should negotiate every home you buy, Bill is telling everyone that he needs to sell quickly and would consider taking much less than the asking price.

This type of ad does not guarantee anything. Bill may be a slick real estate agent who does not even have a $40,000 house; he just wants to gather as many names of buyers as possible so he can "move them up" to higher-priced homes. Most real estate agents would never be this devious, but you should approach all real estate transactions with caution and with one goal in mind: buying the cheapest house you can in a good neighborhood that will be attractive to renters.

When first looking through newspaper ads for a house, ignore everything but the prices. Set a maximum amount that you will pay. There is no one right price for the entire country. For instance, in parts of Oklahoma and elsewhere in the Midwest, you can buy a two- or three-bedroom house for as little as $15,000. In Hawaii and San Francisco, the same "great deal" would cost around $100,000 and even then the house would be located in surrounding smaller suburbs and require quite a bit of fix-up in many instances. Whatever the rock-bottom prices are for your area, stick with the bare minimum that fixer-upper houses sell for.

TIP

Look for your price first, then the address, then the home.

A good strategy (mentioned in Chapter 9) is to choose the five lowest-priced houses in the newspaper. If you have no idea how low the prices can go, choosing the lowest five will teach you a lot. Do this for several weeks and you will become an expert at low-priced housing in your area.

Only after finding the cheapest houses, then and only then should you look at the addresses. Since you narrowed the search to the most important buying consideration, price, you can now look for the second most important attribute: location. Attempt to find houses that are located in good neighborhoods. If you see a house in an unsafe neighborhood, cross it off the list. If you see a house in a neighborhood that floods every winter, cross it off the list.

Only after finding cheap houses in good neighborhoods should you consider looking any further. Relax and enjoy the search. Treat it as a hobby. You may not find a good investment deal the first week you start looking. You may not find one for many months. You will, however, run across a good deal eventually, and you will be surprised at how inexpensively you can purchase such a home.

The houses you are interested in are not the ones Realtors push with pictures and fancy descriptions. The houses you are interested in do not make high commissions for real estate agents, which is why they do not take the time with them that they do with much more expensive houses.

INVESTORS' SECRETS

Rental property investors obey a few rules. Over the years, you will establish some of your own. Rather than attempt to give you an exhaustive list of house-buying tips, this section will present some of the more common philosophies that underlie property buying. Buying a rental house is very different from buying a house for your family to live in for-ever and ever. The investor's goal is always to maximize his or her return. But to be a hands-off landlord, price, location of the property, and the home's fix-up potential are almost equally important—because you want to pro-vide a home that both you and your tenants will be proud of. Remember, too, that the worst time to purchase a house is in the spring when everybody else is buying. Purchasing in the dead of winter helps ensure that you are purchasing in the dead of sell-ing season as well.

> **TIP**
>
> You want the houses that other people don't think they want.

Drive the Price Lower

Everybody who offers a house for sale, no matter how much the asking price, expects to bargain. If a house sells for $500,000, the owner knows that he or she will get less before the final deal is made. The same holds for a house selling for $15,000. The asking price actually means very little except to put a cap on the highest price you would pay for a given house.

Do not even think about making an offer on a house until you have seen it. Even then, it is best to walk away first, leaving the seller wondering if you plan to make an offer. Never mention anything about price the first time you look at the house.

You are being a wise investor when you attempt to get the asking price much lower. Do not fear offending the seller. As a matter of fact, your goal *should be* to offend the seller with your offer. You need to see just how far this seller is willing to go before he or she will part with the house. You are not out to win a personality contest, and if you go too low, the seller will simply tell you that the price is un-

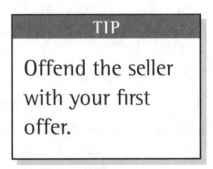

TIP

Offend the seller with your first offer.

reasonable and either make a counteroffer or tell you to find a house that is more in your price range. Many investors have been turned down on a low offer, only to be called a few days later with an acceptance. Of course, you then would be less interested and should make an even lower offer to see what happens. You can always move back up if your first offer was reasonable.

Remember that verbal real estate contracts are not binding. (Verbal contracts other than real estate contracts are binding, however.) For your offer to be valid, you must submit it in writing. Most real estate contracts also include an earnest money check that the seller keeps if you fail to uphold your end of the bargain. You get the earnest money back immediately, however, if the seller does not accept your offer. If both of you agree to the deal, the buyer will apply the earnest money check to the selling price at closing.

You can use some bargaining judgment with earnest money. For example, giving an earnest check for $5,000 on a $30,000 property shows you are serious, looks very appealing to the seller, and helps strengthen your buying position. Nevertheless, such a large earnest check is uncommon. A more standard amount is $500, which ties up much less of your money during the purchase phase, which might last a couple of months.

TIP

Put your offers in writing.

If you work with the seller directly, you can mention your verbal offer to see how he or she responds, but most sellers rightly expect all offers in writing. A real estate contract for purchase is available at any local office supply store and is relatively easy to fill out. Buy several of them. You might make ten offers on ten properties before one is accepted. If you have a friend in real estate (everyone knows *somebody* in real estate), your friend can help you fill out your first real estate offer-to-buy contract.

To effectively buy investment properties, you need to be able to bargain. This means you must be able to look at a house with as much disdain as possible, no matter how great a deal it seems. When walking through the house, say absolutely nothing positive about it. Point out every negative flaw you can find. Do not commit yourself in any way to the possibility of offering something the seller might consider reasonable.

You are doing this as much for yourself as for the seller. It is too easy to get wrapped up in one house, deciding that it is the house you want to buy, before you get the price nailed down. Being disdainful is not being cruel, although at first this approach may not come easily to you. If you walk away from this house without buying it, there will be another one, even better, that you will find later. When buying property, especially low-priced property that nobody seems to want, you hold all the cards.

Locate the Previous Selling Price

Land records are public information. The most important tool you can have in your investor's utility belt is an understanding of the land records at your county courthouse. Given the address of any house in your county, you can go to the courthouse and find out how much owners throughout history paid for that house. The owner you are most interested in is the current one, the owner selling the house right now. As the Internet's information banks continue to grow, such information is becoming available online on sites such as KnowX.com where you can, for a fee, access public land records such as appraisals and selling prices.

Liens and mortgages are also recorded at the courthouse. You can find out whether the current owner has a mortgage on the property; if so, with a little guessing, you can estimate that mortgage's current balance. For example, if the owner bought the house with a thirty-year mortgage two years ago, you know that very little of the house is paid for. If the current owner paid less for the house than he or she is asking, you know the owner wants a profit (although owners do not always get profits).

If a mortgage is still on the house, the owner probably will not be willing to go below the balance of the mortgage. For instance, if an owner still owes $28,500 on the house, he or she will be very reluctant to sell the house for less than $28,500. If there is a mortgage, check to see whether it is assumable. If so, it would be very easy for you to step in and continue the payments.

It is common to ask the seller for the current loan balance on the house. Sellers will not always tell you the balance, but many will. Sellers rarely accept offers below their mortgage balances,

> **TIP**
>
> Earnest money can negotiate for you.

since they would have to pay money to release themselves from the mortgage. In recessions, however, distressed sellers have had to take less for the home than they owed on the mortgage, or they wouldn't have been selling the property.

Whatever you find out at the courthouse is information you can use to make a better offer. The first time you visit the courthouse for land information, ask one of the clerks for help. As long as you are courteous and do not hurry the clerk, he or she will be happy to assist you. Many courthouses now have computerized property records that allow you to search for the information yourself at a computer terminal. Even if you are computer illiterate, finding property information is often as easy as typing an address to start you on your way.

If the seller accepts your offer, or if you and the seller agree on a counteroffer, you should hire an attorney to check the house abstract to make sure the title is not cloudy. A cloudy title means that the owner does not own the property outright, but that the property is legally tied up in a custody battle or lien of some kind. The seller's attorneys can usually clear up a cloudy title, but make sure you can get a clear title before pursuing the house any further.

> **TIP**
>
> Sellers can, during hard times, accept offers that dip below their mortgage balances.

Do not buy a house on contract. That means that the seller retains the house title until you pay off the house in full. There are many problems with this approach; there is even a chance that you could pay many years on the house and still not own it in the end. Often, sellers will be easier to bargain with if they sell the house on contract. But pass it up, no matter how good the deal is, if the seller refuses to sell other than on contract. When you buy a house, be sure that you can get full title and deed to the house when you purchase it. Your attorney can tell you whether this is possible.

The Current Status of the Property

Wise investors are able to quickly size up a seller's situation. From a newspaper advertisement, it is not always easy to see why a house is being sold. The seller's reason for selling is important information that you can use to determine the lowest price possible. The best way to find out why the house is for sale is to ask.

Sellers who are transferred out of town are more willing to bargain than those staying in town. They need to get out from under their current mortgage because they will soon have to start payments on their new one.

Almost without exception, real estate agents get a commission (usually around 7 percent) on every house they sell. In many cases, they work hard and deserve their commissions. However, if an agent is involved in the property you are interested in, you automatically know the house must sell for more than the owner wants. Both the owner and the agent must make their money

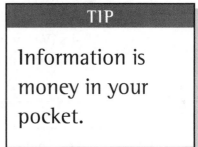

TIP

Information is money in your pocket.

from the sale. Therefore, houses for sale by owner are almost always better deals than those commissioned through agents.

Another thing to remember about the property's real estate agents: They work for the seller and not for you, the buyer. Although your money pays the agent's commission, the agent is solely responsible, by law, to be loyal to the seller. The agent is required to disclose certain facts about the home to you, including flood insurance requirements and special problems such as fresh termite damage. Nevertheless, the agent does not work for you and you must treat the agent with caution when discussing your buying plan of attack.

Now that I've discussed the negative aspects of sellers' agents, I must tell you their advantages. Listed properties certainly make up the majority of houses for sale. If you look only for by-owner properties, you are limiting your inventory considerably. Often, home sellers will put their own homes up for sale just to test the waters, and they are not always extremely motivated to sell. The extra commission paid to Realtors often means the difference between selling a property and sitting on it, so the sellers with agents could actually be more motivated than those who sell their own homes. In addition, if you buy through state foreclosures, Housing and Urban Development (HUD), or Veterans Affairs (VA), you *must* use the services of a real estate broker.

> **TIP**
>
> Realtors can be your friends.

Although a property's agent works for the seller, in many states you can usually get your own agent to represent you. Buyer's agents are more and more common and can often negotiate and find more negotiable deals than you might be able to find on your own. In addition, two people looking on your behalf are better than one.

Although the agent that you use must have all the proper licenses and training, run through the agents and brokers that you know, and the ones who are referred to you, until you run across someone who is more of a negotiator than a salesperson. When your agent walks into the seller's house or to the seller's agent with an offer, your agent must put on a negotiating hat and begin the bargaining. The agent needs to do more than present a contract to the seller; the agent must convince the seller that your offer merits attention and response.

A friend of mine once shared a home-buying experience that confirmed for me the importance of a negotiating agent. He wanted a property in the country. He had looked at several and found one that was distressed; the owners did not live in the property and the property had not had one interested buyer in at least several weeks. The owners had already come down on the price. He called his agent and asked the agent to present immediately an offer that was below the already-reduced asking price. After a few minutes' thought, the agent gathered his strategy and presented the offer to the sellers. He told the sellers that his client made an offer without his wife seeing the property and that wives often don't like properties the husband selects. He told the seller that they'd need to accept his offer quickly, before the buyer's wife saw the property and told him to rescind the offer. The sellers took the offer on the spot. In fact, the buyer had described the property to his wife—it was an investment property he was going to renovate and resell at some later point—so the fact that she hadn't seen the property was not really a problem. The negotiating agent was smart to jump on this point, however, because he closed the deal at his client's asking price. If you plan to use a buyer's agent, be sure to find one who is fast on his or her feet, like the agent in this example.

TIP

Look for a negotiator, not a real estate agent.

The vacancy of the house is critical. If the sellers still live in the house, they are not as desperate to sell it as those who are already in their next house. The longer sellers sit with an empty house, the more eager they are to sell it, the less profit they expect, and the more control you have as a buyer.

With a corporate-owned house, one owned by a business, you sometimes have a little more bargaining power. Perhaps an employee was transferred to another city and the employee's company bought the home to expedite the employee's move to the new location. Sometimes banks own homes, too. They may have foreclosed on a property and want to sell it for the remaining loan balance.

Corporations and banks generally do not want to be in the real estate business. They want to get rid of any properties in their inventory so they can get on to the business they do best. Therefore, you sometimes have a little more bargaining power when buying corporate-owned homes; the seller (the corporation) is more willing and able to sustain a loss on the sale than an individual seller might be. As with motivated sellers who fail to sell their own homes, corporate real estate sales almost always involve a seller's agent, so do not be discouraged if you must go through a Realtor when purchasing such a home.

Perhaps some of my reluctance to buy a listed home is that the homes I buy generally are in such decrepit shape that no agent will list the property. Remember that I want to buy the worst-looking home in the neighborhood, and the homes I want have less curb appeal than most homes in the Realtor's multiple listing book. I want homes that are structurally sound but cosmetically unappealing—homes that nobody else wants and that no Realtor wants to list. Often, the fact that a real estate agent lists a property makes the property in better condition than my cheap instincts allow me to buy.

THE CONDITION OF THE HOME

The kind of homes that investors prefer generally would not be owner-occupied or agent-sold homes. Generally, good investors are interested in rental houses that have not been lived in for at least a year. Either the house did not sell or it was so physically run-down that real estate agents did not want to take on the selling responsibility for such a small return. Or maybe, for whatever reason, the owner was simply not in a hurry to get rid of the house.

As discussed in Chapter 9, you want a house that is structurally sound, in good physical shape outside, looks terrible both inside and out, and is located in a clean, safe, owner-occupied neighborhood. Buy the worst-looking house on the block and turn it into the best-looking one. This philosophy works extremely well and makes more sense than just about any other rental advice you can get. You want houses that are ugly.

Although not always the case, you can usually fix up the inside of a house for less money than the outside. The inside walls and ceilings may have holes in them, the electricity and plumbing may be in terrible shape, the appliances may be ripped out, but drywall, paint, and carpet are relatively easy and inexpensive to replace.

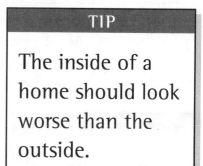

TIP

The inside of a home should look worse than the outside.

If the home's wiring and plumbing are in bad shape, most buyers stay away from the house. Bad plumbing and electrical wiring lower the selling price tremendously; yet wiring and plumbing are not extremely expensive to have redone or repaired considering your long-term investment. Take care of these problems at the start. When you begin renovation, get the plumbing and wiring in shape first. You will need to count on these utilities as you remodel the rest of the house. In addition, you may have to run wires through walls and you don't want to cut into a wall you just finished painting. Expect to replace as much or all of the wiring and plumbing as necessary in order to get it in shape for the next twenty years.

Most areas require that licensed electricians and licensed plumbers do all the wiring and plumbing work on a house. In many areas, you are not allowed to work on your own home's wiring unless you are licensed. Hiring licensed personnel is expensive, and these two expenses will be the most costly part of the home's renovation. But think about the future savings. Good wiring lowers the chance of fires, good plumbing helps avoid water damage, and you and your tenants will sleep better knowing that these important parts of the home are in perfect order.

Since you will do most of the remaining renovations yourself or with low-cost hourly employees (see the next chapter for more information on home renovation), you can afford to get the most important factors, wiring and plumbing, taken care of properly.

Brand-new, no-frills, generic white appliances are very inexpensive. Instead of messing with a ten-year-old stove that works half the time, invest in a new one. A new stove, oven, and refrigerator look nice and you will know their history. If the house you buy has old appliances that look like they're about to stop working, replace them when you renovate to give yourself years of maintenance-free landlording.

> **TIP**
>
> # Fix the wiring and plumbing first.

Today, termite damage is relatively easy to fix. Contrary to popular belief, termites damage houses very slowly. It takes a long time for termites to infest a house so terribly that the house becomes structurally unsound. A few years ago, the government banned the use of chlordane, an extremely effective termite treatment. There is talk of allowing its use again because of its effectiveness. However, even without chlordane, pest control services can rid most properties of termites.

Houses with active termite damage are extremely difficult to sell. Most buyers want to stay away from them at all costs. If the house you are considering has termite damage, ask a licensed pest control agent to give you a bid on getting rid of the termites. Many pest control services also fix any wood damage that termites cause. You might be surprised at how cheaply the pest control service can get rid of the problem.

> **TIP**
>
> In almost every case, houses with termite damage sell for a much bigger discount than the damage costs to fix.

Houses that sell with structural damage rarely have suffered damage beyond repair. Sellers are required by law to disclose such problems. In many cases, structural damage is nothing more than a brick wall that is loose or a floor that sags. But the words *structural damage* automatically scare buyers away from houses, thereby lowering the price considerably. Most of the time, you can repair structurally damaged houses easily and with very little expense. If you feel that the damage might be costly, ask a framing carpenter to look at the problem. Generally, framing carpenters can shore up sinking timbers in a matter of minutes.

THE TYPE OF PROPERTY

Throughout most of the country, it makes sense for investors to buy freestanding, three-bedroom houses. Such homes easily compete with apartment buildings if bought for a good price. But there are parts of the country where this type of home is not practical. For instance, in New York City, high-rise and brownstone apartments take precedence over freestanding houses.

Try to find homes with a garage or at least a carport. Nobody likes to leave their automobile out in the elements. A garage also gives tenants a place to store their lawn and garden equipment.

Keep your eyes open for other types of housing in your area. As mentioned in the last chapter, duplexes and fourplexes are a landlord's dream, since they rarely cost twice or four times as much as single-family houses, but they return two to four times the rent. You may miss these jewels when scouring your paper for low-priced homes, since they will be priced slightly higher than single-family homes. Therefore, once you select the five lowest-priced houses, read through the rest of the ads to make sure you did not miss a multi-unit building.

Two-bedroom houses generally sell for much less than comparable three-bedroom houses. Buyers often shy away from two-bedroom homes since they are difficult to resell. However, wise investors know the rental value of a two-bedroom house. Investors are interested in a house's rental appeal, not its future selling price. Two-bedroom homes compete wonderfully well with one- and two-bedroom apartments. They offer many advantages (such as a yard, garage, and privacy) over apartments, so renters seek them out first. I have found the most success with two-bedroom homes and you may also.

In some areas, mobile homes are attractive rental investments since they offer less depreciation than houses and are very inexpensive to fix up. However, mobile homes do not last as long as permanent homes. In some areas of the country, a two- or three-bedroom mobile home commands as much rental income as a house and is much cheaper to maintain, but you must find a place to put it, with utility hookups. Often, you must pay a small fee to park it if you can't put it on property you own.

Condominiums and cooperatives sometimes make good rental buys, but their appeal has waned since the early 1980s. Remember that they almost always have association dues, which are subject to change and will always rise if they change at all. Some have rental restrictions. Generally, their resale value has not been historically as strong as that of the single-family home or duplex, although resale value is a secondary consideration to you.

LOCATION

You already know to buy homes in good neighborhoods. Nobody wants to rent a house in an unsafe neighborhood. Your competitors have plenty of houses in nice places.

Besides the neighborhood, you must also consider how far you want the rental property to be from your own home. If you buy the house next door, you may see your tenants more often than desired. Buying a home too far from your own also causes problems. Long-distance landlording can be a headache. Most landlords who live farther than fifty to seventy-five miles from their rental property eventually

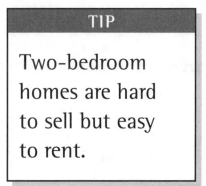

TIP

Two-bedroom homes are hard to sell but easy to rent.

hire a service to take care of the property and to find tenants. As soon as a rental service takes over, you lose profits and control, the two most important parts of successful landlording.

A good strategy for some landlords who live in large cities is to buy rental property in the surrounding smaller towns. Your rentals will be close enough for you to handle all problems but far enough away so your tenants do not bother you with petty requests. In addition, you will not be competing with your larger town's apartment complexes, and taxes are generally lower in smaller towns. Almost every rental property I own lies outside my hometown's city limits. I live in a rather large town (Tulsa) and I find that the smaller towns within thirty minutes from my home make great rentals and sell more cheaply than the houses in my city.

MOVING A HOUSE

Never overlook the possibility of moving a good home to a good vacant lot. Buildings in some areas of your town are likely being demolished for new construction; you can buy homes for the cost of demolition and have them moved inexpensively (from $2,000 to $5,000, depending on the size of the house, its location, and its structure). If you find a great deal on a nice home in a poor area, consider moving it to a better one.

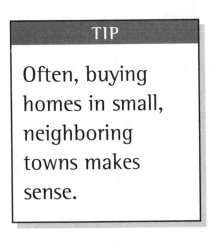

TIP

Often, buying homes in small, neighboring towns makes sense.

The biggest key to moving a house is finding a vacant lot. There are more good lots than you might realize, and you would be surprised at the number of vacant lots in good housing tracts. Houses burn down and the owners often choose not to rebuild at the same location. By moving your home to such a lot, you'll make the neighborhood happy, increase tax revenue for the city, and put more rental income in your pocket than if you had bought an existing home in the same neighborhood.

The amount of money you make during your landlording career greatly depends on how much you pay for your houses. Buying and moving a home to a good neighborhood is almost always more cost-effective than buying an existing one in a good neighborhood.

Building movers know how to move homes and keep them intact during the move. Houses require very little work to prepare before moving, and the moving company can do the work for you. Talk with the movers to determine how much they will do and how much you will do. A straight lift-and-move job is a lot cheaper than having the movers also get the house back to its original condition once it's in place. Ask the movers what the house will need once it is moved to prepare it for living. You may be able to do all the work yourself (sometimes, only painting is needed, depending on the condition of the house before the move).

You would be surprised at how well houses can be moved and still remain intact. Some home movers actually recommend keeping the furniture in place when moving an existing house and family, instead of taking the furniture out before the move and putting it back in afterward. Structural damage rarely occurs with movers who know their job. There are many homes in the country that have been moved and did not even need a touch-up paint job.

WAYS TO BUY

Your newspaper's "For Sale" columns are not the only places to look for good rental deals. Let your friends know that you are always interested in good bargains. If you have a good relationship with a banker, ask the banker about any foreclosed properties that the bank holds. Many times, banks are willing to let houses go for very little money, simply to get rid of them.

Banks are not the only institutions that foreclose on properties. Savings and loans have many more properties than they care to admit. Mortgage lenders may also be able to direct you to a deal.

Ask at your county courthouse about home auctions and tax sales. If you go three years without paying your property taxes, guess what happens to your property? The government steps in and takes it from you. Of course, this won't happen to you, but it does happen every day to hundreds of other people around the country. Usually, these government-foreclosed properties do not have families in them; rather, they are homes that have been abandoned because of divorce, death, or other reasons.

> **TIP**
>
> The government always has more houses than it wants.

In many instances, the government will sell its inventory of houses for the back taxes due. Very few people take advantage of this situation. Although some legal work is involved, and buying a house for back taxes is not always a straightforward process, isn't a $750 house worth a little effort? Ask your county court clerks for more information about these homes.

The government often holds auctions for tax-sale houses. To attend an auction, you only have to know its date, time, and location. Many times, very few people show up to these auctions, so be sure to ask your county clerk's office about them.

Many states around the country have government-run house-selling services for houses that were abandoned or seized. HUD and Veterans Affairs are two offices that regularly sell homes below market value.

SUMMARY

Let's say you have followed this book's suggestions so far. You have streamlined your rental properties to the point where they practically take care of themselves, you have quality tenants, and your landlording business is on autopilot. What is your next step? *Buy more properties.*

Empires are made one step at a time, and twenty-five rental properties, properly managed, are not a lot more time-consuming than two or three. The bulk of your time will be devoted to fixing up the property so you can move good tenants in.

With more properties, the odds are greater that you'll have a vacancy—but with more properties, the vacancy's loss of rent is covered by rents from the others. By now, the risk of more vacancies should not concern you, especially since the open house approach makes vacancies easy to fill.

This chapter discussed the types of homes to look for, the neighborhoods to look in, and how to find good deals. There are great deals all around you. You only have to find them. Nobody seems to want to get into the rental business when real estate is in a slump, but that is the only time to buy! Buy when nobody else seems interested because that is when prices are lowest.

The importance of buying several low-cost houses instead of one or two higher-priced homes cannot be stressed enough. To be successful in the landlording business, your rental return is the primary consideration. Buy your houses right—that is, *cheaply*—and you will compete successfully in the rental property business.

CHAPTER ELEVEN

Renovating Your Rental Properties

EVEN IF YOU'RE not the "fix-it" type, you can remodel or effectively manage a remodeling. Renovating rental properties does not have to be expensive or extremely time-consuming. You should spend the majority of your time preparing the house to rent it.

As you now know, smart landlords buy rental properties that are run-down, look awful, and are located in good neighborhoods. Getting the home looking its best on the outside often takes a good coat of paint, some shingles and shutters, and a thorough yard cleanup. The inside of the house should feel like new once you're done with it. Fresh paint, new wallboard where needed, new (but generic and no-frills) appliances, and go-with-everything carpet spruce up the inside like you would not believe.

This chapter gives the owner of a newly purchased rental house some tips and ideas for turning that shack into a renter's dream. Renters do not expect palaces. They only expect and deserve an attractive, cozy, clean, and safe home that they can be proud of. Chapter 2 explained how inexpensive extras such as ceiling fans, miniblinds, and outside shutters add elegant but inexpensive touches to rental houses that attract good tenants. Attempt to maintain a clean and fresh look and care about tenants' needs without becoming too extravagant in your spending. Simplicity and uniformity are the keys to keeping more than one rental property maintained and in tip-top shape.

I am often surprised at how easy remodeling can be. When I see something that needs to be done, my first thought is that I must get someone to do it. Once I see it done, I wonder why I did not tackle the job myself. Home renovations are easy. If you never thought you could hammer drywall, you've never watched someone else do it. You take a hammer and pound in the nails, and that's about it. The sanding and painting take time, but again, anybody can do the work. This chapter cannot possibly give you an in-depth tutorial on home renovation. The details require many more pages and are better left to the books and television shows completely dedicated to the subject. (An extremely well-written book for home remodeling is Dan Lieberman and Paul Hoffman's *Renovating Your Home for Maximum Profit*, published by Prima Publishing.)

Instead of teaching you how to use a hammer, this chapter focuses on helping you determine a rental property's needs. Every home renovation is different because every home is in a different state of disrepair. After reading this chapter, you will know which renovations are necessary, which are not, and which cost little but add lots of rental appeal.

KEEP THINGS SIMPLE AND UNIFORM

The best renovating advice you can have as a landlord is to keep things simple and uniform. Do not paint the walls a different color in every room of the house. Choose a neutral color and stick with it. If you want to break the monotony, paint the kitchen and bathrooms a different color from the rest of the house. (These rooms require a different kind of paint anyway, if you want to keep steam from peeling the paint.) Flat paint does not last very long on rental property walls. Stick to a semigloss for a longer-lasting paint that is also easier to clean.

> **TIP**
>
> Make your rental homes mirror images of each other.

If you have more than one rental house, use the same colors on all your houses. This single tip will save you a lot of time and effort over your landlording career. Actually, the home you live in can be a guide to the color schemes you use on your rental properties. If your taste in color is not too extravagant, paint the outside of your rentals the same color as your own home, so you will always be able to match the paint whenever you need to touch up something. You are more likely to have the right color in your garage, and you might get bulk discount rates from your local paint store.

Sticking with the same color scheme lets you save in other ways as well. You can then use the same shutters, carpet, fixtures, and everything else. Once your houses match, it's easy to replace broken or worn items (you can keep on hand spare shutters, light fixtures, and carpet squares for patching holes).

Keep Colors Neutral

Keeping colors neutral does not mean they have to be dull. But if you paint every room in a rental white, your tenants will tire of the walls quickly, and the walls will show dirt faster than if they were another color. Instead of white, paint the walls a light cream color. This color will never go out of style, and any furniture your tenants own will fit right in.

If you do not mind spending a little more time, paint the baseboards and all the trim, inside and out, a lighter color than the walls. White works well. This "colonial style" adds an expensive look to any house. Never paint trim or baseboards a darker color than the rest of the walls. This tends to box rooms and makes the house seem smaller. When painting an already dark trim a lighter color, you may have to first apply a primer coat of white paint. Dark colors are difficult to cover otherwise.

Many homes built in the last twenty-five years have no ceiling molding. If yours doesn't have trim, install some. A small trim around the ceiling, painted white, adds an elegant but inexpensive touch to any room. Ceiling trim is a one-time, inexpensive outlay that produces good-looking results forever.

When choosing colors, pick pale ones. Virtually any color works, all through a house, as long as it's light enough to accent the house's furnishings. The color of the walls should be unobtrusive so that tenants' pictures and furniture stand out. You can paint the walls yellow or eggshell blue as long as the

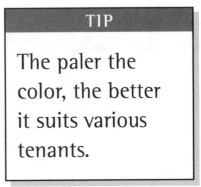

TIP

The paler the color, the better it suits various tenants.

paint is pale enough to stay in the background. I prefer a cream or extremely light tan as such colors seem to complement any tenant's furniture.

Wainscot Living Areas

An inexpensive trick that really impresses tenants is wainscoting, which is the process of paneling the lower half of the walls and painting the upper half. Cap the joint between the paneling and the painted wall with a thin wood trim painted the same color as the wall. When would-be tenants walk into a wainscoted living room during open house, they will be greeted with a rich-looking living area instead of the stark plasterboard walls they saw at your competitor's place.

Wainscoting is easy and requires only inexpensive paneling. Since the paneling only goes up half the wall, you need to buy only half as much as the room would need for a complete paneling job. The paneling has the added advantage of protecting the walls as well. When a tenant scoots a chair too close to the wall, paneling can absorb the scrape better than painted wallboard.

TIP

Buy extra paneling to make future repairs a snap.

Plan ahead—purchase an extra sheet of paneling and keep the paneling in the house's attic. Paneling is difficult to match years later. Between tenant occupancies, wainscoted walls require less maintenance than painted walls, too. Often, a little furniture polish brightens the paneling's shine. Since the paneling took most of the dents and scuffs from the former tenants, you do not need to repaint the room as often. Many times, touch-up paint here and there is all that is needed. If you need to replace a section of paneling, use the extra paneling that you have in storage.

THINK ABOUT THE FUTURE

Renovate for the future, not just for the present. Every renovating decision you make should be with long-term ownership in mind. Assume that you will keep this rental house for the rest of your life. This will help you make wiser decisions.

For instance, if the plumbing and wiring need replacing, do it. The previous chapter describes how an initial investment in wiring and plumbing saves you lots of headaches over the years and also pays off in safety as well. Replace shingles if they appear loose. It is a lot cheaper to do so now than to fix a leaky roof later.

Do not paint a room one crazy color just because you had some leftover paint. Someday, that room will need repainting, and you will have to start all over, because you'll never be able to match the first color. When you put up shutters or install carpet, buy extra. Later, when something needs replacing, you won't have to settle for a "close match," as many landlords would. Often, buying in bulk brings prices down, too. Don't hesitate to ask the manager of a home remodeling store for quantity discounts. The managers in many of these stores have the authority to strike deals with good customers.

> **TIP**
>
> Doorstops and wallpaper guards pay for themselves again and again.

Put doorstops on every wall on which a door opens. A doorstop is a lot cheaper and easier to install than fixing a hole in the wall later. As you walk through the home, consider every little thing you can do now to avoid big problems in the future. Your landlording career is a long one, and you can make it hard or easy on yourself.

If the house has wallpaper, install clear plastic wall guards on every exposed corner. Corners never seem to like wallpaper and the wall guard will keep the paper glued down, even if tenants rub against the corner every time they pass it.

Wallpaper

Wallpaper is an attractive addition to a rental house, but many landlords do not install it because of the time and expense. However, if you know how to hang paper and enjoy the work, by all means add this extra touch. Do not paper all the rooms—walls that look "too busy" get old fast. Only put wallpaper in the kitchen and bathrooms, and be sure to get paper that is water- and steam-resistant.

Papering the walls of a rental property certainly has its drawbacks, so weigh the advantages before you hang the paper. Do not feel that you need to do it. Smooth, well-painted walls look just fine. Some people mistakenly believe that wallpaper covers up problems, but they are wrong—wallpaper *accents* problems. If your wall has holes or loose drywall or cracks, fix them before you put up wallpaper.

> **TIP**
>
> Wallpaper borders are much easier to hang and take down than full wallpaper, and they add almost as much decorative appeal.

If you do decide to hang wallpaper, you must first remove any old paper and then size the walls. Sizing prepares the wall for paper and makes the paper a little easier to remove later—often a difficult task. Someday, you will have to remove the paper, so taking the time to size the walls now translates into a lot less scraping down the road.

A nice touch that any landlord can add is to put a wallpaper border around the ceiling of a painted wall. Even the highest-quality borders are very inexpensive and most are preglued; with a little water, you will have them up in no time. Wallpaper borders are another example of an extra touch caring landlords can add to turn a house into a home, and yet, the paper costs little and is easy to install.

If you sell your home after a good career of landlording, wallpaper seems to help sell the home faster. Therefore, you may want to add wallpaper before you sell the house even though you'd probably not want the wallpaper in the house when renting the home because painted walls are much easier to touch up than damaged wallpaper. If you plan to sell the home, or offer the home on a lease-purchase plan, wallpaper makes more sense than if you are only renting the property.

Safety Always Comes First

Never skimp on safety precautions. Install handrails on the stairs, safety bars in the tubs, and smoke alarms on each floor. If safety is not your number one priority, do not become a landlord. Someday, an inadequate wiring job or other unsafe aspect of a rental home will cause you much grief.

During renovation, think about ways to minimize damage. A plumber can add water shutoff valves below each sink, tub, and toilet to save you lots of money on water-damage repair bills later. When a sink begins to overflow, your tenant has only to turn off the shutoff valve to stop the water. Once the water is off, there is plenty of time to fix the problem that caused the overflow.

The alternative to individual shutoff valves is to show the tenants where the main water shutoff valve is. Located outside, it requires a key to access and activate. But even if you give your tenants a key, the water will overflow and damage your carpet and any first-floor ceilings long before tenants get the water turned off. Shutoff valves on each faucet can protect your home better than the outside shutoff valve.

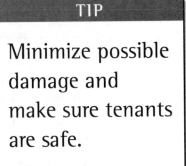

TIP

Minimize possible damage and make sure tenants are safe.

If your home uses a septic tank, ask your local plumbing supply store for the crystals that help maintain proper septic balance. You cannot count on your tenants to keep out of the drains chemicals that will harm the useful bacteria inside your home's septic system. The crystals, added every month or two, will help ensure that your septic tank remains trouble-free for years.

If your home uses well water, make sure that you have your water tested every couple of years. In addition, either you or your tenants will have to change the water filter regularly. Show the tenants how to do this and post the process right next to the well pump inside your well's closet. Changing the well's filter is simple, but it must be done whenever the water pressure gets sluggish. Your tenants probably won't mind being responsible for the filter because they have to live with low water pressure when the well filter gets old. Decide if you want to supply the filters or if you want to supply only the first one. If you want the tenants to change the filters regularly, you should probably supply the filters.

Make sure the house is wired with ample electricity. Two hundred amp service is the least you should have these days, and three hundred amp is best. Otherwise, tenants' hair dryers and large televisions will trip the circuits too often. Even if the house wiring is adequate, replace any fuse boxes with circuit-breaker boxes. When a circuit trips, your tenant will easily be able to turn the electrical service back on instead of searching for a fuse. Label each circuit clearly so the tenant can find the right circuit without having to try them all.

You can purchase an electrical circuit tester for a few dollars at your local radio and electrical supply store. These testers have red and green lights that tell you whether an outlet is wired properly. Most important, they warn you when an outlet is not properly grounded (the ground is the third prong on many electrical plugs). If even one outlet has problems, get an electrician to fix it. This is another safety-first expense that you should never have to repeat.

CONSIDER YOUR TENANTS' NEEDS

Every time you walk through the house, think about the needs of the people living there. What would you need in each room if you lived there? Tenants want and deserve any conveniences you can give them. Landlords who plan for the long term consider the tenants' needs first, knowing that small investments up front reap large dividends in the future.

Make sure the kitchen has plenty of cabinet space for the home's size. If the bedroom closets are small, consider installing extra shelves at the top for more storage. You want to keep tenants as long as possible. Installing adequate storage pays off. Every time your tenants put dishes away in a kitchen without ample storage space, they will want to move.

Extra phone jacks are extremely easy to install. They don't carry harmful electricity, so you don't need an electrician's license to wire them. A trip to your local phone supply store will produce all the tools, outlets, and wiring you need. Most phone wiring parts come with hookup instructions. You need to extend and connect only two wires (the red and green ones—just remember Christmas colors) from any existing phone outlet in the house to the new ones.

Make sure the master bedroom has a phone outlet. Since these outlets are so easy to install, consider putting them in each bedroom, in the kitchen, and in the living room. If your tenants have the phone company put in extra outlets, the cost is extremely high.

If the house is wired for cable television, make sure you put outlets in places where tenants need them. Most cable television companies are not as lenient as the phone company regarding extra outlets. You may have to pay the company a one-time charge to install an extra outlet. Although tenants will not need as many television outlets as phone outlets, one in the master bedroom is a special treat. If your tenants want more than two cable television outlets, tell them they will have to foot the bill themselves.

Check every lightbulb and replace the dead ones. Once your tenants move in, it is their responsibility to replace bulbs that burn out, but every bulb in the house should be working when they move in.

Install dead bolt locks on all outside doors and make sure all windows lock from the inside. Get a locksmith to key the dead bolts to the same key as the front and back doors. One key per house makes it much easier for you and your tenants to keep track of keys. Make sure every door opens easily. If a door drags on the floor, a hinge is usually loose. Tighten all hinges. Because door hinges are notorious for stripping their screws, you may have to remove the screws and fill their holes with wood filler before tightening them again. If tightening the hinges does not stop the sagging, plane the bottom of the door so it no longer drags.

For added security, buy an inexpensive peephole for the front door. You can install it in five minutes with a drill. Tenants will appreciate being able to see who is at their front door before they open it.

Make sure the kitchen and bathrooms have adequate towel bars and paper holders. Sometimes it is difficult to remember these little extras when you are not living in the home. But without them—adequate storage space, outlets, and towel racks—your tenants will have a difficult time living in your rental for a long period of time. They will never notice the extras when they have them, but they will surely miss them when they do not.

When you install towel bars, shelves, or anything else on the walls, be sure to secure the screws into the wooden studs in the walls. Studs are the wood beams that frame the walls. If you have ever seen a house in its midconstruction phase, you have seen the framework of wooden studs that forms the basis of the walls. Purchase an inexpensive stud finder at your local radio and electrical supply store to help you find wall studs.

When you first renovate the house, install enough insulation in the walls and attic to keep the home protected from the elements. Insulation is not expensive, and it saves your tenants lots of money on their utility bills, leaving more money for your tenants and therefore more money for the rent. Weather stripping around all outside doors is also a must, especially for cold-winter areas.

The electrical outlets and switches in the outside walls lose lots of heating and cooling energy. Most home supply stores now sell small packages of insulation already cut to fit electrical outlets and light switch covers. A packet of ten or twenty insulating pads costs only a few dollars, but the pads efficiently fill in the holes in the outside walls.

While insulating the outlets and switches, consider replacing all the switch plates and outlet covers in the house. Over the years, these get painted and papered over so much that they look cheap and old. Switch and outlet plates are extremely inexpensive and their neat and uniform look adds even more to a freshly renovated home.

More landlords are moving away from gas water heaters to electric ones, even though electric heat is more expensive. Heating water is one of the few places a landlord might want to put his or her cost before the tenant's. Every year, more restrictions are placed on gas water heaters. They must be enclosed and properly ventilated, sometimes requiring two or three ducts several inches thick. When you replace a water heater, look at the electric ones instead of going straight for the gas.

Electric water heaters require much less ventilation, cost less, are much easier to install, and are safer than gas heaters. All these factors add up. To lower the tenant's electric bill, put an insulating blanket around the water heater. These blankets are inexpensive at most home improvement stores and pay for themselves the first year. Water heater blankets are a good investment for both gas and electric water heaters.

> **TIP**
>
> Eliminate all pests while the house is vacant.

Utility companies now offer huge rebates if you purchase a specific energy-saving water heater or furnace. At first, I was skeptical about such rebates because I could not understand why such companies would want to help you bring them less business. It turns out that your utility companies do not want to pay the costs of increasing their capacity, and they find that it's cheaper to give you energy-saving advice and rebates than to upgrade their plants to meet higher demands.

Spraying for bugs in a vacant house is much easier, usually cheaper, and much more successful than spraying after tenants move in with their furniture and other household belongings. Call an exterminator to thoroughly spray the house, attic, and crawl spaces, both inside and out. No tenant likes to see bugs the first day in a new house. Get rid of pests now, completely, and the house will have fewer troubles with insects later.

BATHROOMS AND KITCHENS

Cleanliness is nowhere as important as in these two rooms. Get rid of stains, smells, and mildew. If you buy a house with cracked porcelain, replace it. Quality counts when replacing fixtures. Do not buy the latest style; instead, buy traditional fixtures that will hold up with heavy use. Install the positive stop faucets that turn off completely at a fixed point instead of tightening down until the water cuts off. Positive stop faucets save you lots of time in washer replacements and save your tenants the cost of dripping water.

Sometimes white porcelain gets chipped. When this happens, there is little you can do. If the damage is small, ignore it; otherwise, replace the entire fixture. Do not recoat the porcelain. The second coat will chip even easier than the first, and you will be out money and time.

Use latex paint on the bathroom and kitchen ceilings. A thin coat is better than a thick one; the thick coat will peel easier than a thin one since moisture condenses regularly on bathroom and kitchen walls. In the bathroom, consider installing an exhaust fan that vents upward through the roof. Make sure the fan is connected to the light switch so it always comes on when someone enters the bathroom (make sure you get a quiet fan). The fan will help eliminate odors, but more important, it will carry steam out of the bathroom and away from the paint, plaster, and drywall.

Caulk is one of the landlord's best friends. Caulk around all sinks, tubs, toilets, windows, and floors. Nowhere is caulking more important than in the bathrooms. Water damages houses very quickly. Even the best tenants get water on the floors and walls. The last thing you need is water running behind a tub or into floorboard, causing wood to rot and inviting termites.

Caulking ahead of time saves you lots of time, money, and effort in the long run.

Be sure to use twenty-five-year caulk. It is slightly more expensive (about 30 percent more) than the cheaper kind, but lasts much longer and applies more smoothly. Almost all white caulk can be painted. Use indoor/outdoor caulk instead of worrying about different kinds for inside and outside. Do not be afraid to use a case or two of caulk when you first renovate your home. The bathrooms and kitchen need a lot. Also, use ample caulk around all outside windows to insulate them well.

If the shower has doors, consider replacing them with a rod and a shower curtain. Not all showers work with only a curtain, but many do, especially tub/shower combinations. The shower doors get very dirty and are extremely difficult to clean. They often crack, need lots of caulk, and are generally a pain. You can buy a shower curtain at discount stores for a few dollars. Put up a fresh curtain before each tenant moves in.

> **TIP**
>
> Use high quality, indoor/outdoor caulk.

If the bathtub has old decals on its bottom, you can remove them by first applying a heat gun or hair dryer to soften their adhesive. Once the adhesive softens, you will be able to peel or scrape the decals off. Be sure you do not scratch the tub surface; a plastic car-windshield scraper works nicely. Whatever adhesive residue remains can be taken up with fingernail polish remover or paint thinner.

CARPETING

When renovating the house, install the carpet last, only after you are through painting and drilling and have moved the appliances in. If you are replacing old carpet, leave it down until you are ready to install the new carpet. The old carpet can catch all the sawdust, loose nails, and paint scrapings; you can then remove all this debris when you remove the carpet. Never install carpet in the bathrooms or kitchen. Spills can easily ruin a carpet; in these rooms, hard floors make cleanup easy.

Make sure you buy a neutral-colored carpet that does not show dirt easily. Stay away from sculptured carpet. Choose a traditional carpet with average-height nap that is easy to clean and looks good.

You might be surprised at how cheaply you can buy carpet. Go to several different carpet supply stores and check price tags before you look at the carpet's color and texture. Most of the home improvement stores sell generic carpet at very competitive prices. Be sure to measure how much you will need before shopping for estimates. Although most stores quote a price per square yard, many will discount further when you buy several rooms' worth.

Do not be afraid to let salespeople at the store know that you are a landlord and will do business with them in the future if they will give you a good price. It's a good idea to deal with the manager.

Wise landlords know that good carpet padding is even more important than good carpet. A good carpet will not last very long without adequate padding. In fact, a good padding under an average carpet makes that carpet feel like the top of the line and also makes it last for a long time. Buy padding when you buy carpet. When cutting extremely good carpet deals, many companies offer to throw in padding free of charge. But it may be better in the long run to pay a few cents more per yard for the higher-grade padding than to take the free padding.

The first time you install carpet, hire someone who knows what to do and offer your help so you will learn how it is done. Carpet is not difficult to lay, but it must be stretched properly onto tacking strips. Once you watch and help someone else lay it, you should be able to do it yourself the next time. Laying carpet almost always requires two people because it is difficult to stretch it by yourself. You also need several special tools: A knee kicker stretches the carpet as you crawl across it. A carpet that is not properly stretched wrinkles and wears out quickly. A hot glue seamer glues two pieces of carpet together. But you don't need these tools very often and they are expensive. Most rental supply stores carry all the carpet-laying tools you need, so rent instead of buying your own.

THE HOME'S EXTERIOR

The outside of the house gives would-be tenants that vital first impression. The first step in preparing any home is to pick up trash around the yard, trim trees and shrubs, and mow the grass. It is not uncommon for low-priced houses to have overgrown lawns, so the odds are good that you will have to do some yard work before starting on the house itself. Clearing away extra growth around the house gives you easier access when painting and repairing the outside.

The yard is both the tenants' friend and enemy. Typically, tenants love the freedom and space of a yard. Yards create a better family environment than do tight apartment dwellings. Despite this, tenants dislike yard work. Sometimes, you must nag tenants to get them to mow the lawn. You might as well trim hedges and trees, since tenants will rarely get around to it.

When cleaning the yard, consider its future upkeep. Keep trees for shade and keep bushes to accent the house, but get rid of all other growth. Too many bushes and unkempt trees make the house look messy. The more trees and bushes you leave, the more work you make for yourself in the future. Don't leave high bushes in front of windows; such cover causes security problems.

Once the yard is clear, you must begin on the house itself. Scrape all loose paint off the wood. Although you do not have to remove all paint before putting on a new coat, make sure to scrape and brush off any loose and peeling paint you find. Old windowsills are notorious for loose paint, so be thorough.

Help your future paint job to last longer by repairing all loose gutters and downspouts. Gutters protect a home's foundation, especially those with basements. Clean out the gutters so water flows through them freely. Unfortunately, gutters need cleaning about twice a year (after spring and fall). To make future maintenance easy, install screens to keep leaves and debris from clogging the gutters. Home improvement stores have plenty of gutter screens, which are easy to install.

> **TIP**
>
> Tenants like yards, but not yard work.

Make sure the downspouts point far enough away from the outer walls of the house. You can buy some inexpensive concrete splash guards so the water at the bottom of the spouts gets carried even further into the yard and away from the house. Not only do these splash guards help carry water, but they protect the downspout from being damaged by weed-cutting machines.

Once you get the gutters clean and repaired, paint them to match the trim on the house. The paint helps lengthen the life of the gutters and makes the house look better.

If the house has no gutters, you can save this maintenance work by doing without it. Keep in mind, however, that gutters do help protect the paint and foundation, and your tenants may require a gutter over the front door so they stay dry while looking for keys. Many gutter installers offer lifetime guarantees, so the money you spend on guttering today will be a lifetime investment.

Make sure that the roof shingles are all in place. Loose or missing shingles can become very expensive someday should a heavy rain soak through to your ceiling and damage your tenants' possessions. Secure any loose shingles with roofing nails (proper roofing nails do not rust). If you have to replace the entire roof, buy the materials and hire the labor instead of calling a commercial roofing company. The last section in this chapter describes how to find reliable roofing help if you know nothing about roof repairs.

If the roof needs heavy repair, check with your city building office to see whether a building permit is required. Many times, you need a permit to repair framing beams or change the structure of a roof. In extreme cases, you might have to resort to hiring a licensed roofing contractor.

Step back and take a good look at the windows of your house. They should all be in good shape and look uniform. On most houses that sell for a low price, the windows need a lot of work. Often, they do not close well, offer little insulation, and look terrible from the outside. Work on the windows, chiseling away where needed, so they open and close with relative ease. After scraping them, paint them carefully. You want them to open and close easily without chipping the paint.

Placing storm windows over the regular windows improves the home in several ways. Storm windows give your tenants added security and insulation. Older windows often let cold air in. Storm windows also give a uniform look to the front of most houses. Older homes, especially those with wood sashes, often look more modern after you place single- or double-paned storm windows over the old windows. Although tenants have to open the inside window and the storm window every time they want fresh air, the advantages of security, insulation, and appearance will make up for the extra effort. Most storm windows come with their own screens, so your tenants can open the windows without letting insects in. Since the windows on homes vary in size, measure each window on the house and go to a construction supply house to buy the storm windows.

> **TIP**
>
> Storm windows insulate and look good.

Aluminum-frame storm windows are very easy to install. These windows fit on the outside of your home's current windows. Typically, one person holds a window up on the outside of the house while another drills eight screws through the storm window frame into the house's original window frame. Each window takes about four minutes to install. Once you secure the window, put a bead of caulk around its four sides. Be sure to drill two or three seep holes in the bottom frame at windowsill level, so that any water that does get into the window will leak outside.

I find that old windows add lots of time to renovating. In addition, I must scrape and repaint windows every few years. I have considered replacing older wooden windows with new two-pane windows, but I just haven't made the leap. Completely new replacement windows cost a lot of money, and you are better off to leave such a job to the pros. I believe that such windows will pay for themselves over the years by making my rentals look more attractive and, most important, greatly reducing my renovating time between tenants. Again, I am still pondering the benefits, but you might want to compare prices to help you decide.

Storage is important outside as well as inside. If the house has no garage, consider installing a small storage building in the backyard. Tenants can keep their garden tools and barbecue grill there. This keeps yard clutter down and protects the tenants' tools. Small storage buildings are relatively inexpensive, but they are a must if your home has no garage.

If you install a portable storage building (a metal building that sits on blocks of some kind), you will save money. If you go to the trouble and expense of installing a permanent building (one with a foundation), it will last longer, and you can match the building to your home's exterior. Generally, you must get a building permit to add a permanent storage building.

Make sure the front and back porches have adequate lighting. Outside lights deter burglars and help tenants feel more secure. If the garage is not attached to the house, install a light outside the garage so tenants can see at night.

Once you've painted and fixed up the yard, gutters, roof, and windows, your rental home should look wonderful. A few little extras, which most landlords would fail to do, can set your newly renovated home apart from the crowd.

> **TIP**
>
> Add some inexpensive frills to welcome your open-house guests.

Large, freshly painted wooden house numbers over or next to the front door provide a welcoming look. A new mailbox, or even a freshly painted old one, spruces up the front door even more. If the mailbox is out by the street, paint the post and consider planting a few flowers around it. Put stick-on house numbers on the mailbox so the postal carrier and the tenants' guests will have no problem locating the house. (Neither will your open-house guests.)

Clean and sweep the porch well. If drops of paint have spilled, clean them up with turpentine. Paint any outside light fixtures and replace damaged ones. Paint the porch light fixture (and the mailbox, if it's attached to the front of the house) the same color as the house numbers.

When your open-house guests arrive, the quality and attention to detail they see will impress them instantly. They will be greeted by a house that says, "Welcome and come on in."

THE LANDLORD'S TOOL KIT

Most good books on home remodeling and renovation list the tools you need for different jobs. Over the years, you will build a tool collection suitable to regular landlording maintenance jobs. Once your rental home is finished, you need very few tools. But even if you hire out the renovation work, there will be times when you must fix certain things, so be prepared with the right tools.

Begin with the basics. Buy a hammer, a set of screwdrivers and wrenches, a tape measure, a plane, and a saw. You probably already have most of these. Over the years, you will add to this basic set of tools as needed. Nobody has to be an expert carpenter to hang a new shelf or tighten the hinges on a screen door.

If you have never used a cordless, battery-operated, combination screwdriver and drill, you do not know what you have been missing. Today, master carpenters would rarely leave home without one.

The first time you install ten or twelve miniblinds without a cordless drill will convince you that a cordless is the only solution. It saves you hours of manual drilling and screwdriver turning. Get a good cordless drill that can hold a charge for thirty minutes to an hour under heavy use and has ample power (called "torque"). Buy a spare battery pack so you can drill while the other battery charges.

This chapter already discussed buying a circuit tester for electrical outlets and an electronic stud finder for the walls. They both pay for themselves in safety and time saved. Without a circuit tester, you will not know if outlets are wired incorrectly; without a stud finder, you may have to drill (and patch) several holes in the walls before finding a wooden stud.

> **TIP**
>
> Get a heavy-duty, cordless, combination drill and screwdriver to save hours.

If the house has screens or screen doors, buy a screen repair roller. Most screens that pop out will go right back in. Unless a broken screen is actually ripped, you can usually repair it in a few minutes without spending a dime. To make screen repairs even more infrequent, install a screen guard on every screen door (children and pets are the biggest threat to screen doors). Screen guards are decorative metal bars that help protect screens from hands and feet.

Do not scrimp on tool quality. It is an old adage that work is only as good as the tools used. Buy the best tools you can find. Several tool manufacturers offer lifetime warranties, so you'll only have to pay for a particular tool once.

The nice thing about tools is that they are usually tax-deductible items, and you have to buy them only once. When you renovate your second or third house, you will already have all the tools you need.

GETTING HELP

Houses are extremely difficult for one person to renovate. Two people can work at more than twice the speed as one, so hire help whenever you think you need it. The less "handy" you are, the more you need experienced help. The money you pay hired help is tax-deductible, and the sooner you finish the house, the sooner you can rent it. You do not need to hire a professional contractor, only someone who has worked on home renovations in the past. Since the house building/renovation market changes so often, there are always people looking for honest temporary work.

Over your landlording career, you will meet several people who are good at different aspects of home repair and renovation. Keep their names and phone numbers so you can call them when you need someone. A roofer's helper is always a good name to have. Generally, you can buy shingles very cheaply and hire a roofer's helper to put them on, even if it means tearing the old roof off completely first. By putting the labor and supplies together yourself, you save a great deal over what you would spend to pay a roofing contractor to do the work.

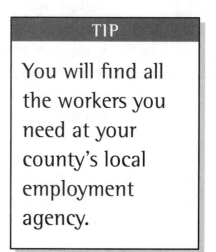

TIP

You will find all the workers you need at your county's local employment agency.

At any one time, there may be several carpenters, electricians, plumbers, roofers, or general repair workers looking for temporary work at your county's local employment office. These people will be happy to have some work because their incomes fluctuate with the whims of the local economy. Not only can you usually get any help you need there, but you can make some good contacts with people who can help you in the future.

If you just need strong backs to carry, load, and unload materials and to work in the yard, contact colleges in your area. Most have job-finding services for students who need extra money. A college fraternity is also a good place to find many strong hands for a short amount of time and money.

Be courteous and fair to your workers, pay them daily, and buy pizzas for lunch. This way, you will be able to get good help whenever you need it.

FINANCIAL HELP

The U.S. Department of Housing and Urban Development (also known as HUD, a landlord's mixed blessing) and the Small Business Administration (the SBA) often offer low-interest, long-term loans for single- and multifamily housing renovations. Expect lots of paperwork, approvals, and the usual red tape, but the money might be a better deal than you can get at a bank. One of the best reasons to get such a loan, if you think there's a chance that you'll ever sell the property, is that the loans are often assumable and a future buyer can take over the loan as part of the selling agreement if desired. You can find HUD on the Internet at *www.hud.gov*; the SBA is at *www.sba.com*. Both HUD and the SBA have local offices, so check your phone book's Government pages for the HUD and SBA offices nearest you.

SUMMARY

Not good with a hammer? No problem—you will have more fun and learn more the first time you renovate a rental property. Besides getting and keeping good tenants, your property's renovation is vital to its long-term maintenance. This chapter presented some common landlording ideas to start you thinking about renovation in the right way.

The key to successful and easy rental maintenance is simplicity and uniformity. Keep your colors neutral and your houses consistent. If you have more than one rental house (and you will once you are successful with your first one), keep the same styles and paint in all of them. When you need an extra hand, do not hesitate to hire one. It is difficult to renovate a house by yourself, and sometimes impossible, even for home do-it-yourselfers and professionals.

Whatever renovation you do, always keep the future in mind. Invest up front so you reap dividends later. Make sure the wiring and plumbing are in good shape. Scrape old peeling paint away before applying a new coat. Properly stretch carpet and install good padding underneath so it lasts a long time. Install storm windows over existing older windows to improve appearance and insulation. Everything you do now makes your rental home more attractive to good tenants and keeps them there for a long time.

In the next chapter, you'll learn how you can make record keeping a snap thanks to some handy shortcuts and use of a computer and the Internet.

CHAPTER TWELVE

Record Keeping and Computerizing Your Rental Properties

DESPITE THE HYPE, not everybody "surfs the Internet" these days. If you are not already computer literate, you don't really *have* to understand computers to achieve landlording success. Usually, most people who dislike computers do not understand them and are, therefore, afraid of them. As a landlord, your record keeping is so simple that you may never need a computer. You have to keep track of only two items: expenses and income. If you have only one or a handful of properties, you can probably do all your record keeping by hand.

Nevertheless, since computers are getting less expensive and easier to use every day, you might consider getting one. Computers can help with word processing and tax preparation, which even one-house landlords can appreciate.

Whether to use a computer or not is up to you. They are nothing more than tools to help you do your work. Just as the typewriter improved the work of scribes years ago, computers simplify many paperwork tasks. This chapter describes landlords' record keeping tasks and how landlords can integrate computers into their business.

This chapter is no replacement for a good introduction to computers. There are many computer books for beginners on the market these days. Once you have decided on the kind of software you want to use with your computer, select one of the many helpful guides available at your bookstore to make the most out of your new software.

LANDLORDS AND RECORD KEEPING

If you're like me, you loathe record keeping! You would rather be working with a paintbrush and sandpaper than recording mileage credits and filing receipts. If so, the following sections may help ease your record keeping burden.

Keep All Receipts

The IRS loves details. If you do nothing else, *keep all rental property receipts*. Receipts give you an expense trail at tax time and provide proof during an audit. If you have more than one rental house, write the address of the house to which the expense pertains on each receipt. To save time, create a one- or two-character code for each property you own, and write that code on each receipt. If the receipt has few details, write the store name and a list of the items purchased. As far as the IRS is concerned, detailed record keeping is more important than just about anything else you do.

As Chapter 8 pointed out, a separate checking account for your rental properties shows the IRS that you made a serious effort to separate your business funds from your personal funds.

Today, competition among banks has given customers a range of checking accounts that are free or very inexpensive. Whether or not you have a separate account, get a receipt for every check you write to help support every penny you deduct. Canceled checks on their own do not make good detailed records, and the IRS may want all related receipts to support the checks you write.

> **TIP**
>
> A canceled check is not always enough proof during a tax audit. Receipts support the checks you write.

Keeping track of receipts is not everyone's idea of fun, but it is a necessary evil. If your organization skills are terrible, you can still be a successful landlord; but you *must* keep all your receipts (if only in a shoe box or whatever else is handy) in case you ever have to support the deductions you took at tax time.

I like to use an accordion file folder that I got at an office supply store. I empty the folder on December 31 and start the new year putting receipts in the folder. The folder sits on my desk and remains open. Each of its file folder pockets (there are about thirty-five pockets) holds that year's receipts for a property's repairs, contract labor, supplies, rent receipts, and so on. At the end of the year, each pocket refers to a separate line on the tax form schedule for each property. In addition to the folder, I keep everything on the computer—I like computers—but if you don't use a computer, the accordion folder keeps things separated so you can easily add tax totals at the end of the year.

Give Your Tenants Rent Receipts

Every step you take to show concern for details is another step toward supporting your tax position. If your tenants pay by check, you do not have to write receipts because the tenants' checks serve as their receipts. Nevertheless, many landlords purchase cash-received receipt booklets from an office supply store and give their tenants a rent-paid receipt each month. Or, you can easily type up and print a stack of blank receipts from your computer that you fill out as your tenants pay the monthly rent.

Not only should you be able to back up your expenses with receipts, but you should be able to back up deposits to your checking account as well. Having a rent-paid receipt for every rent deposit you make not only shows concern for record keeping, but it also gives you a clear payment history, in case you need to recommend a tenant to another landlord some time in the future.

Keep a Car Log

Automobile mileage is a deductible business expense as long as the mileage is directly related to your rental property and as long as you *keep a detailed written log in the car*. The IRS is a stickler about mileage records. Producing a two-year-old, frayed car log showing each mile you drove for rental property business is very important if you get audited. Make an entry every time you go out that shows where you went, why you went, and how many miles you drove.

Some landlords just guess at mileage, but guessing, no matter how conservative, will rarely hold up at tax time. You might be surprised at how many miles you actually drive. For most people, keeping a log in the car actually increases the mileage reported. It is too easy to fail to record mileage if you have to wait until later. A log in the car is handy and encourages you to record the mileage right after the actual trip.

If you drive to collect rent, you can deduct the mileage. If you drive to buy supplies for your rental houses, you can deduct the mileage. If you work on the rental house, show it during open house, or go to the bank to deposit the rent check, you can deduct the mileage. The mileage allowance adds up, so be conscientious about recording it. Each year, the dollar amount per mile that you can deduct changes (it usually rises in your favor as auto costs increase). Mileage is an important and legitimate way to offset rental income for tax purposes.

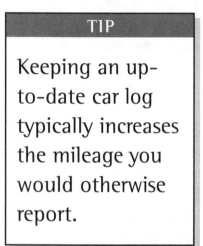

TIP

Keeping an up-to-date car log typically increases the mileage you would otherwise report.

In addition, the IRS prefers to see a handwritten journal of recorded trips to and from your rental properties and related business rather than a lump sum of miles that you estimate. Quite honestly, I don't follow that advice, although I do believe I follow the spirit of that advice; I keep a laptop computer with me and record my mileage and expense every time I do rental property business. Will the laptop's records hold up as well as a handwritten log if I'm ever audited? My accountant doesn't know for sure, but he advocates the handwritten log because it shows age, whereas I cannot prove exactly when I entered a certain transaction on the computer. I take my chances in exchange for the ease of record keeping on the computer, but you'll have to decide for yourself.

LANDLORDS AND ACCOUNTANTS

Rarely does a landlord with only a few properties need the services of an accountant each month. Unless you incorporate, the odds are good that you keep records on a cash basis (as opposed to the accrual basis required for corporations and incorporated landlords); that is, you record expenses when they occur and record income when it arrives. A single log (in addition to the car log mentioned earlier) is all you need, showing the date, description, and amount of each transaction. You do not need anything fancy; a simple spiral notebook will do nicely.

At tax time, even one-property landlords should consider using an accountant. The tax laws change too often for you to keep up with them, unless tax work happens to be your specialty. A certified public accountant (CPA), an accountant, or a tax preparer will be able to find deductions where you may not have known to look and identify problems before they get out of hand.

The type of help you get depends on your confidence in your own work and the amount of money you want to spend. Tax preparers will produce accurate tax returns, but they are limited as to the extent of tax-planning advice they can give you. Accountants cost more, but they can provide tax-planning services; if you have lots of properties, accountants can help you set up an organized record keeping system to ease your tax-time burden. CPAs are even more expensive; they must meet strict educational requirements every year to maintain their certifications; on the whole, they are the most up-to-date on changes to the tax laws as they affect your property. Some landlords like to do all their own record keeping and tax preparation. There is nothing wrong with that, especially for landlords confident in their abilities. A computer can help here, but it can never replace the abilities of a trained accountant or tax preparer. When you hire another person to take over your tax-preparation responsibility, that person can act as an objective party in the

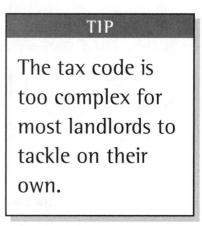

TIP

The tax code is too complex for most landlords to tackle on their own.

event that you are audited. Before accountants put their signatures on a tax return, they scrutinize it for errors and fraud. Most accountants take full responsibility for errors they cause and will pay the penalty fees for you if they make a mistake that causes you more tax liability.

In most cases, the fees you pay a tax preparer or accountant are deductible. When you consider how much accountants save you in missed deductions and how much they protect you in case of an audit, hiring them makes a lot of sense, even for the most budget-minded landlord. If the government sends you an audit notice, contact your tax preparer (after you recover from the sickening shock) and see if the preparer will represent you at the audit. Unless you work in taxation, a tax preparer will be better skilled than you at handling your audit, and you can give the preparer limited power of attorney to handle the entire matter.

> **TIP**
>
> Tax time is not the time to save money for taxes—do that during the year leading up to it.

The most important time to ask your accountant for tax advice is *before* tax time. The beginning of the tax year is when you should start planning your tax-saving strategies. People often want to lower their taxes at the time they pay them, but by then it is too late. An accountant can provide you with lots of tax-saving help if you ask early enough in the tax year. Start planning your year's taxes on the first of January so your tax bill will be as low as possible at the end of the year. Ask your accountant to study your tax records from the previous years, and give him or her the details about your current year's business, to determine the best tax plan for you. You'll want to establish one-year, five-year, and twenty-year tax plans to maximize the service of the tax expert. Follow those plans, but keep in mind that since tax laws change virtually every year your plans will have to be updated.

If you have a lot of rental property income, you may be required to file quarterly tax returns. Quarterly tax payments became more difficult than ever starting in 1992, because each quarter you are required to re-evaluate your current financial status for the year. An accountant's help with quarterly payments is almost a requirement these days. If you are required to file quarterly tax payments, you almost certainly will need some help computing the totals.

LANDLORDS AND COMPUTERS

A computer is not the solution to every problem. For the small-time property owner, it could be more of a burden than a help unless the owner is already familiar with computers. Although computers are cheaper now than ever before, you will likely spend several hundreds and maybe more than one thousand dollars for a new one with a printer and adequate storage capacity. Read as much as you can about the current computer market before buying one. They differ greatly in price and capabilities.

Many community colleges offer short courses for new computer users. These courses usually include hands-on demonstrations and helpful advice, even for people who are just beginning. Computers can be easy to use and a lot of fun. Children have known this for several years now, but adults sometimes are slow to realize it. I highly recommend a short, four-night community college introductory computer course if you know little or nothing about computers now. Supplementing these courses with books from the wide range of

TIP

Many computer manufacturers make deals with Internet services to offer a deeply discounted computer if you agree to sign up for the Internet service for a specified length of time. If you know little or nothing about the Internet, this is an easy and inexpensive way to learn.

teach-yourself PC books that are offered will help get you ready to use a computer.

Choosing a Computer

Although there are many different kinds of computers on the market, PCs generally fall into one of two broad categories: Macintosh and Windows. Apple Corporation is the main source for Macintosh computers, although several other companies make add-on products. Many companies make PCs that use Microsoft's Windows operating system. A Windows PC is almost always guaranteed to work exactly like any other computer that uses that operating system.

To confuse matters, Windows comes in different versions. Two of the most popular are Windows 98 and Windows NT. A new version of Windows NT may be available by the time you read this under the name Windows 2000. For most home and small business users, Windows 98 is more than adequate. NT and Windows 2000 are designed for the small to medium-size office environment.

Despite the impressive technical abilities of Macintosh computers, Windows PCs dominate the market. A vendor at a recent COMDEX computer convention told me that Apple holds only 6 percent of the PC market share, and this share is not likely to increase significantly, at least in the near future.

In the world of computers, it is much more convenient to own the same type of computer as other people with whom you might want to share files. There are many more software programs available for Windows than there are for Macintosh. If you have friends who highly recommend the Macintosh, you might consider purchasing one if you want to keep your records the same way. But for most first-time computer buyers who want to use the computer for record keeping, word processing, and tax preparation, Windows PCs generally offer a wider assortment of programs and capabilities.

Whatever computer you decide to buy, purchase it from a distributor who has been in business for a while. Over the last few years, there have been many horror stories about computer companies going in and out of business quickly. You do not want to buy a computer from a vendor only to find that nobody is around to help you in six months if something goes wrong. If you buy from an established company, you should have no problem with repairs or add-ons in the future.

> **TIP**
>
> Buy your computer from an established business. Many mail-order and small computer distributors have gone out of business over the years.

Fortunately, many of the large electronic discount houses that sell computers, stereos, and appliances now set the standard in pricing. A Sunday newspaper flier is almost guaranteed to offer numerous computers on sale. These stores offer little or no technical advice, but they do have service areas that can repair or upgrade the computers purchased there. I like these discount stores, and as long as you stick with a store that's been around awhile and has many other stores around the nation, it is probably safe to buy a computer there.

In addition, there are several large, established mail-order companies. Many of the major PC vendors such as Compaq, Dell, and Hewlett-Packard also sell PCs via mail order and the Internet. When you order from established vendors it's possible that you'll lower your purchase price, too, because you may not pay local sales tax. Nevertheless, you don't have a chance to try out the computer before you buy it. In addition, repair is not as simple as taking your PC back to the store where you purchased it. Fortunately, many of the established mail-order PC vendors now offer on-site repairs for a specified period of time after the sale, and you can extend the time for that on-site repair with additional warranties.

To give you an idea of what you can accomplish with computers, the rest of this chapter focuses on key applications that will help you in your landlording career.

Word Processing

Nothing the computer can do other than connecting to the Internet will help you more than word processing. Word processing programs turn your computer into a computerized typewriter that makes writing, editing, printing, and changing documents easier than you would ever think possible.

Unlike typewriters, nothing you type using a word processor goes to paper until you are completely finished editing and proofreading. Figure 12-1 shows a computerized word processing program, Microsoft Word, in action. The words typed at the keyboard appear on the computer screen, where you can easily change, move, or delete them. Only after correcting any mistakes you see on the screen do you print the document to paper. If you still see mistakes in the printed version, you can correct them and print a fresh copy without having to retype the entire document.

Today's word processing programs check spelling and grammar, provide a thesaurus, and offer so many more features that there are literally hundreds of books dedicated solely to word processors on the market today. Despite their power, word processors are extremely easy to use and range in price from $20 to a few hundred dollars.

The word processing program is the mainstay of any computerized landlording activity. Usually when a new tenant moves into a house, the lease is only slightly different from that of the previous tenant. Only the names, amounts, and dates change; the rest of the lease generally stays the same. With word processing software, you can call up the old tenant's lease on the screen, update the information, and print a new lease in a matter of

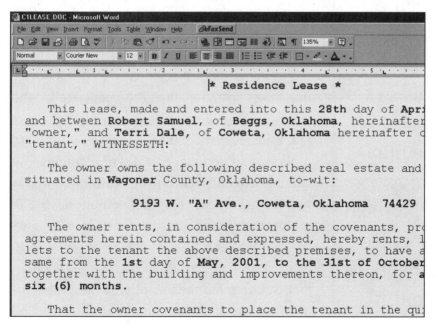

FIGURE 12-1. An example of a screen in Microsoft Word

minutes. The old lease is still safely tucked away on the computer's hard drive, and the new lease is always available in case you need it. You can make as many printouts of the lease as you like. With a word processor, every copy is an original.

At the time of this writing, Microsoft Word is the best-selling word processor, and it's likely to stay that way. I use Word myself. Word is a little pricey, ranging from under $100 to $300 depending on where you buy it (mail-order prices are generally the best), but often it is part of the software bundle that comes with a new computer. I've written more than sixty books about computers and I've used Word for the last thirty-five or so. A less expensive word processor will not have the features that Word has, but you may not need all of Word's bells and whistles, so be sure to read the product information before you purchase.

If you purchase a scanner, which is a device that takes a digital image of paperwork, you can scan any document into your computer and transfer that document's text to your word processor so you can edit it. For example, you can use a scanner to transfer current contracts and forms to your computer without having to retype everything. As an alternative to purchasing a scanner, you can go to your local print shop and hire them to scan your documents. But given the low prices of scanners today ($40 to $400), I wouldn't pay someone else to scan my documents. A low-priced scanner

TIP

Word processors allow landlords to easily store and retrieve old leases, write new leases, file and keep correspondence by property, and maintain lists of workers' names and phone numbers. A word processor acts like a file cabinet for your paperwork as a landlord.

should suffice for virtually anything you'll ever want to do with it, including scanning documents to create text files (called OCR, or optical character recognition) and scanning photos of your family and friends.

Digital cameras can also come in handy for landlords who want to photograph potential properties to buy as well as rental houses (for community bulletin boards or rental ads). They also make it easy to snap photos of your properties to give the real estate agent when you decide to sell. The advantage of a digital camera, besides the scanning capabilities that they are beginning to offer, is that you can easily transfer the images to your computer and modify them, print pictures on a color printer, or send the pictures to others over the Internet. In addition, you can have your digital prints developed just as you now do with your other cameras.

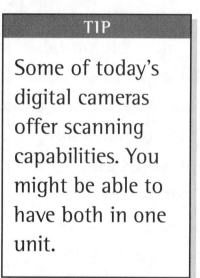

TIP

Some of today's digital cameras offer scanning capabilities. You might be able to have both in one unit.

Record Keeping

Computers are wonderful tools for storing and retrieving information. Managing financial information is a breeze with the calculation capabilities of various software programs. They keep track of your expenses and income, storing them under any department or budget title you prefer and summing year-to-date totals in an instant.

The problem with computerizing your record keeping is that many landlords may not have enough record keeping needs to warrant the computer's use. Unlike word processing, which helps almost any written task, computing may be an overkill for the small-time landlord's financial records alone.

Consider what happens when you get a rental house key duplicated for $1.25. Is that small amount worth turning on your computer; starting the record keeping program; entering the date, description, and amount; saving the information to the computer's hard drive; and turning the computer off? Probably not. The truth is that the recording of most expenses and income for many landlords is still best done, even in today's high-tech times, with pen and paper in a journal. Further, if you write a check for most or all of your property-related expenses, you already have a good record of each expense. Entering the expense into the computer becomes a time-consuming duplication of effort.

Before you dismiss a computer as overkill for your landlording needs, however, consider that you can use one for so much more than monitoring your rental properties. Your rental expenses will not be the only expenses you record on your PC—you'll use it for personal financial management as well. You can use it to write personal letters, support other business ventures, and track your household and investment expenses and income. You'll use the Internet—which you'll learn more about in the next chapter—for e-mail and information gathering, for your landlording business as well as other interests. You and your kids can use the computer for education and entertainment.

As you use your computer more and more and buy more properties, the computer becomes a much more viable record keeping tool. Keeping a variety of financial records becomes difficult without a computer's filing capabilities. The more you use

TIP

The more properties you have, the more you need a PC to maintain records and streamline end-of-the-year tax computations.

your computer and the more you learn about it, the more ways you'll find it can streamline your daily landlording tasks.

There are lots of software programs available that track your income and expenses; keep personal and business income and expenses separate; keep track of bank balances, rental income and expenses, and depreciation; and maintain tax records. Figure 12-2 shows one such program, Intuit Quicken, a financial manager. Instead of writing checks by hand and then entering duplicate information into the computer, you can actually print checks and manage your checking, savings, and investment accounts electronically.

Some people do not like to convert their records to the computer's required format. Over the years, these people may have maintained excellent records by hand. After becoming successful landlords, they want to computerize their records, but they do

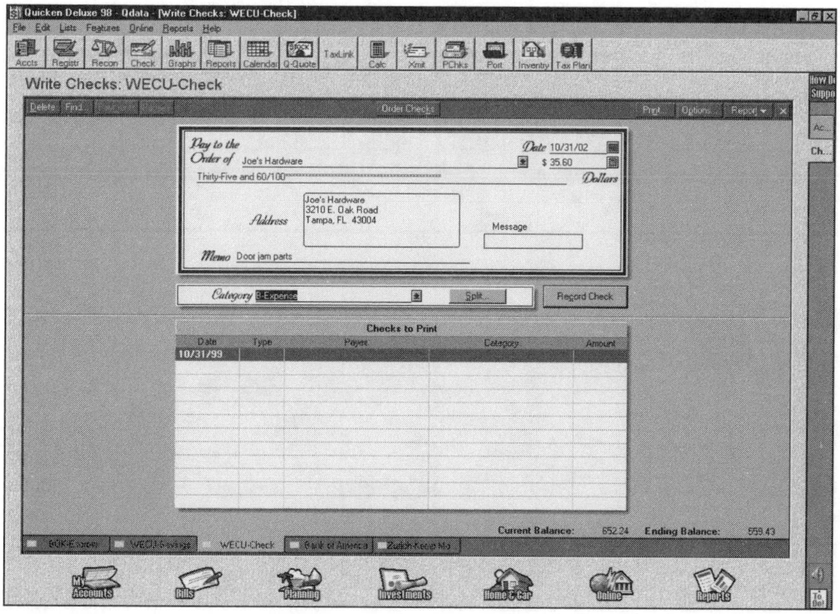

Figure 12-2. A screen from Intuit's Quicken

not want to change the way they keep track of things. Although a personal and business finance program like Quicken is very flexible, some people cannot make it do exactly what they want.

If you are willing to learn a little more about using your computer, you may feel more at ease using a spreadsheet program rather than a program like Quicken. An electronic spreadsheet is sometimes called a "word processor for numbers" because it allows you to write, manage, and print rows and columns of numbers as easily as a word processor manipulates words. The most popular electronic spreadsheet today is Microsoft Excel. Figure 12-3 shows a computer screen from a landlord's customized Excel program. Notice that instead of a fixed format for the data (as Quicken requires), Excel is able to display the numbers and descriptions any way the user desires, even duplicating the look of a handwritten journal, if that is what you want.

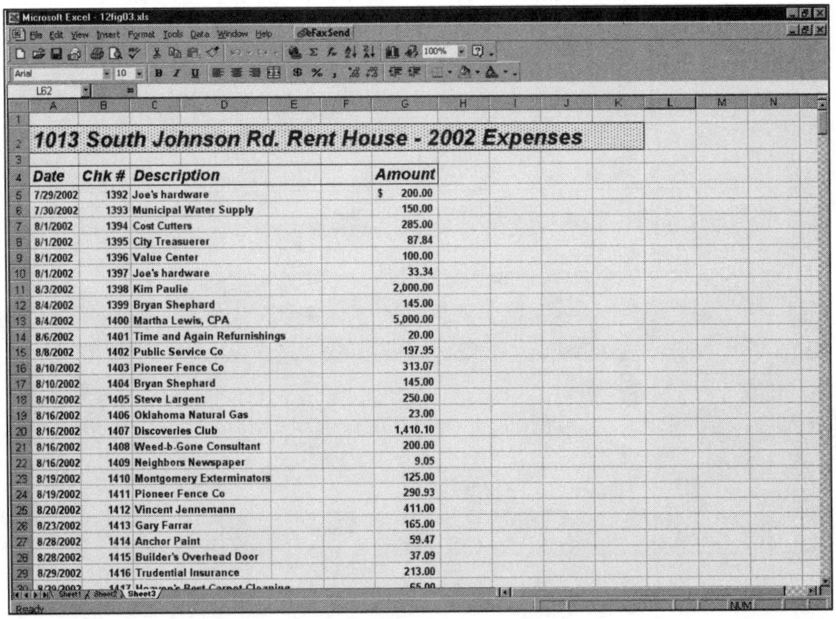

1013 South Johnson Rd. Rent House - 2002 Expenses

Date	Chk #	Description	Amount
7/29/2002	1392	Joe's hardware	$ 200.00
7/30/2002	1393	Municipal Water Supply	150.00
8/1/2002	1394	Cost Cutters	285.00
8/1/2002	1395	City Treasuerer	87.84
8/1/2002	1396	Value Center	100.00
8/1/2002	1397	Joe's hardware	33.34
8/3/2002	1398	Kim Paulie	2,000.00
8/4/2002	1399	Bryan Shephard	145.00
8/4/2002	1400	Martha Lewis, CPA	5,000.00
8/6/2002	1401	Time and Again Refurnishings	20.00
8/8/2002	1402	Public Service Co	197.95
8/10/2002	1403	Pioneer Fence Co	313.07
8/10/2002	1404	Bryan Shephard	145.00
8/10/2002	1405	Steve Largent	250.00
8/16/2002	1406	Oklahoma Natural Gas	23.00
8/16/2002	1407	Discoveries Club	1,410.10
8/16/2002	1408	Weed-b-Gone Consultant	200.00
8/16/2002	1409	Neighbors Newspaper	9.05
8/19/2002	1410	Montgomery Exterminators	125.00
8/19/2002	1411	Pioneer Fence Co	290.93
8/20/2002	1412	Vincent Jennemann	411.00
8/23/2002	1413	Gary Farrar	165.00
8/28/2002	1414	Anchor Paint	59.47
8/28/2002	1415	Builder's Overhead Door	37.09
8/29/2002	1416	Trudential Insurance	213.00

FIGURE 12-3. An Excel spreadsheet customized for a landlord

Electronic spreadsheets such as Excel are more flexible than financial programs such as Quicken, but the learning curve is greater. Although they are not difficult to use, you must be able to know enough about the program to create your own spreadsheets. Finance programs such as Quicken are more rigid in the way they present the information, but you have to know less up front to use them. The more you learn about your computer, the more you may want to control the look and feel of your records. You might want to start with a financial program, then switch to a spreadsheet program as your needs and computer knowledge grow.

You will probably need both. The spreadsheet program is handy for special calculations, such as those you may make when deciding between two properties to purchase. You can list both properties in the spreadsheet and modify the values to see, in different rental income scenarios, which property makes the best financial sense. You can use a spreadsheet to estimate the remodeling costs associated with a property you need to renovate. The spreadsheet's generic nature does not make it as simple to use for recording financial transactions as a program such as Quicken does, but the spreadsheet offers more flexibility and options.

Whatever route you decide to take with your computerized record keeping, your primary goal should be accuracy. The computer does not make sloppy mistakes. If a computer produces an incorrect result, the odds are extraordinarily high that the person using it typed a wrong total or gave the computer an incorrect instruction. The computer will help you produce more accurate records as long as you carefully enter the amounts into the computerized files.

After accuracy, the primary advantage to computerized record keeping appears at tax time. Depending on how your record keeping system is set up, at the end of the year you may be able to press a button and print out your tax returns or at least print all the information your tax preparer will need to produce an accurate return.

Tax Preparation

Setting up the computer so it produces instant tax returns is not always as easy as the computer magazines and dealers might lead you to believe. Nevertheless, it is possible to produce automatic tax return information—as long as you diligently record all income and expenses properly throughout the year and as long as your computer is set up to format the data properly.

If you recently bought a computer and are unsure about where to begin computerizing your property's records, ask your tax preparer for help. The tax preparer will either be able to recommend appropriate programs or will know someone who can.

Do not expect to have an instant tax return the first year you computerize your record keeping. In fact, there may be cases where it would be better not to get an instant return. No computer is better at spotting tax problems than a trained tax preparer. Your accountant should always review your computerized records. Just because the computer printed it does not mean the information is accurate; you may have made a mistake while entering some of the data.

Your accountant may want you to use a record keeping program that ties directly into his or her own tax preparation program. As the familiar tax return appears on the screen, the accountant directs the program to search the appropriate files for your records. After all the data is entered, the program automatically computes totals, looks up the appropriate taxes, and prints a return.

Letting your accountant produce the final tax return is probably the best solution for most landlords, even those landlords who are computer literate and heavily computerized. You can use your computer for word processing and record keeping throughout the year. When tax time comes around, give your computerized files to your accountant instead of handing over a shoe box full of disorganized receipts (as many noncomputerized landlords might do). From your files, the accountant produces a tax return, after reviewing all the information for accuracy and finding extra deductions where appropriate.

Rental Property Computer Programs

Some programs are specifically written with the landlord in mind. These track rent expenses, tenant information, property descriptions, income, and expenses. Check out local computer stores and software catalogs to see what's available. Generally, programs specifically written for property managers are inexpensive, running from $25 to $75.

Such programs are wonderful for landlords who don't have the time or interest but who still see the need for computerizing the property's records. There are drawbacks, however, to using programs dedicated to a single business. You almost always have to adapt the way you work to the program's requirements. Such programs are rarely flexible enough for you to modify the way the data is stored. Another drawback is that they rarely share data with other programs, a vital consideration at tax time, if your accountant has a tax preparation program that cannot communicate with yours.

Before purchasing a rental property program, check out spreadsheet programs such as Excel, which is so general in nature that you can often make it do exactly what you need done. For example, with Excel you can track remodeling costs, produce graphs and charts, and show trends. Analyzing the details of a remodeling job will help save you money and time for subsequent jobs.

Since there are so many good programs available, you should shop around and ask a lot of questions before buying. Understand from the start that software is updated all the time. A program you begin using today for your record keeping may be made obsolete by a much better one from a different manufacturer tomorrow. Ask the software seller if you can try the program before you buy it. See if you can borrow a spare program manual for a weekend to read about the program's features. You may also be able to download software on a trial basis, or for free to keep forever, from the Internet. Applications that are free to download may or may not cost money. The free programs are called freeware; the programs that cost money (after a specified free trial) are called shareware. If you decide to keep a shareware program, you can send the distributor a check to register it legally under your name. This way you receive program updates as they become available.

Law Programs

Check your local software and office supply store for legal software—the range of such software is growing all the time. You can get programs that contain forms, letters, and advice that may not eliminate your need for an attorney but may lessen your reliance on attorneys. While you're browsing the legal software in the computer store, look over the will and living trust software; such programs can benefit landlords and other property owners considerably.

The Internet

The Internet is the computer industry's most explosive area of growth. When this book's first edition appeared not all that long ago, the Internet did not even exist in its current form and few people even knew about it. This book's second edition devoted a few paragraphs to the Internet due to its budding popularity. In the third edition of this book you'll find an entire chapter devoted to the Internet! (See Chapter 13, "Can the Internet Help Landlords?".) If you don't have Internet access, or if you've never thought you'd use the Internet, you still owe it to yourself to find out what it's all about. This is a rental property management book, not a computer book. However, the Internet has impacted so many areas, including rental property management, that you owe it to yourself to learn more.

The next chapter tells you enough about the Internet to decide if it's worth looking into. If you are already online, you'll learn new ways to use the Internet that will benefit you as a landlord.

SUMMARY

Record keeping is a necessary evil for landlords. As far as the IRS is concerned, record keeping is the most important part of your business. Whether you keep your receipts in a shoe box or logged on a computer, receipts and detailed logs provide your backup and alibi if you ever get audited.

Only you can decide whether you need a computer. Before ruling one out, make sure you have looked at computers, seen what they can do, and understand how easy they are to operate. Record keeping alone is not a good enough reason to buy a computer, but word processing and tax preparation programs can save you more time than you might have thought possible.

Before using computers, however, you must learn a little about them. Although they are getting less expensive and easier to use all the time, computers are not yet for everybody.

This chapter gave you an overview of some programs that might help you as a landlord. Only a limited survey of programs is possible here, but there are thousands on the market today. Stop in at your local computer store to see what it has to offer. Be sure to shop at established stores, and trust your tax preparer for software advice more than the computer sales clerk. Arm yourself with knowledge before going into the store. The more computer books you read, classes you attend, and knowledge you gain, the more effective you will be with one and the better deal you will make at the computer store.

One of the most powerful landlording tools you can get is Internet access. The Internet puts a world of information at your fingertips. As the next chapter explains, landlord-related Web sites are constantly updated with information, hints, tips, and warnings that can make your life as a rental property owner much easier.

CHAPTER THIRTEEN

Can the Internet Help Landlords?

THERE IS AN amazing volume of information on the Internet, including resources for rental property owners. You just have to know where to look. Before we go over how to find landlording information on the Internet, here's a quick rundown on how it works in case you are not familiar with the technology. If you already use the Net regularly, skip to the section, "Internet Help for Landlords."

If you have a computer with a modem (a device that connects your computer to the telephone), you have access to all kinds of information on the Internet and can send and receive e-mail to anyone else connected to the Internet. Most computers sold today come with modems that provide this capability. These days it seems the entire world is online, and almost everyone has an e-mail address.

Once you get a computer and modem, you must sign up with an Internet service provider (ISP). Many companies, both local and national, provide Internet service; You should find several ISPs listed in your local yellow pages under "Computers." National ISPs such as America Online (AOL) and the Microsoft Network (MSN) provide access from anywhere in the country and even around the world. You must also have a Web browser. Most ISPs will provide a browser if you don't already have one installed on your computer.

On the Internet you can shop, trade stocks, read news, join clubs, exchange recipes, review movies, play games, and, most important for the readers of this book, get rental property information. Most Realtors have home pages on the Web that describe them and provide hyperlinks ("clickable" text links that allow you to jump to another Web page) to pages that describe properties for sale in almost every town.

For the rental property owner, the Internet provides a wealth of information. Figure 13-1 shows a Web site called

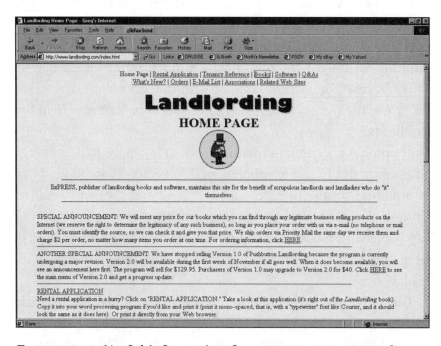

FIGURE 13-1. Useful information for property owners on the Internet

Landlording.com, from which you can get information and order software related to rental property management.

When you want to access information on the Internet, you must know a site's Web address (also referred to as the URL, which stands for *uniform resource locator*). You must type in the address correctly for it to work. For example, Landlording.com's full address is *http://www. landlording.com/index.html.* For the sake of simplicity, Web addresses in this book leave out *http://.* The most current Web browsers will automatically add this bit whenever you type an address.

Companies and individuals who maintain Web sites change the information on their sites regularly. They know that they have to keep the information fresh and timely to keep people coming back. The most current versions of Web browsers provide many shortcuts that help you navigate the Internet. You can search for information across the entire Internet, select from your list of Favorites or Bookmarks, and click on buttons and links that take you to other Web pages you want to view.

Figure 13-2 shows a Web page that contains all kinds of information about landlording and also offers products and services that you might find useful. The address is *www.rental-prop.com/~rpr.*

TIP

To view information related to the Web page you have accessed, click the available links on that page. You can also bookmark your favorite Web pages so you can come back to them later. In Microsoft Internet Explorer these are called Favorites. In Netscape Navigator they are Bookmarks.

INTERNET HELP FOR LANDLORDS

Given the vast amount of information available on the Internet, you may wonder how such a resource can help you. So far you've seen examples of two useful Web sites, but how much better can they be than this book? Can the Web do more for you than just provide landlording tips?

Would-be and struggling rental property owners often ask me:

- Can the Internet be useful to me?
- Can I advertise for new tenants on the Internet?
- Where do I look for building supplies?
- How do I hire help over the Internet?
- Can I sell my house on the Internet?

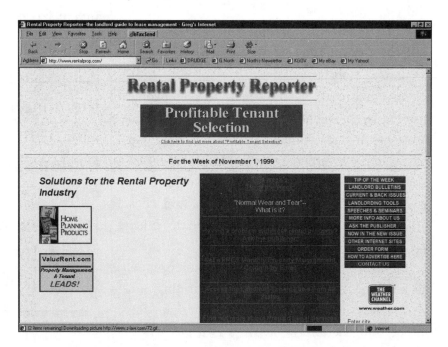

FIGURE 13-2. Another example of a helpful Web page
for landlords

If you've used the Internet much before now, you probably already have a good sense of how the Internet can benefit you as a landlord. I have found the 'Net to be a poor source of landlording tips. But you'll find many other kinds of resources for the rental property owner.

This chapter describes many ways you can use the Internet to augment your rental property experience. Not all of these resources make sense for all landlords—and not even a fraction of the Internet's helpful topics reside here—but this chapter should give you a good idea of the number of ways the Internet can benefit you. If you don't like computers, if you've never used one, or if you do not want to connect to the Internet, you'll still do just fine if you follow the advice in the rest of this book. Nevertheless, the Internet is an additional tool that can aid your experience.

Buying and Selling Property on the Internet

Throughout this book, you've seen tips for locating good properties to buy, renovate, and then rent to others. You also learned ways to sell a property when it no longer provides the income you require. The Internet is becoming the place to buy and sell many items people used to buy and sell in more traditional outlets. Before the Internet connected people across the country and around the world, you used to have to live in a relatively large city to ensure that goods were quickly available when needed. Today you can live virtually anywhere—as long as you have Web access and delivery services can reach you—and have just about any item on your doorstep the next morning.

As of this writing, however, buying and selling properties online is still more difficult than using a real estate agent. Locating information from all over the world on the Internet is fairly simple, but locating information about your town still can be difficult unless you live in a major real estate market. Established real estate companies are experimenting with selling property online. You can see how some of these sites work by visiting some of the following: realestate.yahoo.com, homeadvisor.msn.com/ie/default.asp, and www.aol.com/webcenters/realestate/home.adp. Finding a property in a specific area and narrowing the sites down to the neighborhood and price range that interest you is not always easy while online. Although you can search for real estate for sale in your town or general area, the properties you'll find are almost always higher-priced homes and commercial sites. On the Internet you won't often find properties that a landlord would be interested in—low-priced homes in need of some work in good neighborhoods.

> **TIP**
>
> If you use a newspaper to hunt for properties, find out if your newspaper has a Web site. If so, it probably posts its classified ads online, too.

One tool you *can* use to narrow your search down to the area and price range that interests you is your local newspaper's Internet site. Many newspapers post some or all of their content and offer other services online. In almost all cases, you can access the paper's contents on the Net for free. (A few papers charge a fee for full access to news stories or archives, but in almost all cases classified advertising sections are free.)

Suppose you are looking for a property within ten miles of your home within a certain price range. Although a national real estate site may not list items in your desired range, your local newspaper's online classified advertising and real estate sections should contain every house for sale that appears in the daily printed version of the paper. The advantage is that you can often search the Internet site for specific criteria that narrow down the list of properties you have to view. Many newspapers update this classified section a few times a day, so you may locate properties that have yet to appear in the print copy. You'll see the listings before your neighbor who may not see the newspaper until the next morning.

Figure 13-3 shows a newspaper's online classifieds, with new additions that many papers are adding to attract customers (and higher advertising rates). Viewers can click on links such as *New Homes*, *Buy/Sell*, and *Communities* to see the Web pages that offer those services. Each page provides search capabilities so that you can specify a range for a price and location. The Web site will then produce a list of properties that meet your requests. In addition, the *Mortgage* and *Tool Kit* links provide services that you can use to compute loans, compare interest rates, find

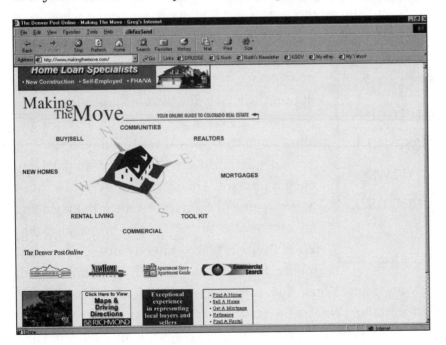

FIGURE 13-3. A local newspaper's online ads for homes for sale

moving companies, and decide how much home you want to purchase.

Finding Tenants on the Internet

To reach the widest local audience possible, it makes sense to advertise in the local newspaper's classified sections that will also appear on the Internet. Keep in mind, however, that this may not boost the number of potential renters you get. It depends on where you live, but in my experience few potential renters use the Internet to locate homes to rent. People still rely primarily on the printed version of the local newspaper. Even if they don't subscribe, most people purchase a paper to use as a reference as they drive around looking at properties and to make appointments to see houses. Although it's possible to print out the Internet listings, the newspaper still seems to be the medium of choice for locating properties to rent.

> **TIP**
>
> Use the Internet to place classified ads if your newspaper offers this feature.

That said, when you advertise in a printed newspaper's classifieds, you're often advertising on their Web site also. Almost all newspapers put their classified ads on the Internet and allow anyone to view them free of charge.

I now prefer to use the Internet to place my open house ads. This is not for everyone, but I prefer to use the Internet rather than placing my ad over the phone for one primary reason: What I type is placed directly in the paper and online. If an error appears in the published ad, it's my fault. When you call in an ad there are more chances for mistakes. You might read your ad copy incorrectly, and the customer service representative may type a mistake. In most cases, you won't see the mistake until it's printed in the paper.

Would-be tenants usually overlook such typographical errors, but correcting the mistake for everyone who walks in the door at the open house is just another task you'd rather avoid.

When I place an ad over the Internet, I type the text myself. I can proofread and edit the ad then send it to print with a click of the mouse. Many newspapers will call to verify the ad copy and take your credit card number over the phone. But you can often pay for the ad online by entering your credit card information. If you do this, make sure the newspaper's site uses a secure server. You can tell you are on a secure page by looking at its Web address, or URL: If there is an *https://* (note the *s*) in front of the address, it is secure. If you are uncomfortable giving out your credit card information over the Internet, you can place the ad and pay later by phone. Although fraud can occur, Internet credit card transactions are extremely secure and reliable. Which is less secure—entering a credit card number at your keyboard to pay for a classified ad or giving your credit card to a teenage waiter at the corner restaurant? The bottom line is that you need to pay for your ad in a way that makes you the most comfortable.

Buying Building Supplies on the Internet

Recently, a friend asked me if it is a good idea to order building supplies over the Internet. I had never thought about this before he asked. Although I am a strong advocate of the Internet, I suspect it would be difficult to get a good deal on home renovation supplies online. Heavy items such as building materials are difficult and expensive to ship. Today's super-size home and building supply stores are far better suited to shopping for sinks, lumber, and windows. You can see what you want and buy the merchandise immediately. I usually purchase building supplies as I'm renovating a place because I cannot always know what I'm going to need until I get into a job. Perhaps a wallboard needs replacing, perhaps not, but I don't always know until I remove the trim and begin to sand.

On the other hand, the Internet is a good place to study online store catalogs of remodeling items, such as drapes and wallpaper. The larger home repair chains all have Web sites that let you browse their catalogs from the comfort of your home. But no matter how comfortable you are with the Internet, in most cases it makes more sense to buy renovation and redecorating supplies at physical stores. If you're like me you'll want to see what you're getting when you buy a door or kitchen faucet—and an online catalog just doesn't cut it. Shop for books and music CDs on the computer, perhaps, but leave the larger rental-related items to in-store shopping.

One area where Internet shopping sites and online catalogs can come in handy is looking for hand tools, fire extinguishers, and other necessities. Online catalogs often provide descriptions of tools and other items that you may not have known you could use if you passed by them in a store.

Some of the more popular sites to visit where you can scour for the latest decorating ideas, materials, and advice, are

www.homedepot.com
www.lowes.com
www.sears.com
www.sutherlands.com

For tools, I recommend an online auction site like eBay (*www.ebay.com*). As of this writing, eBay (see Figure 13-4) is the world's most popular site. It lists several million items up for auction at any one time. You can locate the tools you want using a handy search feature. If you find what you're looking for, you can place a bid for that item (after registering with the site, which is free). If your bid is the highest at the end of the auction, the item is yours. You pay extra for shipping, of course.

Online Banking

The world of banking is changing rapidly and the Internet is helping lead that change. You now can pay bills online—without writing a check, stuffing an envelope, or licking a stamp. You can check your bank balances twenty-four hours a day. You can transfer funds between accounts, apply for loans, and compare loan rates.

But the most important reason you as a small landlord should consider online banking is to help you balance your checkbook

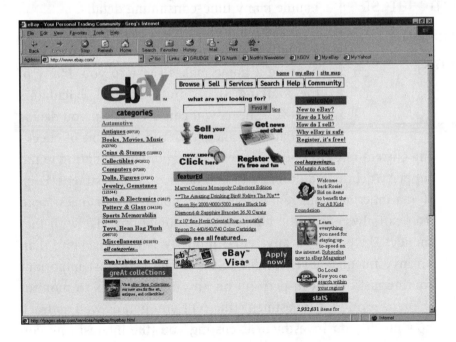

FIGURE 13-4. Place a bid for tools you need for your rental
properties on an auction site like eBay

at the end of the month. With the click of a button you can compare your register to the bank's records and then reconcile them, showing any errors you may have made. This dramatically decreases the time you'll spend reconciling your accounts each month. And while you may go many months with very few rental property bills, remodeling or freshening up a home can create a sudden spike in expenses. By combining the online services of your bank with financial management software such as Quicken (see Chapter 12, "Record Keeping and Computerizing Your Rental Properties"), you will get a clearer picture of your financial situation through the years and save time by letting your computer handle many time-consuming details.

> **TIP**
>
> Regularly check your bank's Web site for the latest loan rates and refinancing charges.

By comparing your current loans with available ones, you can decide whether refinancing a home makes sense to you. Many of the banking sites offer financial calculators and worksheets you can use to help you decide on loan refinancing. Get in the habit of checking current rates to find out if refinancing or consolidating rental property debt could do more to maximize your investment. Even if you inherited your rental house, that house is *your investment*. You can always sell the house and do something else with that money. The equity in any rental property is nothing more than an investment you've decided to keep. The two most important routine tasks you can perform on any investment is to monitor the return on that investment (the rent you get) as well as track how much your investment is costing you (the interest rate you pay on the mortgage).

Online Credit Checks

The major credit-reporting agencies such as Equifax provide on-line services for individuals, employers, and small and large businesses that enable subscribers to receive credit reports at reasonable fees. Generally, unless you order your own report, you must have a valid reason for ordering someone else's credit report, but a landlord has every right to know a potential tenant's credit history.

Depending on the cost of the report, you may want to run a credit check for several potential renters, or only for your top one or two candidates. Because the information is all in the credit bureaus' electronic databases, the results of a credit report may come back to you almost instantly. Many of these agencies require you to buy a subscription, while some charge a fee for each individual report. They typically have toll-free numbers that you can call to get an introduction to the process if their Web sites do not provide the answers you need. Some of the more well-known bureaus are:

Company	Phone	Web site
Equifax	800-556-4711	www.equifax.com
Experian	888-397-3742	www.experian.com
Trans Union	888-567-8688	www.tuc.com

Keep in mind that credit-reporting services such as Equifax (*www.equifax.com*; see Figure 13-5) do not tell you whether a potential tenant will be a good tenant or a bad tenant. The credit report does not even tell you directly if the potential tenant has good credit. The report simply gives you a profile of the potential tenant's financial situation (debt) along with his or her credit history. Then it's up to you to decide how to interpret that information. The agency should give you more information about interpreting credit reports when you first sign up for service.

Some agencies require the potential tenant to give you permission before you can obtain the report. The easiest way to do this is to include it on the rental application that potential tenants will fill out at the open house. Tenants with a good credit history will want to provide the necessary information so you will rent to them.

E-mail

I strongly suggest that even if you do not use the Internet to access information you still set up an e-mail account. Some e-mail providers, such as Juno (*www.juno.com* or 800-654-5866) and

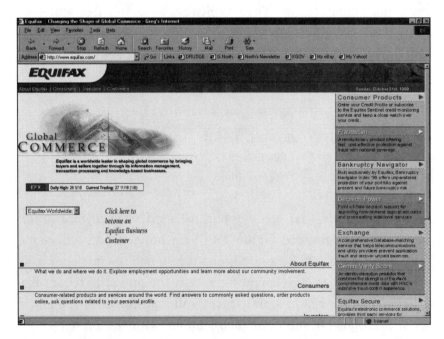

FIGURE 13-5. Get credit reports online

NetZero (*www.netzero.com* or 888-279-8132), charge nothing. In exchange for free e-mail and Internet services, you see small, unobtrusive ads whenever you check your mail. E-mail can come in very handy for a landlord. So many people have e-mail today that it's very likely that your tenants do, too. If you encourage your tenants to e-mail you with questions and problems that are not urgent, that is less time you spend on the phone or calling tenants back. E-mail also lets you check with people you hire to work on your property while you are away to make sure things are going smoothly.

> **TIP**
>
> Ask the credit agency what information your potential tenants must provide so you can obtain reports online.

E-mail doesn't replace the phone, of course. E-mail does, however, let you stay in contact when you're out of town or difficult to reach. Perhaps you are in a different time zone from your tenants. You might be awake when they are asleep. This has happened to me several times over the past few years when I was traveling in another country for a conference and needed to check on my properties back home. Having e-mail means I can stay in touch without inconveniencing myself, my associates, or my tenants. Having e-mail also saves you money on long distance. All you need to do is find a local dial-up number for your ISP and you'll still be able to communicate with anyone in the world who has e-mail for free. Finding a local dial-up number is not always easy and usually depends on how large your provider is. But even if your ISP does not offer overseas access, you can still send and receive e-mail through most hotel business centers. Some hotels are even starting to offer Internet and e-mail access right in your room.

Helpful Web Sites for Landlords

Rental property owners can use the Internet to their advantage to get information and help, or to conduct business and communicate via e-mail. Table 13-1 describes some key Internet addresses that you might find useful as you search online for information. Internet addresses change and go dormant frequently, so don't be surprised if you occasionally arrive at a dead end. Most Internet browser programs offer searching tools you can use to find the most up-to-the-minute landlording information.

TABLE 13-1. Internet Addresses for Rental Property Owners

Internet Address	Description
www.gis.net/~spoa	Small Property Owners of America's helpful hints and warnings on property ownership and management.
www.hud.gov/fhe/fhehous.html	Information from the U.S. Department of Housing and Urban Development (HUD) on the Fair Housing Act.
www.law.cornell.edu	Complete online legal reference, including fair housing laws.
www.mrlandlord.com	Mr. Landlord has a newsletter as well as links to numerous resources and services for rental property owners.
www.landlording.com	A rental owner's collection of helpful tips, warnings, and advice.
www.smallpropertyowner.com	Resources for landlords from the American Association for Small Property Ownership.

A Laptop for the Landlord

Today's laptop computers can be just as powerful as full-size desktop PCs—but you can take laptops, which can weigh as little as 3 pounds, anywhere you go. Instead of buying two computers—a laptop for travel and a desktop computer for work at the office or home—many people now use the laptop for both.

Consider purchasing a laptop so you can carry it with you while working on your properties. You can easily keep track of your mileage (every trip you make for your rentals, even if you do not go to the property itself, is deductible but only if you record the expense and the number of miles traveled) and rent received in person. It is also handy for recording to-do notes; scheduling meetings with renters, bankers, and workers; keeping your contact information handy; and even accessing the Internet using a wireless modem.

I would never have suggested a laptop in the previous edition of this book. But prices on portable computers are so low, and the information available on the Internet is so pervasive and timely, that I now believe that a computer and Internet access are an amazing help to any property owner who wants to be as efficient—and profitable—as possible.

Index